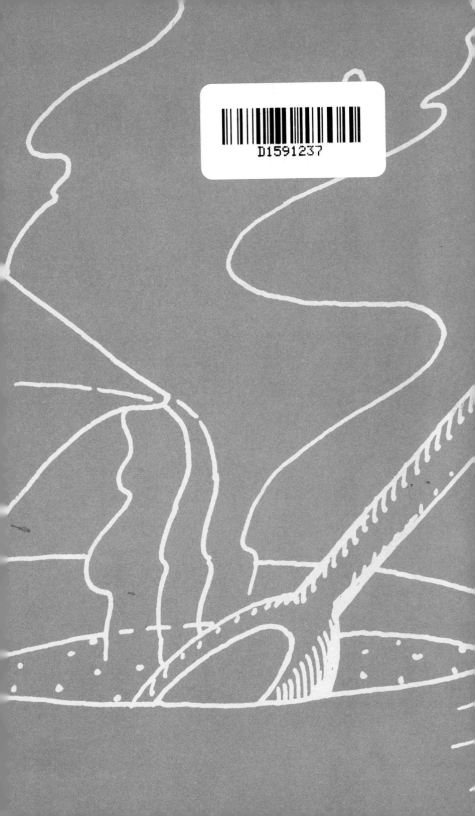

D1591237

The Chef Gregory Cookbook

with Lois Rosenthal

Illustrated by Michael Dektas

F & W Publishing Corporation
Cincinnati, Ohio

Library of Congress Catalog Card Number 72-91472
ISBN 0-911654-27-5
F & W Publishing Corporation, 22 East 12th St., Cincinnati, Ohio 45210
Copyright © 1972 by F & W Publishing Corporation
Printed in the United States of America. All rights reserved

Acknowledgments

Thanks to Mona Pointer, Marianna Woodward, Marge Haller, Jody McClay, Sylvia Schwab, and Janet Kendall for their help in collecting my recipes and gathering notes taken in class.

Bouquets to Marge Valvano for wine advice.

Thank you, thank you Judy Bergman, Rose Reis, and Suzanne La Boiteaux for reading recipes for editorial content.

And special thanks to Babs Marcus and Toni Tobias for not only reading recipes but also acting as culinary counselors to the editor.

The Hyde Park merchants have provided invaluable information and Nat C. Reis has walked a million miles to the phone to answer questions. We are grateful.

And last — but certainly most important of all — the book happened because Richard Rosenthal, whose patience and ideas and perseverance pulled it all together.

May 16, 1973

To the Monday night Gourmet Girls.

To. Peggy

Best wishes - Hope you enjoy the book - Good food always -

Chet Snagg

North Christian

The Chef Gregory Cookbook Ingredients

1
The Philosophy of Cooking

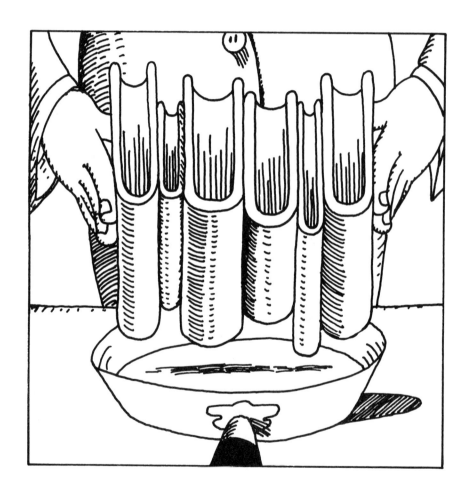

It's so easy to say "Drop over for a drink" or "Come for dinner so we can get together and talk," especially when you look forward to being with people you enjoy. You may have to entertain business associates or visiting firemen or prepare festive family gatherings. These occasions should be fun for you. But so often the fun disappears, and you are overwhelmed with the work and worry of preparation. Perhaps not knowing just what to do and where to begin are the biggest problems. When you are uncertain how to proceed with any task, the job takes on mountainous proportions. I want to help you turn the mountain back into a molehill.

The purpose of this book is to simplify cooking and entertaining. I want fear never to strike your heart again after you've issued an invitation. By putting the whole picture in perspective, you'll be able to not only enjoy the people you entertain, but enjoy the cooking and entertaining, too.

It all begins — and ends — with organization.

You begin by planning menus, making shopping lists, deciding the kind of party you are going to have, and selecting the china, silver and serving equipment you need for the particular occasion. The whole picture of the party has to be laid out in advance.

Since the shopping often takes as much time as the cooking, plan exactly what you need ahead of time. If some of the food must be ordered in advance, make certain how far in advance this must be done. You may have to go to a variety of stores to gather all your ingredients, so make sure you know exactly what you are looking for and where its available. What greater catastrophe is there than beginning to cook, getting halfway into a recipe only to find that a crucial ingredient is missing?

To be a successful entertainer takes a great deal of practice.

A good way to start is to take small groups of people that you can handle easily — preferably people you know well — and practice with them. Repeat your party menu several times with and without guests to get the feeling of accomplishment and confidence. Then approach another more difficult menu. Start with simple recipes. A complicated menu produced badly embarrasses both you and your guests and can badly shake your confidence. Start simply and work your way up the ladder, step by step toward more sophisticated menus.

One of the most important things to remember about cooking is that people "eat with their eyes," too. If your food is not attractively arranged and presented, you lose half of its effectiveness. If you have artistic inclinations, these help add beauty to food presentation. But if art is not one of your fortes, look at magazines and newspapers for ideas. Not only are interesting menus given, but you can get ideas on table settings, flower arranging, and zillions of other party hints. Be a clipper; keep a file of ideas and use them.

There really is no excuse for people saying that they don't have time to entertain. The busiest person, through organization and proper planning, can produce lovely parties. Many parts of the meal can be cooked ahead of time and frozen so that you can have a party without all the rush of last minute preparation. One of my basic aims is to show you how to plan successfully so that you can cook and spend very little time in the kitchen while your guests are there. After all, you should have a good time at your own parties, too!

I feel that it is very important for people to have some type of training in cooking, whether it is formal schooling or watching a friend or relative who cooks extremely well. If these are not available to you, watch one of the cooking shows on TV. Many techniques are easier to understand when you have seen them done rather than trying to figure them out from a cookbook. Watch a recipe being prepared, then practice the procedure yourself and learn by doing. (Grandma's favorite old recipe may be the hit of your next party and a new surprise to all your guests.)

I am going to show you how to be a better cook, and how to feel comfortable and confident in entertaining. You will become successful doing what suits you best, whether you use simple techniques or tackle more advanced recipes.

But most important, be yourself. Do your own thing. There are really no strict do's and don't's in entertaining any longer. Suit your own personality, your budget, and the occasion. Use our basic information and our techniques, but above all, use *your* imagination. Happy cooking!

2
The Chemistry of Cooking

All the bubbling and boiling and bustling that goes on in your kitchen produces a multitude of chemical reactions in food that are very important for you to know about. Many changes in food are so subtle they occur without your ever noticing them. I am going to point out some basic reactions so you will know exactly how food changes under various conditions. We have all been stunned by our cooking disasters especially when we have followed recipes to the letter and can't imagine what in the world has gone wrong. This chapter is a sure fire disaster preventer. Let's really get down to basics and look at the ways we cook our food.

There are vast differences between cooking on a gas or an electric stove or over a charcoal or an open wood fire. Each of these sources of heat always gives the food you are cooking a completely different flavor, quality and texture.

I prefer a gas stove. It provides the best control of the heat and you get better flavors by cooking over an open flame.

Electricity tends to dry the food out more than gas because it cooks so much more quickly. Food burns easier, too. So use more liquids when you are stewing or boiling with electricity to counter the much greater rate of evaporation.

When you cook over a wood fire, remember to use hard wood. The soft resinous variety causes food to wind up tasting like hemlock or pine. The only exception to this rule is when you are smoking food or using a campfire. Apple or cherry wood is marvelous for roasting game or fowl and gives it a great flavor.

The size and depth of your charcoal fire will depend on the amount of space you need between the fire and the piece of meat you are grilling. The thicker the piece of meat, the farther away from the fire you place it. In this way your meat cooks slowly through, without burning on the outside.

A basic rule to remember when you are buying meats, is that you cannot take an inferior piece of meat and make something good out of it, but you can take a less expensive cut of meat of good quality and make something very good out of it.

Predetermine the cooking method you plan to use to bring out the best qualities of the piece of meat you are cooking, whether it is roasting or broiling or pan frying or stewing.

Most of my recipes advocate using fresh meat and vegetables. The flavor of the ingredients in a recipe often depends on their freshness. When fresh meat and vegetables are not available, you must compensate for the lack of freshness and flavor in canned and frozen food. One good way to liven them up is to add a few drops of lemon juice after cooking and draining, but before serving. This will bring them back to life and make them much more tasty.

Fresh herbs and spices are so important to cooking, that you should always try to buy them from a supermarket or store that has a good turnover. If you are doubtful about their freshness, open the jars and smell the ingredients. This may not endear you to your friendly grocer, but by smelling the spices you will be able to determine just how fresh they really are. (If the smell is bold and pungent and makes your nose tickle, it's fresh!) Many households never recycle their herbs and spices and use them for years. You can't do this and expect them to retain their flavor. Buy them in small quantities, replenish them, and you will have much better results. A cooking rule for herbs and spices: generally use lesser amounts of a dried herb than fresh, but vary the quantity a little depending on how fresh the dried ones are.

Buy food as you do spices — in quantities that you will use in a reasonably short period of time. Don't buy a large quantity of something just because it is a bargain. Chances are you'll never use it all and eventually you'll throw it out, a good part of it anyway. Also, it almost always deteriorates in quality so that you can't or shouldn't use it.

Try to store canned and packaged food in areas that are fairly cool — from 65° to 70.° They will keep for a longer period of time. Opened foods should be stored in airtight containers, to keep the flavor and freshness in and the bugs out.

When you are using anything that has been frozen, remove it from the freezer and put it in the refrigerator about 24 hours before you're ready to prepare it, so that it can slowly defrost. When the temperature of an ingredient is quickly changed from a very low degree to a high degree it destroys its texture. Meat, for instance will retain its juices when allowed to defrost gradually. When your meat is defrosted, remove it from the refrigerator and place it on the kichen table and let it come to room temperature or approximately 65° before cooking. This usually takes one to two hours in the normal portions you'll be using.

Almost all ingredients can be frozen. Exceptions are foods heavy in pork products and pork itself. These only keep a limited amount (about 30 days) of time in the freezer before they dry out badly. Never freeze foods heavy with cheese or mushrooms. Most everything else can be frozen and kept well with happy results.

One of our biggest headaches — and helps — is the self-defrosting refrigerator. We no longer have the sloshy job of defrosting it, but it does cause other problems. One is the havoc it raises with fresh vegetables and lettuce. Make sure that any time you store salad greens or vegetables in the refrigerator, you have them properly covered (in plastic bags or other containers), and keep them on the damp side. When refrigerators defrost, they warm up and the food inside then warms up and begins to decompose. Consequently the length of life of everything inside is shortened a great deal.

Here are some specific examples of chemistry at work in the kitchen.

When you are stirring thickened sauces, for instance, use a wooden spoon rather than a metal one. The metal spoon tends to break the sauces down, while the wooden spoon has a much softer reaction, keeping the consistency and texture of the sauce.

Another big problem is determining the best time to add wines to cream sauces. When you do the basic cream sauce, you must have the sauce up to the boiling point before you add the dry white wine or sherry. Then the lactic acid in the cream sauce is able to accept the acetic acid in the wine and this will keep the sauce from curdling.

When you beat egg whites, to be really successful, whether you are making cakes or meringues or souffles, a copper bowl is essential. It is the reaction between the copper bowl and the egg whites that gives the marvelous stability to the meringues. When you beat the egg whites by hand with a large wire balloon whisk in a copper bowl, always add a pinch of salt to help create the reaction. If you do not have a copper bowl for the egg whites, and you beat them in a conventional mixer, add a teaspoon of cream of tartar for every 6 to 8 egg whites, and this will create the same reaction you get from a copper bowl.

Various kinds of metals cause different reactions to the various kinds of foods that are cooked in them. For instance, aluminum pots are not good for cooking light or white stocks or sauces, because the aluminum tends to grey the sauce and make it come out a dirty laundry color instead of a bright white as it should. It is better to do these sauces in tin-lined copper pots, stainless steel, or enamel iron casseroles or magnalite ware. Beware of cooking in copper pots that are not tinned on the inside, for there is a danger of contamination from the food. A poisonous reaction occurs.

Never cook dishes heavy in wine in cast iron pots. You get a very bad reaction between the cast iron and the acetic acid in the wine and the flavor produced is quite disagreeable.

So, you can see what you cook, in what pot, over what heat, by what method, after being defrosted or bought fresh, are all links in the chain of events that produce good food. More specific reactions will be discussed in my recipes. Read on.

3
Basic Cooking

The Four Friends

There are four ingredients that I use so often and find so valuable, I call them my four friends. So, instead of listing them individually on each recipe I will refer to them as "the four friends".

They are:

1 tsp. garlic salt
1 tsp. accent or msg
1 tsp. liquid maggi
1 drop tabasco sauce

When I refer to the three friends in a recipe, it is always garlic salt that is omitted.

Defining Acidulate

Another term I often use is acidulate, especially when I am preparing mushrooms. This simply means to squeeze lemon juice over the mushrooms to keep them from turning dark.

Peeling tomatoes and peaches

Many of my recipes call for peeling tomatoes and peaches. The easiest method is to dip them into boiling water for three to five seconds and then immerse them in cold water to chill. The skin should come off easily with a paring knife.

Julienne

To julienne vegetables or meats means to shred them finely. I often call for this to be done in my recipes, too.

Egg Wash

Egg wash is the coating brushed on pastry surfaces to give it a beautiful brown color when the pastry is baked. Egg wash also acts as a glue so that you can stick decorations on pastries and cookies.

In a bowl put:
> **1 whole egg**
> **1 Tbl. milk or cream.**

Beat together until well blended and brush on the pastry with a pastry brush. Always let the egg wash dry for a few minutes before baking.

The double boiler heating method

When I say to place the bowl in which you are beating something in hot water over the heat, I mean that you should prepare a double boiler-type arrangement. What you are preparing needs gentler heat than placing it directly on your burner, so place it in a pot of water to protect it from overheating.

Hot water bath

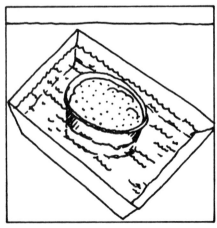

When you need a gentle heat for cooking fish and meat mousses, custards, certain souffles, molded rice and vegetable dishes, a hot water bath does the trick.

Place the mold in a layer pan and add enough hot water to the pan to come up two or three inches on the sides of the mold. Place this whole arrangement in the oven and bake as directed.

Puff Pastry

Puff pastry can be ordered in four or five pound batches from a bakery. Wrap the pastry in one pound packages in your freezer so that you will have some handy when you need it. Also, your baker will be more agreeable to supplying your pastry needs if he can make them for you in five pound batches rather than smaller quantities.

You can also use Pepperidge Farm frozen patty shells. Soften them, and roll them out together. Two packages equal one pound of puff pastry.

Basic White or Cream Sauce or Bechamel (6 to 8 servings)

> ½ cup butter (1 stick)
> ½ cup flour
> 3 cups milk or light cream
> Four friends
> Pinch nutmeg, freshly grated
> Medium-size onion, chopped (½ cup)

Melt butter in a heavy saucepan (stainless steel or enamel to keep sauce from greying). Add the chopped onion and saute. When onion is transparent, add flour. Add rest of seasonings and stir in milk or light cream with wire whisk. Stir and bring to boiling point. Reduce heat and simmer 25-30 minutes. Strain through wire sieve if a more delicate sauce is desired.

Poulet or Enriched Cream Sauce

Prepare cream sauce adding:

> 1 Tbl. chicken base to seasonings and 1 cup dry white wine after the sauce has been brought to boiling point. Reduce heat and simmer 25-30 minutes.

Newburg

Prepare cream sauce adding to seasonings:

> 2 tsp. dry mustard
> 1 large Tbl. sweet Hungarian paprika

Add 1 cup dry sherry to the sauce after it has been brought to boiling point. Reduce heat and simmer 25-30 minutes.

Curry Sauce

Prepare cream sauce adding:

1 large Tbl. curry powder to butter and onions after onions have been sauted. Heat briefly to release flavor of curry. Proceed with white sauce recipe.

Brown Sauce or Espagnol (6 to 8 servings)

½ cup butter
1 medium-size onion, chopped
½ cup flour
Four friends
1 bayleaf
½ cup tomato puree
3 cups beef stock or consomme
1 cup dry red wine

Melt the butter in a heavy saucepan and saute the onion in the melted butter until it is transparent. Add the flour, stir and cook until light brown or noisette. Add the remaining ingredients, stir and bring to boiling point. Simmer 25-30 minutes. Strain through wire sieve if a more delicate sauce is desired.

Leftover **mushroom stems** may be added to the simmering ingredients for an extra spark.

Mayonnaise

Can be made in blender or in a bowl, beating with a wire whisk.

4 large egg yolks
1 tsp. dry mustard
1 tsp. salt
Juice of one lemon
Pinch of white pepper
1 cup vegetable oil or combination ½ cup olive oil,
½ cup vegetable oil

Place egg yolks, mustard, salt, lemon juice and pepper in bowl or blender jar. Stir together. While stirring or blending on low speed, gradually add the oil in a steady stream until all the oil has been absorbed and the mayonnaise has been made.

Vinaigrette or Basic French

> ½ cup red or white wine vinegar
> Salt to taste
> 1 tsp. ground black pepper
> 1½ cups vegetable or olive oil or combination of
> both.

Place ingredients in blender jar to blend or can be shaken together in a glass jar.

This dressing may be used as a basis for meat marinades also.

Country French Dressing

> ½ cup red wine vinegar
> Four friends
> 1 tsp. dry mustard
> 1 tsp. salt
> Ground black pepper
> Juice of one lemon
> ½ to ⅔ cup olive oil

Place ingredients in blender to mix or may be shaken together in a glass jar.

Never-Fail Hollandaise Sauce

> 6 Grade A large egg yolks
> 1 Tbl. water
> 1½ cup clarified butter (melted butter with sediment removed)
> Juice of 1 to 2 lemons
> Salt and pepper
> Pinch cayenne

To clarify butter melt it over low heat, let stand for a few minutes until milk solids settle to the bottom. Skim the butter fat from the top and keep warm, ready to use.

Warm egg yolks and water in double boiler arrangement, or any pan placed inside another containing hot, not boiling, water. Stir yolks with wire whisk until they are light and fluffy about three to four minutes. Gradually add warm clarified butter in small additions, beating after each addition until egg yolks absorb butter.

Caution: do not overheat mixture. It must be brought to about 180° or directly underneath boiling. If the sauce is too hot, it will separate or curdle. If bowl is too warm, remove from heat.

Season with salt, pepper, cayenne and lemon juice.

To save curdled or separated sauce, immediately remove sauce from heat, take out of the hot water and place in refrigerator or set in cold water to quickly reduce heat for three to four minutes.

Then do one or more of the following:

1. Stir with wire whisk. This will sometimes bring sauce back together.
2. Add a small piece of ice.
3. Beat in another egg yolk.
4. Add 1 tablespoon whipping cream.
5. Add one tablespoon mayonnaise.

One of the above or a combination of these measures should work.

If your sauce looks like scrambled eggs, no amount of patching will work, and I'm afraid you'll have to begin again.

Hollandaise sauce should be served warm, not hot. Whatever you serve it on should be very hot.

It can be frozen or stored in glass containers in the refrigerator up to one week.

Pan frying

Pan frying is a quick frying or short order method of cooking vegetables, fish or meat. Place a small amount of fat in the bottom of a pan and heat until the fat is hot. Add, for example, a steak that has been brought to room temperature, and heat over high heat quickly turning once or twice, searing the outsides, keeping the juices in. Fry until the degree of doneness you desire has been reached.

In Chinese cooking, using the frying technique, vegetables are quickly cooked over high heat in a small amount of fat.

This gives you crisp vegetables that retain the vitamins and color often lost in longer cooking methods.

The most popular way to prepare fish in America is pan frying. According to your preference, you may or may not coat them with breading, flour or cornmeal. The fish should always be cooked in a small amount of fat. A good thing to remember about using butter as a fat is that when butter is heated, it burns. To prevent this, add a small amount of cooking oil to raise the temperature of the butter. You will have the butter flavor but prevent the burning that results in pan frying.

Boiling

Place the food you wish to cook in a pot of cold liquid and together bring them to the boiling point. Then reduce the heat and simmer the meat or vegetable until it is tender. It is always better to bring the cold liquid and the meat or vegetable to a boil together than to drop food in already boiling water or broth. This preserves flavor and tenderness. There are some exceptions to this rule, but in general this is a must.

Roasting

A good general rule for roasting is to preheat the oven to a high temperature before placing the meat (which should be at room temperature) in the oven, and then turn the temperature down to a lower heat immediately. More definite temperatures depend on the cut and variety of meat and will be given in specific recipes in the book.

Beef Tenderloin

Have the beef at room temperature. If you want to keep the meat on the rare side, fold the small or tail ends of the meat underneath the roast so that you have the same thickness throughout. Coat the outside with **butter or cooking oil.** Add the **four friends** and **ground black pepper.** Preheat the oven to 425° to 450° and place the tenderloin in the oven. Turn the heat down to 350° and roast 15-20 minutes for pink, tender results.

Standing ribs of beef or English roast beef

Your butcher should prepare your roast beef to the oven-ready stage by removing the chine bone from the back of the rib as well as the tough back strap. The ribs from the under side of the roast are also removed. The butcher then trims the roast to an 8″ cut, measured from the eye of the rib down the rib bone so that when you are slicing the roast for serving, the slices will fit nicely on each dinner plate without hanging over the edges. The chine and the ribs are now tied back on the roast in their proper place and it is ready for roasting.

The ribs should be at room temperature. Coat the heavy fat side generously with a fourth of an inch covering of coarse **kosher salt.** Place in a roasting pan rib side down so that the ribs will act as a natural rack to support the meat. The oven

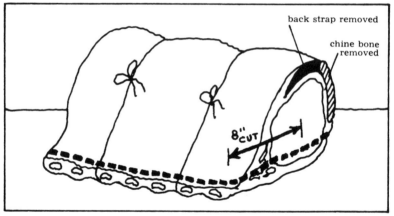

back strap removed

chine bone removed

8″ CUT

should be preheated to 450°. When the roast is placed in the oven, turn the heat down immediately to 350°, and roast the desired length of time. The high temperature in the oven will sear the outside of the meat and close the pores so that you don't lose the juices and the end result will be a heavy charred effect you see so often in good restaurants.

After you remove the roast from the oven, cover it with a kitchen or turkish towel and let it stand 15 to 30 minutes. This stops the cooking action and prevents the beef from "bleeding" or losing all of its juices when you slice it.

Cooking Guide for Standing Rib Roast

Preheat oven to 450° then turn down to 350° when roast is placed in the oven. Use Grade A - U.S. Choice meats.

2 rib (4 to 6 servings)

Rare 1 to 1½ hrs.
Med. 1½ to 2 hrs.
Well done 2 to 2½ hrs.

4 rib (10 to 12 servings)

Rare 1½ to 2 hrs.
Med. 2 to 2½ hrs.
Well done 2½ to 3 hrs.

5 rib (12 to 15 servings)

Rare 1½ to 2 hrs.
Med. 2 to 2½ hrs.
Well done 3 to 3½ hrs.

7 rib (whole standing rib)
about 22 lbs. 18 to 20 servings.

Rare 2½ to 3 hrs.
Med. 3 to 3¾ hrs.
Well done 4 to 5 hrs.

If a meat thermometer is used to determine cooking time, insert the thermometer into the thickest part of the meat before you put it in the oven. Do not have the meat thermometer tip near or on a bone or it will not register accurately. Reading should be as follows:

Rare	120 degrees
Medium-rare	130 degrees
Medium	140 degrees
Well done	150 degrees or more

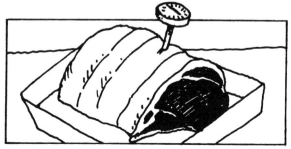

Don't be fooled into over-cooking larger poundages of meat. They really don't take much longer to cook than a small roast because the thickness of the meat is the same whether it is a 5 pound roast or a 25 pound roast.

A 25 pound roast rib of beef is cooked 2½ hours at 350°.

A 5 pound roast takes approximately the same length of time, perhaps varying ½ hour less.

Meat should be kept on the rare side to preserve flavor and tenderness. The more you cook meat, the tougher it becomes.

Cooking times also vary according to whether the meat does or does not have a bone. With the bone left in the meat, cooking time is longer. When the roast is boned, rolled, and tied, cooking time is reduced but the flavor generated by the bone is sorely missed.

For example, it takes 2½ hours to cook a 25 pound rib of beef with the bones intact in a 350° oven, while the same boned, rolled roast normally takes 2 hours.

Wild game

When you are roasting wild game such as pheasant or duck or roasts from bear, elk or deer, the outside of the meat should be barded since these animals have very little fat of their own. Cover the outside of the roast with ¼ **inch thick slices of bacon or salt pork or melted butter** to keep the meat tender and moist.

Chickens or turkeys

Stuffed chickens or turkeys take longer to roast than unstuffed birds. Never stuff birds ahead of time or botulism will result. This is one last minute activity that must remain that way. Periodically baste the outsides of the bird with wine or butter or a combination of both to keep the outside tender and to give the bird an appealing color.

To roast chicken breasts see the recipe for Chicken Gregory.

Roasted Chicken

4½ to 5 pound roasting chicken. Wash in cold water and dry well. Rub the inside cavity with **salt.** Place **one or two ribs of celery, one medium size quartered onion, one bay leaf,** and **two tsp. thyme, tarragon or sage** inside the cavity of the chicken. Rub the outside of the chicken generously with ¼ cup softened butter or margarine. Place the chicken in a roasting pan and add enough **dry white wine** to cover the bottom of the pan. Roast in a pre-heated 350° oven for two hours. Baste the chicken every 20 to 30 minutes using the drippings from the bottom of the roasting pan.

When you pierce the leg joint and the juices run clear, the chicken is done. Another way to test is when the tendons on the leg pull free from the drumstick indicating that the chicken or turkey has roasted sufficiently.

If you stuff the chicken, add another 25 to 30 minutes for a 4½ to 5 pound chicken.

Use the **drippings in the bottom of the pan** for the basis of the sauce or gravy to serve with the chicken or use bechamel sauce.

For tender, juicy, carefree roasting, place the prepared chicken, game or turkey in the cooking-roasting bags that are on the market today, but follow the manufacturer's directions on the package for temperature and time. These bags really do work well and do shorten the cooking time.

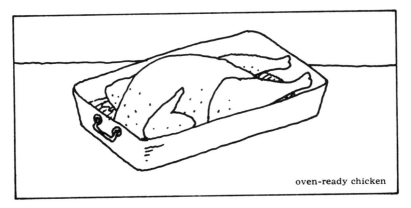

oven-ready chicken

Timetable for Roasting Turkeys

WEIGHT (unstuffed)	ROASTING TIME (unstuffed turkey)	ROASTING TIME (stuffed turkey)
\multicolumn{3}{Use the chicken recipe given above for roast turkey. Preheat oven to 350°.}		

Use the chicken recipe given above for roast turkey. Preheat oven to 350°.

WEIGHT (unstuffed)	ROASTING TIME (unstuffed turkey)	ROASTING TIME (stuffed turkey)
6 lbs.	2 hrs.	2 hrs. 30 mins.
7 lbs.	2 hrs. 5 mins.	2 hrs. 40 mins.
8 lbs.	2 hrs. 10 mins.	2 hrs. 50 mins.
9 lbs.	2 hrs. 15 mins.	3 hrs.
10 lbs.	2 hrs. 30 mins.	3 hrs. 20 mins.
11 lbs.	2 hrs. 45 mins.	3 hrs. 40 mins.
12 lbs.	3 hrs.	4 hrs.
13 lbs.	3 hrs. 15 mins.	4 hrs. 20 mins.
14 lbs.	3 hrs. 30 mins.	4 hrs. 40 mins.
15 lbs.	3 hrs. 45 mins.	5 hrs.
16 lbs.	4 hrs.	5 hrs. 20 mins.
17 lbs.	4 hrs. 15 mins.	5 hrs. 40 mins.
18 lbs.	4 hrs. 30 mins.	6 hrs.
19 lbs.	4 hrs. 45 mins.	6 hrs. 20 mins.
20 lbs.	5 hrs.	6 hrs. 40 mins.
21 lbs.	5 hrs. 15 mins.	7 hrs.
22 lbs.	5 hrs. 30 mins.	7 hrs. 20 mins.
23 lbs.	5 hrs. 45 mins.	7 hrs. 40 mins.
24 lbs.	6 hrs.	8 hrs.

Grilling

Grilling is probably the first method of cooking known to man. There are various ways to grill foods today, although I prefer grilling on charcoal or open wood fires.

Electric grills just do not produce the flavor results you get from an open fire. Electric broilers cannot give the meat the crusty charred outside that you associate with good grilled foods.

For gas grilling in a stove, you must adjust the rack in the broiler according to the thickness of the meat or fish you are cooking.

There should be a space of from three to four inches

between the flame and the top surface of the meat or fish. Timing will depend on thickness.

Using a charcoal or an open wood fire, the meat or fish or vegetable may be cooked by directly placing it onto the coals or suspending the food above the coals on racks.

First build a fire and let it burn down to a white ash which produces good intense heat. Bury the meat (for example) directly in the ashes and cover it with the hot coals. When it has been cooked long enough, remove and brush off the loose ashes that have adhered to the outside of the meat. The lovely crust and the delicious distinctive flavor produced by the fire remains.

If you use racks above the fire for grilling, the thicker the piece of meat, the farther away from the fire the racks should be. In this way you will not burn the outside of the meat, but cook it slowly through.

Baking

Baking is usually done in a controlled heat area such as an oven where you can adjust the temperature. The material to be baked is placed in the oven and cooked until all excess moisture has been removed.

Poaching

Poaching is usually associated with fish and vegetables. Bring what you are cooking to a boil in stock (usually), reduce heat, and simmer in a covered pot. The hardest part of poaching is to not let the simmering become boiling.

If you don't have a fish poacher and want to poach a whole fish, do it this unique way:

Put your **cleaned, washed fish** into a large roasting-cooking bag, add **seasonings,** and **one to two cups dry white wine.** Tie the open end of the bag securely.

Place the fish in the bag on the top rack of your dishwasher. Close the dishwasher, set the dial to the wash cycle but DO NOT PUT SOAP IN THE WASHER.

Start the cycle and let it run. For a small one to three pound fish, one wash, rinse and dry cycle will be enough. A three to eight pound fish needs two wash, rinse and dry cycles.

This is a cool, clean, cooking method and a mighty unique use of the dishwasher as a way to cook. Look around. See what other appliances you can use when you run out of stove space.

Braising

Braising is a technique generally used on less tender cuts of meat although vegetables can be cooked this way, too. The meat or vegetable is placed in a heavy metal or enamel pot and seared on the outside. Liquid is then added, partially covering the meat or vegetable, and this combination is brought to the boiling point. Place a cover on the pot, reduce the heat and cook slowly so the juices will reduce to produce the basic gravy or sauce for the dish you are preparing.

Stewing

Stewing is another form of braising. The difference between the two is that stewing is done in an **uncovered** heavy pot or casserole, while braising is always covered. Usually you stew on the top surface of the stove, but after your stew has reached the boiling point, it may be completed in the oven.

Reheating

Most of the recipes in this book can be prepared several days ahead of time. This is a great convenience, but difficulties may also arise when you reheat food. People tend to recook instead of reheat. To reheat something that has been in the refrigerator, first remove it and let it stand until it reaches room temperature, which will take about an hour or so. Place it in a moderate, 350° oven for about 20-30 minutes and the casserole should be well heated and ready to serve. This is why it is important to buy shallow casseroles instead of deep ones. The deep ones take longer for food to heat through and overcooking may be the result.

Basic Vegetable Cooking

The four distinct methods of cooking vegetables are boiling, steaming, baking and braising.

Boiling

Vegetables should be placed in cold water, salted and brought to the boiling point. Reduce heat and simmer until vegetables are tender or to the degree of doneness you desire.

Steaming

Vegetables should be suspended in a basket over hot water in a covered container. The steam cooks the vegetables.

Baking

Vegetables are placed on shallow trays or casseroles, put into the oven and baked until done. The length of time will depend on the vegetable and the temperature of the oven.

Braising

Vegetables are cooked quickly with fats or stocks over fairly high heat in a heavy casserole until tender.

Basic vegetable cookery using frozen vegetables

When frozen vegetables are used, people tend to cook them much too much. Generally speaking, they have already been pre-cooked during the blanching and freeing process. So rather than recook frozen vegetables, just reheat them to serving temperature and then drain and season. This is just enough cooking to produce a more fresh-like texture and flavor than the normal limp quality associated with frozen vegetables.

Vegetable	How to prepare

Artichokes
    French or
    globe
	Wash. Cut off 1 inch of top, the stem, and tips leaves. Pull off any loose leaves. Brush cut ed with lemon juice.

Jerusalem	Wash, pare; leave whole or slice.
Asparagus	See our special recipe.

Beans
    Green or
    wax
	See our green bean recipe.

Lima, fresh	Shell and wash.
Lima, dried	Rinse; add to 2½ times as much water as bean Soak overnight. Or, bring to boil; simmer 2 minutes; let stand 1 hour.
Navy, dried	Prepare same as dried Limas, but use 3 times as much water as beans.
Beets	Cut off all but 1 inch of stems and root. Wash scrub thoroughly. Do not pare. Or pare and slice or cube. Or pare and shred.
Beet greens	Wash thoroughly. Don't cut off tiny beets.
Broccoli	See Asparagus recipe.
Brussels sprouts	Cut off wilted leaves. Wash. Leave whole.
Cabbage (Green)	Remove wilted outer leaves. Cut in 6 to 8 wedges. Or shred.
Carrots	Wash and pare or scrape. Leave whole, slice, or cut in quarters or strips.
Cauliflower	See our special recipe.
Celeriac (celery root)	Cut off leaves and root fibers. Scrub, but don't peel.
Celery	Cut off leaves; trim roots. Scrub thoroughly. outer branches; cut hearts lengthwise.
Chard, Swiss	Wash thoroughly; if not young, cut midribs from leaves.
Corn	Remove husks from fresh corn. Remove silks stiff brush. Rinse; cook whole. Or, cut off just tips from kernels with sharp k and scrape cobs with dull edge of knife.
Dandelion greens	Discard greens with blossom or bud as they w be bitter. Cut off roots; wash thoroughly.

28

to cook	Time
·r with cold salted water in uncovered pot. ⅃ ¼ cup olive oil and few cloves, garlic, or ⅃n slices.) Bring to boil. Reduce heat and ⅃ner till leaf pulls out easily. Drain.	30-60 min.
·e as above.	15-35 min.
·r with cold salted water in uncovered pot. ⅃g to boil. Reduce heat and simmer till tender. ⅃n and season.	20-30 min.
⅃salt, cover, and simmer in water used for ⅃ing or stock.	About 2 hrs.
⅃ same as dried Limas.	2-3 hrs.
·r with cold salted water in uncovered pot. ⅃g to boil. Reduce heat and simmer till tender. ⅃n, peel and season when done.	Young, 35 min. Old, 60 min.
⅃r with cold salted water in uncovered pot. ⅃g to boil. Reduce heat and simmer till tender. ⅃ and season.	15-20 min. 10 min.
⅃lightly; cook covered without water except ⅃s that cling to leaves. Reduce heat when ⅃n forms. Turn with fork frequently.	5-15 min.
⅃r with cold salted water in uncovered pot. ⅃ to boil. Reduce heat and simmer till tender. ⅃ and season.	10-15 min.
⅃r with cold salted water in uncovered pot. ⅃ to boil. Reduce heat and simmer till tender. ⅃ and season. Or braise. ⅃ok wedges uncovered in cooking liquid from ⅃d beef or ham.	10-12 min. 5-7 min. 12-15-min.
⅃r with cold salted water in uncovered pot. ⅃ to boil. Reduce heat and simmer till tender. ⅃ and season.	Young whole, 18-20 min. Cut up in 1″ pieces, 10-12 min.
⅃ with cold salted water in uncovered pot. ⅃ to boil. Reduce heat and simmer till tender. ⅃ and season.	40-60 min.
⅃ with cold salted water or consomme in ⅃ered pot. Bring to boil. Reduce heat and ⅃r till tender. Drain and season.	10-20 min.
⅃ with cold salted water in uncovered pot. ⅃to boil. Reduce heat and simmer till tender. ⅃ and season.	Young, 10-20 Older, 15-25
⅃ with cold salted water in uncovered pot. ⅃to boil. Reduce heat and simmer till tender. ⅃ and season. ⅃as above.	6-8 min. 5-8 min.
⅃ with cold salted water in uncovered pot. ⅃to boil. Reduce heat and simmer till tender. ⅃ and season.	10-20 min.

Vegetable	How to prepare
Eggplant	Wash; pare if skin is tough. Cut in ½-inch slic
Kohlrabi	Cut off leaves; wash, pare, and dice or slice.
Leeks	Cut off green tops to within 2 inches of white p Wash.
Lentils, dried	Wash. Add to 2½ times as much water.
Mushrooms	Wash quickly in warm water. Do not soak. Dr Trim stems. Acidulate. Saute or braise.
Okra	Wash pods. Cut off stems. Cut large pods in ½-inch slices.
Onions	Peel under water. Quarter, or leave small onions whole.
Parsnips	Wash; pare or scrape. Slice crosswise or lengt
Peas, Green Black-eyed	Shell and wash.
Potatoes Irish	Scrub thoroughly. Cook with skins on. Or wa and pare thinly. Cook whole, quarter, or cube.
New	Scrub; pare narrow strip of peel from center o each. Or scrape.
Sweet	Scrub; cut off woody portions. Cook while in
Rutabagas	Wash, pare thinly. Slice or cube.
Salsify (oyster plant)	Wash; pare thinly. Slice or cube.
Spinach	Cut off roots; wash several times in lukewarm water, lifting out of water each time.
Squash Acorn	Wash. Cut in half; remove seeds. Or pare and cube.
Hubbard	Wash; cut in serving pieces; do not pare. Or pare and cube.
Summer	Wash; pare. Slice or cube.
Zucchini (Italian)	Wash; do not pare. Slice thin.
Tomatoes	Wash ripe tomatoes. Plunge in boiling water, cool under cold water. Peel; cut out stems. C (Or cook whole—see recipes.)
Turnips	Wash; pare thinly. Slice or cube.

w to cook	Time
⸱ in beaten egg, then in fine dry bread crumbs or ⸱n-flake crumbs. Brown slowly on both sides ⸱ot fat. Season.	About 4 min. total
⸱er with cold salted water in uncovered pot. ⸱ng to boil. Reduce heat and simmer till tender. ⸱in and season.	25-30 min.
⸱er with cold salted water or stock in uncovered ⸱ Bring to boil. Reduce heat and simmer till ⸱der. Drain and season.	15-20 min.
⸱er with cold salted water in uncovered pot. ⸱ng to boil. Reduce heat and simmer till tender. ⸱in and season.	About 35 min.
⸱l to melted butter and oil in skillet; cook over ⸱ heat. Turn occasionally.	5-8 min.
⸱er with cold salted water in uncovered pot. ⸱ng to boil. Reduce heat and simmer till tender. ⸱in and season.	10-20 min.
⸱er with cold salted water in uncovered pot. ⸱ng to boil. Reduce heat and simmer till tender. ⸱in and season.	15-20 min.
⸱e as above.	15-20 min.
⸱e as above.	8-10 min. 35-40 min.
⸱le and cut up. Cover with cold salted water ⸱ncovered pot. Bring to boil. Reduce heat and ⸱mer till tender. Drain and season.	Whole, 25-40 min. Quartered, 20-25 min. Cubed, 10-15 min.
⸱er with cold salted water in uncovered pot. ⸱g to boil. Reduce heat and simmer till tender. ⸱n and season.	Tiny, 15-40 min.
⸱e as above.	30-40 min.
⸱e as above.	25-40 min.
⸱er with cold salted water in uncovered pot. ⸱g to boil. Reduce heat and simmer till tender. ⸱n and season.	20-25 min.
⸱ covered without water except drops that cling ⸱aves. Reduce heat when steam forms. ⸱ with fork frequently.	3-10 min.
⸱e cut side down at 350° 35-40 min.; turn cut ⸱ up; bake till done.	50-60 min.
⸱ with cold salted water in uncovered pot. ⸱g to boil. Reduce heat and simmer till tender. ⸱n and season.	About 15 min.
⸱e on baking sheet; season and dot with butter. ⸱r with foil. Bake at 400°.	45-60 min.
⸱r with cold salted water in uncovered pot. ⸱g to boil. Reduce heat and simmer till tender. ⸱n and season.	About 15 min.
⸱r with cold salted water in uncovered pot. ⸱g to boil. Reduce heat and simmer till tender. ⸱n and season.	15-20 min.
⸱on and cook covered in butter in skillet 5 ⸱tes; uncover and cook, turning slices, till tender.	About 5-8 min.
⸱ slowly, covered, without adding water. Season ⸱ salt, pepper, and sugar. Add a little minced ⸱.	10-15 min.
⸱r with cold salted water in uncovered pot. ⸱g to boil. Reduce heat and simmer till tender. ⸱n and season.	15-20 min.

31

Three exceptions to general vegetable cooking rules or **Jim Gregory Specials.**

Asparagus

Trim the asparagus to five or six inches in length, wash the stalks, and then lay the asparagus into a shallow frying pan or shallow enamel pan. Lay the stalks in the pan not more than four to five deep and add enough cold water to cover them. Salt generously and cover the asparagus with three to four layers of paper toweling. Tuck the towels around the stalks, going over the top of them and down into the water. Heat to a rapid boil and then remove from the heat and let stand ten minutes. The asparagus is then ready to serve. If the asparagus is cooked ahead of time, place it back on the heat long enough to heat through, but be careful to not let the water boil.

Green Beans

Prepare a large pot of salted water and place on the stove to boil. While you are waiting, trim and snap your beans to the desired length. When the water is rapidly boiling, throw in the green beans and bring back to the boiling point and cook for eight minutes. The beans will float to the surface after this length of time. Drain immediately and wash in cold water to stop the cooking action. Butter and season to taste. To heat for serving, place the beans in a shallow casserole in a 350° oven for 10-15 minutes or quickly saute with butter or oil. Add salt and pepper and they will have a delicious flavor.

Cauliflower

Wash and trim. Remember to cut through the heavy stalk or make incisions so that the cauliflower will cook all the way through. Place cauliflower in a large pan, cover generously with cold water, salt and ½ cup milk for each head of cauliflower. Bring cauliflower to boiling point, reduce heat and simmer 12-18 minutes according to the size of the cauliflower.

The addition of the milk to the water will deodorize the cauliflower as well as keep it nice and white.

4
Kitchens and Equipment

The "old fashioned," large open kitchen had a lot going for it: common sense. An open kitchen makes cooking convenient and efficient because the tools you use most often are within easy reach. Don't bury equipment away in drawers where you have to waste time digging to find it. Arrange pots and pans on a peg board or free standing pot rack where they look gleaming and professional. Having them exposed will make you keep a cleaner kitchen, too, because you'll want to keep them shining if they're out for all to see. And, they give a homey feeling too.

Ideally, you should have a good work table made of wood, stainless steel or Formica with an underneath shelf for storage in the center of the room. Often used equipment and spices should go on trays underneath, ready to use at a moments notice. If your kitchen can't accomodate a center table, make your command center a good cooking counter near the stove or sink.

Store sugar, flour and spices close at hand in easy-to-clean and easy-to-open containers. It is also very useful to have an old fashioned (or new fashioned) basket or standing rack full of onions, garlic, fresh vegetables, oranges and lemons nearby. You use them so often in cooking, they should be handy. Also, keeping them at room temperature instead of refrigerated gives them a much better flavor and they'll last just as long out of the refrigerator, too.

Stand wooden spoons, mallets, skewers, scrapers and the multitude of gadgets you need inside a vase or crock. Put it near your work area so you can reach in and grab what you need quickly.

Knives should be hung on a magnetic rack on the side of your work table or on a wall nearby. This keeps them from becoming dull as well as preventing drawer accidents.

Put your garbage container under your working area. If you don't have a garbage disposal, you can use the garbage can to catch metal cans and glass jars (which can be separated later and recycled. I use a marketing basket, too, when shopping, to cut down on paper bags.)

Plenty of storage areas in your kitchen are essential. Make sure you return each piece of equipment to the same storage area each time you use it. Knowing exactly where everything is is a must, especially when you're on a tight schedule. (See kitchen layouts on pages 58-59.)

Make sure equipment infrequently used such as fish poachers, large soup tureens, etc. is stored in plastic bags (in more out-of-the-way places), dust free but still ready to be used at a moment's notice.

Don't buy "sets" of pots and pans. You do such a variety of jobs in the kitchen, you'll need a variety of equipment made of different materials to accomodate them.

It is very helpful to buy casseroles that coordinate with the decor of your house, your china and your silver. You can cook and serve in them, eliminating the expense of buying two sets of equipment. Make sure the casseroles are not more than three to four inches deep in round or oval shapes. When reheating, these casseroles will quickly warm your food and not overcook it as may happen in deep casseroles.

Care of Equipment

Stainless steel: You may use abrasive pads to remove tough spots when washing. Rinse in hot water to avoid soap film. Occasionally polish with stainless steel polish.

Aluminum: Same cleansing procedure as stainless steel. Do not let foods high in acid stand in these containers as they will badly pit.

Black Iron Utensils: After use, if they have to be washed, scrub with soap and hot water and make sure you dry them well. Heat them in a hot oven or over a burner on low heat until all moisture has been absorbed. Oil the inside of the pot and wipe out the excess with paper towels. This procedure will prevent rusting. Hang these pots rather than stack them so that the air will help them dry. After using black iron over a number of years, you will build up a natural coating and you won't have to be so careful.

Enameled pots and pans: On electric stoves, use a wire grid between the pot and the burner as direct heat will crack the enamel, cause it to fall off or explode. Be careful not to bang enameled utensils as they tend to chip. If the enamel on the inside of the pot discolors, fill the pot with Soilax or a mixture of Clorox and water or oven cleaner to remove the dark spots. Harsh abrasives will rub the enamel off, so never scrub with Brillo pads. These pots need tender loving care, but will provide wonderful service.

Copper: Never put a copper pot on the burner without something in it, or the tin lining will melt. Especially on an electric stove, always start cooking over low heat as copper heats so quickly. Copper polish kept near the sink is a reminder to keep these pots shiny.

Tinware: Can be cleaned with soft abrasive pads, but remember to wash and dry well to avoid rusting. Keep them near the stove if you can. The dryness there helps keep them rust free. If they do rust, scrub with Brillo and oil them with vegetable oil. High heat also melts tinware, so use them as you do copper.

Care of Knives

Carbon steel: Holds a better edge, but the problem is that when you cut food high in acid, the acetic content in the food will start a rusting action. To avoid this, wash and dry well after using. If the knife does discolor, clean with steel wool and scouring powder until the shine returns. NEVER put any of your knives in the dish washer.

Stainless steel: These are shiny and surgical looking, but do not hold an edge as well as carbon steel. These, too, should always be washed and dried well. To sharpen knives, use a flat whetstone or magnatized piece of steel. Most household knife sharpeners do not work. Knives must be periodically ground down to be resharpened. You may do this yourself, or if your butcher is agreeable he may sharpen yours along with his own. Professional knife sharpeners of one kind or another are a periodic must for your knives.

Herbs and Spices

Cinnamon: Comes in stick and ground form. Best from Saigon. Used in pungent flavored stews and sauces, desserts and beverages. Spices up wine punch beautifully.

Curry Powder: Blend of over 100 herbs and spices usually identified with Indian and Middle Eastern cooking.

Capers: Oldest known seasoning. Were used by Egyptians, Greeks and Romans. Capers are often pickled in vinegar to give them flavor and are used primarily to flavor sauces.

Celery: The stalks can be eaten fresh, the leaves used to produce wonderful flavors in soup, and the seeds season sauces, salads, pickles, soups and vegetables.

Coarse Kosher Salt: Distilled sea salt. Milder flavor than artificially iodized salt. Used in salt cellars or grinder. Similar to French gros-de-sel.

Garlic Salt: Pulverized garlic mixed with salt. Most convenient and natural garlic flavor to use Don't buy garlic powders, as they tend to turn rancid and do not store well.

Pepper: Black pepper is from ripened peppercorns while white pepper is unripe or green peppercorns. Many chefs prefer white pepper in white sauces, light soups and stocks since it is less conspicuous. Both black and white pepper have the same flavor.

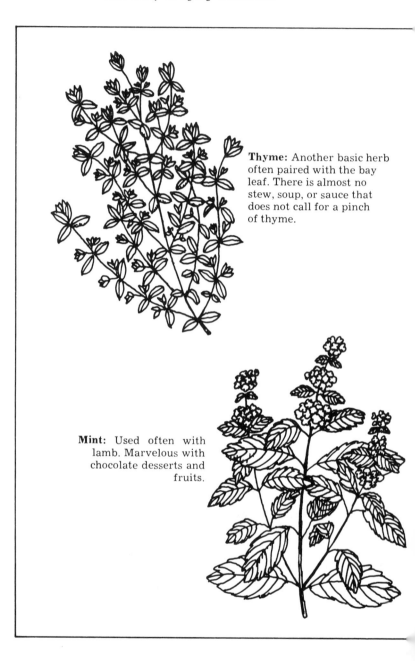

Thyme: Another basic herb often paired with the bay leaf. There is almost no stew, soup, or sauce that does not call for a pinch of thyme.

Mint: Used often with lamb. Marvelous with chocolate desserts and fruits.

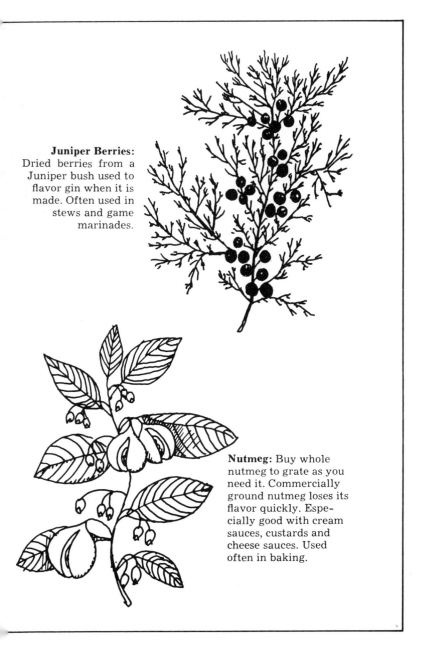

Juniper Berries:
Dried berries from a
Juniper bush used to
flavor gin when it is
made. Often used in
stews and game
marinades.

Nutmeg: Buy whole
nutmeg to grate as you
need it. Commercially
ground nutmeg loses its
flavor quickly. Espe-
cially good with cream
sauces, custards and
cheese sauces. Used
often in baking.

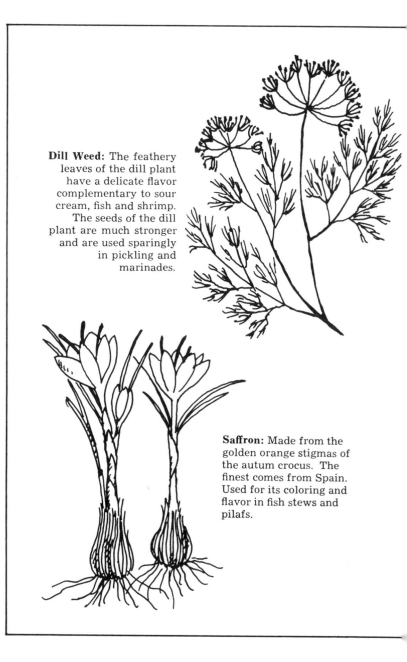

Dill Weed: The feathery leaves of the dill plant have a delicate flavor complementary to sour cream, fish and shrimp. The seeds of the dill plant are much stronger and are used sparingly in pickling and marinades.

Saffron: Made from the golden orange stigmas of the autum crocus. The finest comes from Spain. Used for its coloring and flavor in fish stews and pilafs.

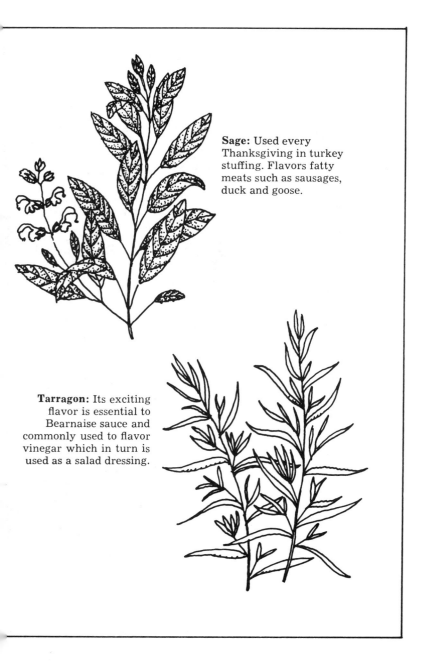

Sage: Used every Thanksgiving in turkey stuffing. Flavors fatty meats such as sausages, duck and goose.

Tarragon: Its exciting flavor is essential to Bearnaise sauce and commonly used to flavor vinegar which in turn is used as a salad dressing.

Sweet Basil: Italian basil used for tomato dishes and Italian cooking.

Bay or Laurel Leaf: One of the foundations of French cooking. Used in almost every conceivable way. It's musty flavor is found often in stocks, sauces and marinades.

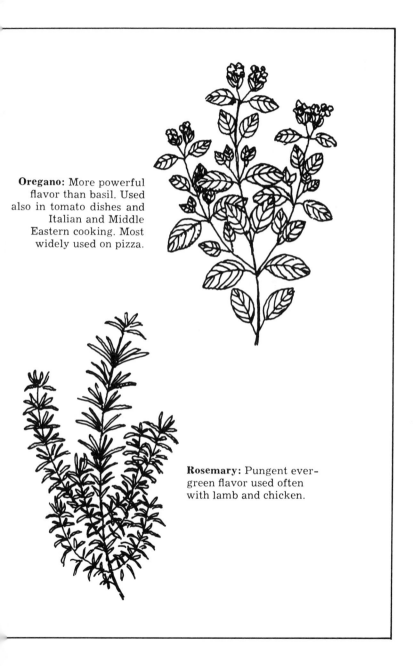

Oregano: More powerful flavor than basil. Used also in tomato dishes and Italian and Middle Eastern cooking. Most widely used on pizza.

Rosemary: Pungent ever-green flavor used often with lamb and chicken.

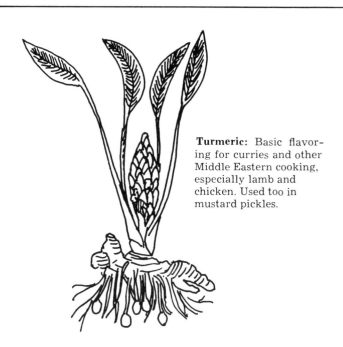

Turmeric: Basic flavoring for curries and other Middle Eastern cooking, especially lamb and chicken. Used too in mustard pickles.

Mustard: Mustard powder is often used in sauces and salad dressings. Flavors newburg sauce. Coleman's is best. Connoisseurs prefer Dijon prepared mustard since it has been flavored with wine and aged.

Allspice: Berry from allspice tree used to flavor marinades. Particularly for game dishes. In ground form it is a delicious baking spice and adds zest to fruit compotes.

Marjoram: Less strong cousin of oregano. It also enhances tomato dishes but is enormously versatile and is used for meat, fish, eggs and a long list of vegetables.

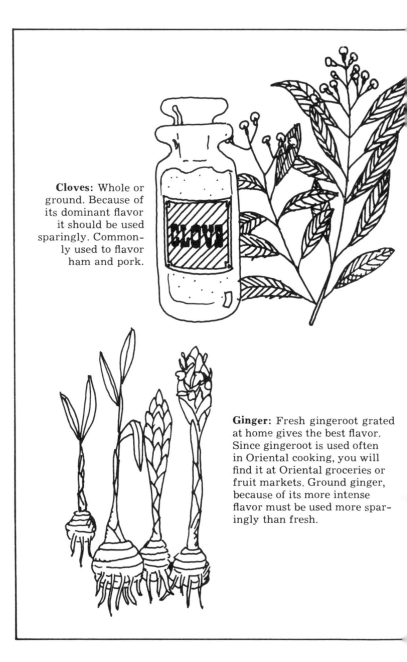

Cloves: Whole or ground. Because of its dominant flavor it should be used sparingly. Commonly used to flavor ham and pork.

Ginger: Fresh gingeroot grated at home gives the best flavor. Since gingeroot is used often in Oriental cooking, you will find it at Oriental groceries or fruit markets. Ground ginger, because of its more intense flavor must be used more sparingly than fresh.

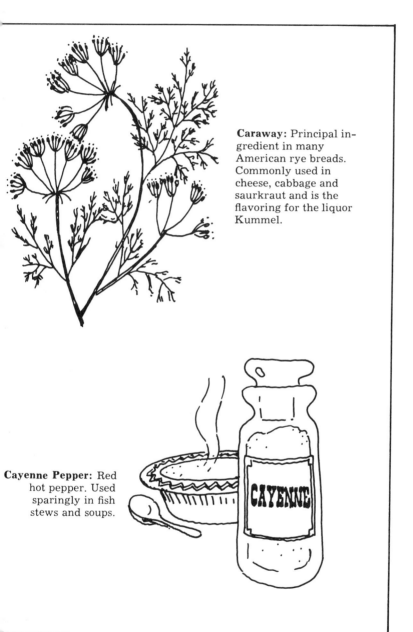

Caraway: Principal ingredient in many American rye breads. Commonly used in cheese, cabbage and saurkraut and is the flavoring for the liquor Kummel.

Cayenne Pepper: Red hot pepper. Used sparingly in fish stews and soups.

Flavorings

Make sure the flavorings you buy are pure extracts. Artificial flavorings taste terrible.

Vanilla extract: Alcoholic distillation of vanilla bean. Used mainly in desserts or sweet cooking.

Vanilla bean: Fruit of the vanilla tree. Split bean and scrape insides to flavor puddings, sugar, and sauces.

Almond extract: Alcoholic liquid flavoring of bitter almond. To flavor pastries, for baking, and Oriental cooking.

Lemon extract: Oil from lemon rind with alcohol added. Used to flavor desserts.

Cream of tartar: Prime ingredient in sugar glazes and syrups.

Seasonings

M.S.G. - Monosodium Glutamate: Helps retain fllavors of cooked foods. Do not use with foods containing egg yolks or sweet dishes.

Tabasco: Pepper sauce. Use with discretion. Acts as a catalyst in bringing out food flavors.

Soy Sauce: Soy flavored sauce used in Far Eastern cooking.

Maggi: Hydrolyzed plant proteins with water and salt added. Emphasizes natural flavors of food and restores flavors lost in cooking.

Vinegar: Taste vinegar before using to test its' acidity because it evaporates when standing. Add water if it is too acid.

> *Cider*: Made from apples. Natural American vinegar.
>
> *Red Wine*: Basic for French dressing. Heavier in flavor than white wine vinegar.
>
> *White Wine*: For light salads, fish and white meat.
>
> *Rice*: Super for fish and fruit salads and Oriental cooking.
>
> *Herb Flavored*: Garlic, tarragon and a multitude of others. Fine for salads and cooking.

Chutney: Mixture of seasoned tropical fruits. Used as a condiment with curries and for cooking. Major Grey's Chutney is the one you'll most likely find in your grocer's shelf and is considered the best.

Starches and flours

Arrowroot: Most delicate starch. Transparent. Used for binding delicate sauces such as hollandaise. Breaks down if cooked for a long period of time. Good for diet cooking.

Cornstarch: Used primarily in puddings and desserts.

Potato starch: For binding sauces, soups and fondues.

Rice: Light textured. Does not break down (as arrowroot will) when used in delicate sauces that must be cooked for a long period of time.

Wheat: Hard or durem: For bread making. High in gluten. Soft: For cake mixing and light pastries.

All purpose flour: Combination of soft and hard wheat flour that has been homogenized for general cooking and baking.

Self rising flour: Used only for baking. Has baking powder already added.

Oils

All oils can be used interchangeably for salads, baking, cooking and frying. Each has a different flavor and one may complement a specific recipe more than another.

Vegetable: Usually a corn oil. To dilute olive oil or used alone for special diet cooking. Low in calories, high in vitamins.

Crisco: Liquid vegetable oil.

Wesson: Combination peanut vegetable and soy oil.

Peanut: Liquid peanut oil. Distinctive flavor.

Safflower: Oil from Safflower seeds. Often prescribed for use in special diets because of its high vitamin content.

Olive: Standby of the world. Flavor depends on the area in which the olives are grown.

Walnut: Used a great deal in England and France.

Fats

Lard: Fat rendered from pork. Used mostly for pastry.
Hydrogenated Crisco: Solidified vegetable oil.
Salt Butter: Made from sour cream. Tart flavor.
Sweet Butter: Made from sweet cream. Sweet flavor.
Chicken Fat: Fat rendered from chicken.

Sugars

Different forms of sweetening perform specific jobs and possess distinctive flavors. They are listed below in order of refinement.

Molasses: Raw form of granulated sugar. Still in liquid form. Has strong flavor.

Dark brown: Early granulated form of sugar. Strong, but milder than molasses.

Light brown: Lighter in flavor than dark brown.

Granulated white: Most commonly used sugar. Refined and bleached.

Granulated Fruit: Very fine.

Confectioners or Four-X: Powdered sugar with starch. Primarily used for icings and pastry.

Lump: Dark brown sugar in loaf shape. Cut or break as needed for use. Used often in Cafe Brilliot.

Honey: Natural fruit and flower sugar in liquid form.

Cooking wines and spirits

Since the flavor of the wine is all that remains after cooking with it, you must use good wines and spirits — never inferior, cheap wines, to get good flavor. Don't go overboard and buy imported vintage wine. Domestic wines will do just fine, and they're inexpensive. Or you can use left over table wines or even a little of the wine you plan to serve with your meal to complement your recipe.

Below is a list of the basic wines and spirits you will need in your kitchen. For a superb wine guide, see *Grossman's Guide to Wines, Spirits and Beers* by Harold J. Grossman, Charles Scribner, Publisher.

Red and White Dry Wine: Dry means little or no sugar content. The basic cooking wines are:

White: Chablis   Red: Burgundy

Dry and Sweet Sherries: Used for soups, seafoods, newburgs, compotes and charlottes.

Madeira: Dry fortified sherry. Wonderful with fruits and game sauces.

Marsala: Sweet and dry. Dry is best known for veal marsala and sweet for sabayon sauce.

Rum: Light and dark are interchangeable according to the mood and spirit of the dish. Wonderful in chocolate dishes and friut.

Kirsch: White liqueur made from black cherries. Best comes from Southern Germany or Switzerland. Used with fruits, pastry and fondues.

Brandy: Used for flaming in many meat and poultry recipes and adds flavor to soups, sauces and desserts.

Grand Marnier: Orange flavored brandy used for fruits, desserts and duck.

Cointreau: Made from Seville oranges. More bitter than Grand Marnier but used in many of the same dishes.

Creme de Cacao: Chocolate flavored liqueur used in chocolate mousse and for after dinner drinking.

Creame de Menthe: Mint flavored liqueur used to make wonderful after-dinner drinks called grasshoppers. Chocolate mint mousses can't be beat either.

Onions

Everybody has a favorite remedy for tearless onion peeling and chopping. Here's our simple solution. Just breathe through your mouth rather than your nose. It's the sulfur fumes from the outer skin of the onion that irritate your nasal passages and makes you tear. Chilling the onions in the freezer for five to ten minutes before peeling also helps, but be sure not to freeze them.

Below is a list of onions and some of their cousins you'll need in your kitchen.

White: Basic, hot-flavored cooking onion.

Yellow: Milder, sweeter flavor than white.

Bermuda: Sweeter than yellow. Known as the hamburger onion.

Spanish or Italian: Red, mild-flavored onion with the exception of those from California which are hotter. Often used as a substitute for shallots.

Leeks: Elongated white onion. Most often used to give soup flavor.

Shallots: Queen of the onions. Their delicate flavor used often for sauces and fish. Should never be browned because they become bitter.

Pearl: Small, white, mild-flavored onions used often in stews and soups.

Spring onions or Scallions: Often mistakenly called shallots. Used in salads and as a relish or braised.

Chives: The green leaves of the bulb are cut and added to soups, sauces, meats, fish and vegetables. Delicate flavor.

Garlic: Universally known onion flavor. Should be used with discretion. Do not expose to high heats and long periods of cooking.

Leafy green vegetables

When you go to the market, look around and see what greens are in season, what is new and fresh, and what you haven't tried before. Be adventurous. Mix combinations of lettuce that you've never put together and I'll bet the tastes you'll get will surprise and please you. The lettuces listed below are not a complete list of all leafy green vegetables, but are those that I use most often. Be sure to buy prime quality. Tired lettuce of any variety tastes like it looks.

Watercress: Peppery taste. Used in salads or soups and sauces. Wonderful with game. When you wash the watercress, be sure to look for and pick off snails that sometimes stick to these greens.

Bibb lettuce: Known also as Kentucky Limestone. Considered the queen of lettuces. Has a delicate nutty flavor, and is good as a salad by itself. Bibb lettuce is especially sandy. To remove the sand, wash first in large quantities of lukewarm water to loosen the dirt. Agitate vigorously. Shake and soak in cold water to refreshen the leaves. Remove excess water, but do not dry lettuce completely. Put in the refrigerator in plastic bags.

Iceberg or Head Lettuce: Most commonly used as a basic salad filler.

Belgian Endive: Its yelow white leaves have a wonderful flavor and complement more bland lettuces. May be cooked as a vegetable.

Romaine: Use tender, inner green leaves. Outer leaves are tough. Pungent flavor. Used for Caesar salad. Wash as you do bibb.

Savory Cabbage: Finest of the cabbage family for salads and cooking. Light green and curly.

Parsley: Chinese parsley is the most often used variety. It is curly and milder than Italian parsley which is flat leafed and stronger in flavor.

Boston: Softer textured lettuce. Used in salads or soups. Braised with French peas is a delightful treat.

Spinach: May be used raw in salads or cooked as a vegetable. Wash as you do bibb.

Refrigerator and freezer — use space on top of refrigerator for large equipment.

Butcher block — knives suspended from hooks on side. Cooking wines and liqueurs on top.

Adequate lighting over working areas.

Exhaust and ventilation system.

Double oven, six-burner gas range with broiler — otherwise known as a restaurant range.

Wooden work table — heavy-duty hard maple. Portable chopping block on work table.

Dining table can also be used as a planning desk.

Hanging pot rack should be close to the stove or sink for easy access. Magnetic Knife Bar.

Decorative crocks and buckets full of wooden spoons, whisks, spatulas, mallets, ladles, et cetera. Have herbs and spices handy on trays nearby.

Shelf underneath work table for convenient storage of often-used ingredients and equipment.

Open storage shelf hangs over the sink for cleaning supplies. Paper towels are under the shelf.

Triple sink with disposal and drain boards. Have garbage can or trash compacter in same location.

Portable Working Cart.

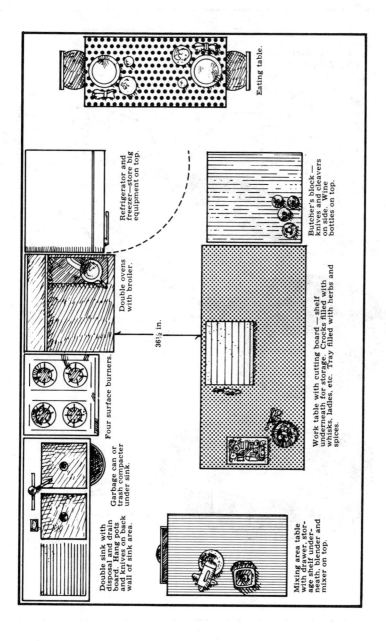

Eating table.

Refrigerator and freezer—store big equipment on top.

Double ovens with broiler.

Four surface burners.

Garbage can or trash compacter under sink.

Double sink with disposal and drain board. Hang pots and knives on back wall of sink area.

Mixing area table with drawer, storage shelf underneath, blender and mixer on top.

36½ in.

Butcher's block — knives and cleavers on side. Wine bottles on top.

Work table with cutting board — shelf underneath for storage. Crocks filled with whisks, ladles, etc. Tray filled with herbs and spices.

Chef's skillet: 10" diameter with rounded sides for sauteing vegetables. fish and meats. May be aluminum or enameled iron. Handy for quick white sauces because these metals never discolor the sauce.

Steel omelet or crepe pan: I prefer a 5" diameter. This pan is a luxury since it is used only for crepes and omelettes. Never, never wash it. Wipe out with paper towels after using.

Black cast iron frying pan: Nothing is better for browning than this good old standby. Gives fried foods a golden brown color.

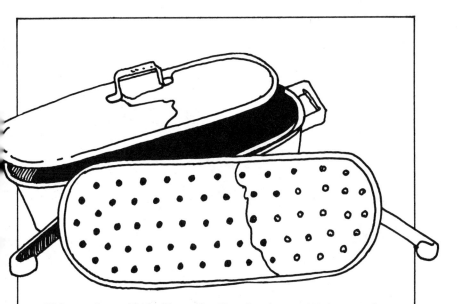

Fish poacher with inside rack: May be tin or stainless steel or copper. Primarily for poaching fish but can be used also for large quantities of vegetables, spaghetti or noodles. It is a good icer for wines at large parties or can serve as an attractive table decoration filled with flowers and fruit.

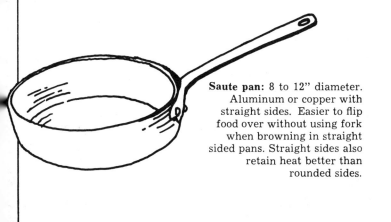

Saute pan: 8 to 12" diameter. Aluminum or copper with straight sides. Easier to flip food over without using fork when browning in straight sided pans. Straight sides also retain heat better than rounded sides.

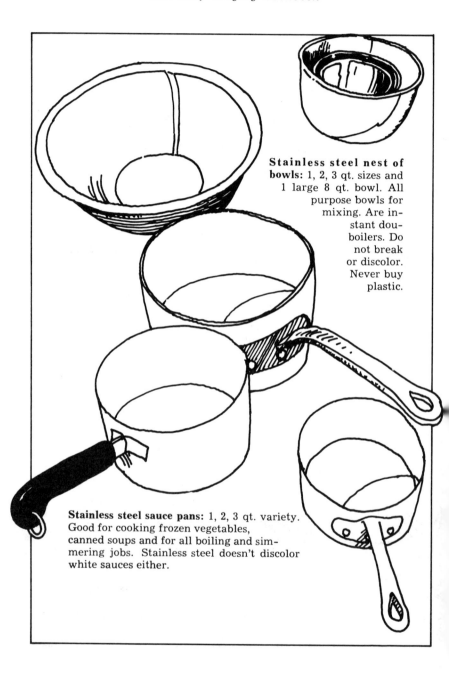

Stainless steel nest of bowls: 1, 2, 3 qt. sizes and 1 large 8 qt. bowl. All purpose bowls for mixing. Are instant double-boilers. Do not break or discolor. Never buy plastic.

Stainless steel sauce pans: 1, 2, 3 qt. variety. Good for cooking frozen vegetables, canned soups and for all boiling and simmering jobs. Stainless steel doesn't discolor white sauces either.

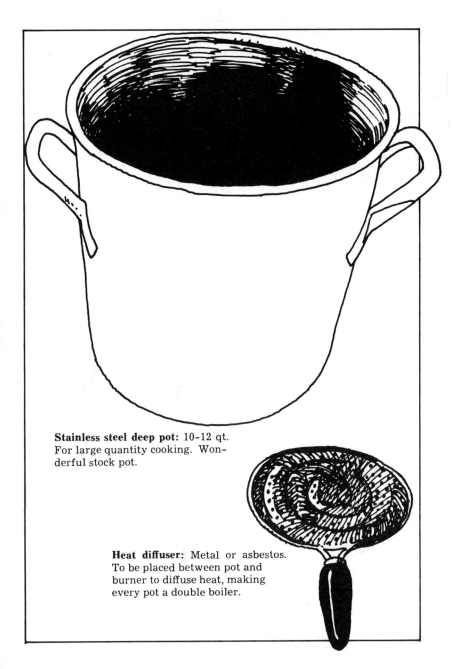

Stainless steel deep pot: 10-12 qt. For large quantity cooking. Wonderful stock pot.

Heat diffuser: Metal or asbestos. To be placed between pot and burner to diffuse heat, making every pot a double boiler.

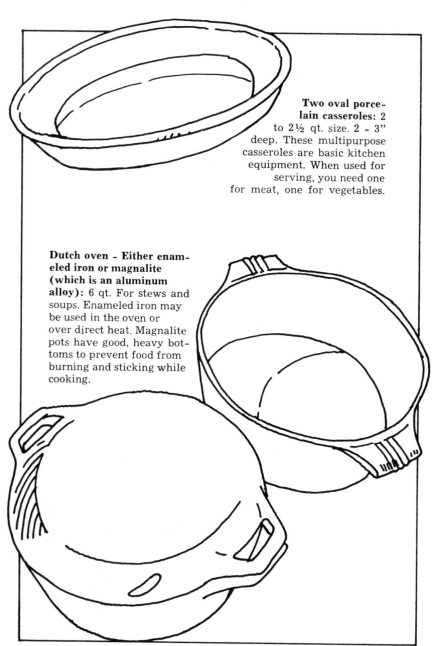

Two oval porcelain casseroles: 2 to 2½ qt. size. 2 - 3" deep. These multipurpose casseroles are basic kitchen equipment. When used for serving, you need one for meat, one for vegetables.

Dutch oven - Either enameled iron or magnalite (which is an aluminum alloy): 6 qt. For stews and soups. Enameled iron may be used in the oven or over direct heat. Magnalite pots have good, heavy bottoms to prevent food from burning and sticking while cooking.

Quiche dish: 10" diameter, 2-3 inches deep. Tin has removable bottom for easy removal of quiche. Porcelain does not have a removable bottom and is a handsome server if you wish to leave the quiche in the pan.

Marmite or earthenware soup pot: 6 to 8 qt. For stews and soups. Earthenware cooks food more slowly, giving better flavor. When new, rub the inside with garlic, fill with water, add an onion, celery and a carrot. Cover and bake in 300° oven for 2-3 hours. This will remove the earth flavor from pottery.

Wire whisks or whips: One 10-12" balloon piano wire whisk for beating egg whites or whipping cream in copper bowl. Heavier wire whisks needed for stirring soups and sauces.

Copper beating bowl: For beating egg whites and whipping cream. Prime requirement for successsful souffles and meringues.

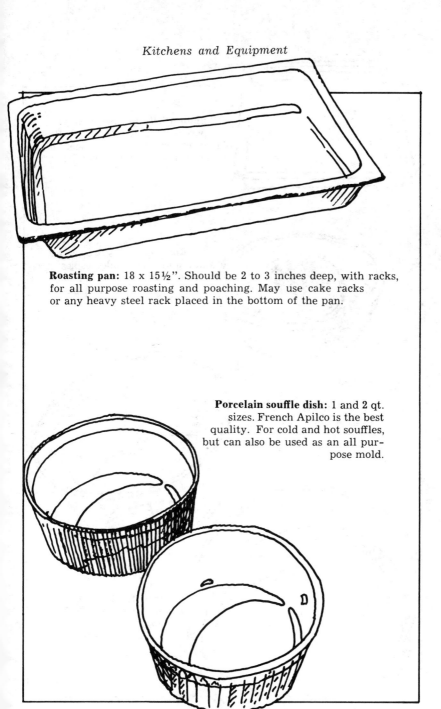

Roasting pan: 18 x 15½". Should be 2 to 3 inches deep, with racks, for all purpose roasting and poaching. May use cake racks or any heavy steel rack placed in the bottom of the pan.

Porcelain souffle dish: 1 and 2 qt. sizes. French Apilco is the best quality. For cold and hot souffles, but can also be used as an all purpose mold.

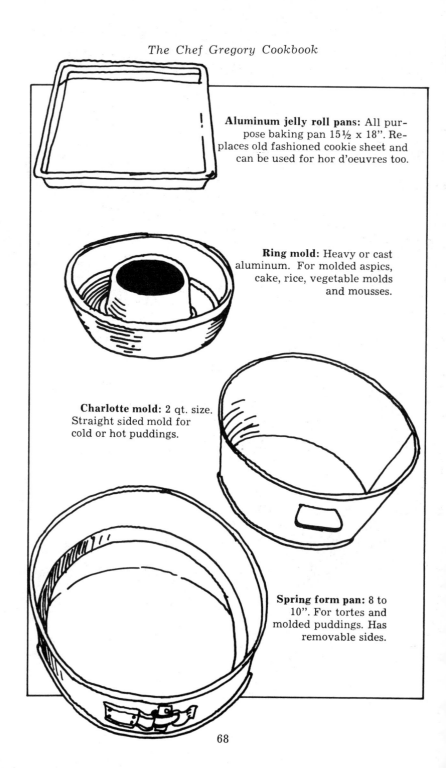

Aluminum jelly roll pans: All purpose baking pan 15½ x 18". Replaces old fashioned cookie sheet and can be used for hor d'oeuvres too.

Ring mold: Heavy or cast aluminum. For molded aspics, cake, rice, vegetable molds and mousses.

Charlotte mold: 2 qt. size. Straight sided mold for cold or hot puddings.

Spring form pan: 8 to 10". For tortes and molded puddings. Has removable sides.

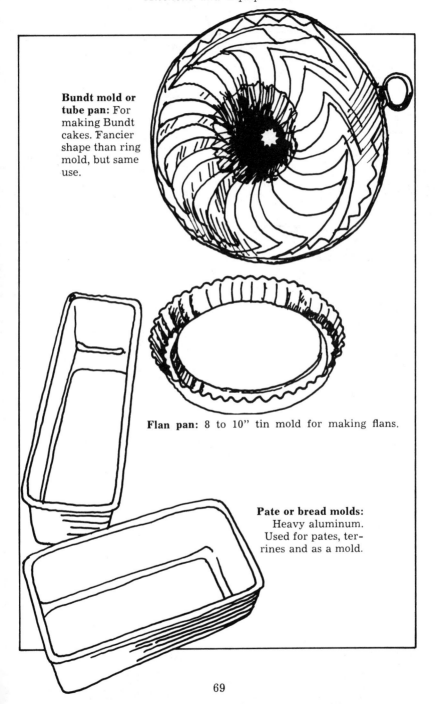

Bundt mold or tube pan: For making Bundt cakes. Fancier shape than ring mold, but same use.

Flan pan: 8 to 10" tin mold for making flans.

Pate or bread molds: Heavy aluminum. Used for pates, terrines and as a mold.

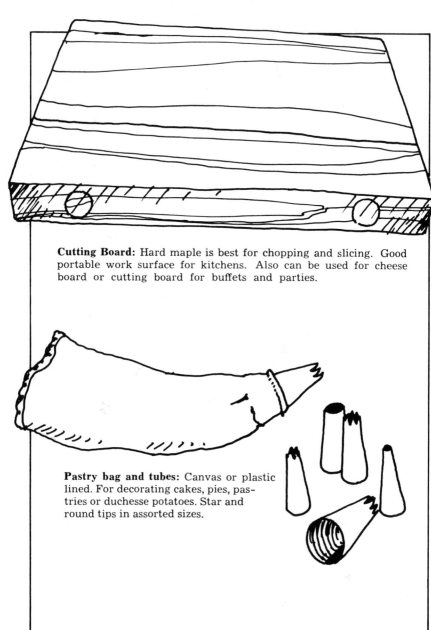

Cutting Board: Hard maple is best for chopping and slicing. Good portable work surface for kitchens. Also can be used for cheese board or cutting board for buffets and parties.

Pastry bag and tubes: Canvas or plastic lined. For decorating cakes, pies, pastries or duchesse potatoes. Star and round tips in assorted sizes.

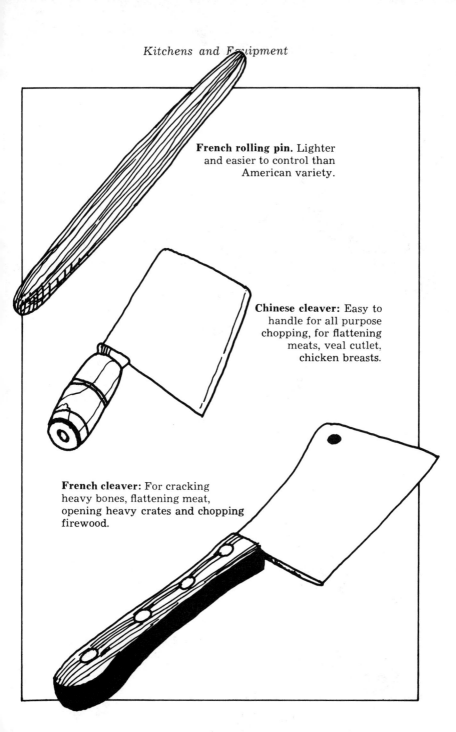

French rolling pin. Lighter and easier to control than American variety.

Chinese cleaver: Easy to handle for all purpose chopping, for flattening meats, veal cutlet, chicken breasts.

French cleaver: For cracking heavy bones, flattening meat, opening heavy crates and chopping firewood.

Chef's knife: 8-10" stainless steel or 10-12" carbon steel. Buy so that the weight and length is comfortable for your hand. It is the basic tool for chopping and slicing. Stainless steel is easier to clean but harder to sharpen. Carbon steel holds the best edge, but discolors or rusts if not washed immediately after using.

Paring knives: Should have at least two for peeling, cutting and trimming.

Serrated knife: For slicing bread, meats, fruit, tomatoes.

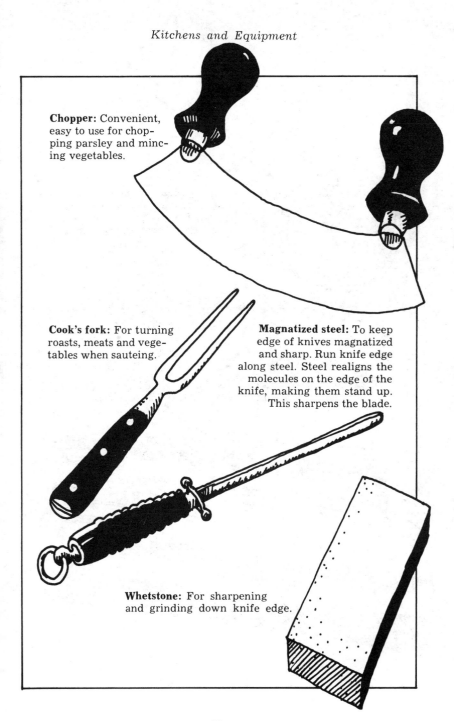

Chopper: Convenient, easy to use for chopping parsley and mincing vegetables.

Cook's fork: For turning roasts, meats and vegetables when sauteing.

Magnatized steel: To keep edge of knives magnatized and sharp. Run knife edge along steel. Steel realigns the molecules on the edge of the knife, making them stand up. This sharpens the blade.

Whetstone: For sharpening and grinding down knife edge.

73

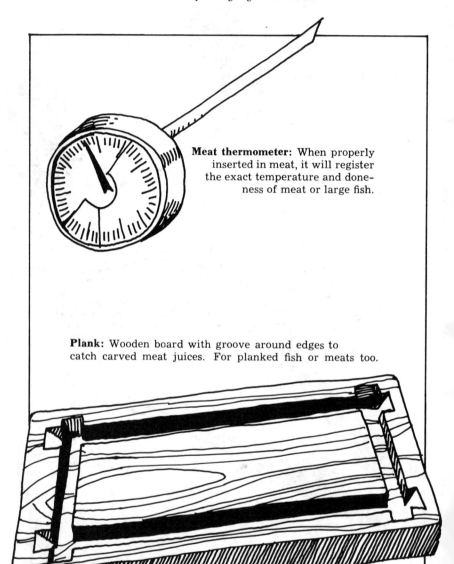

Meat thermometer: When properly inserted in meat, it will register the exact temperature and doneness of meat or large fish.

Plank: Wooden board with groove around edges to catch carved meat juices. For planked fish or meats too.

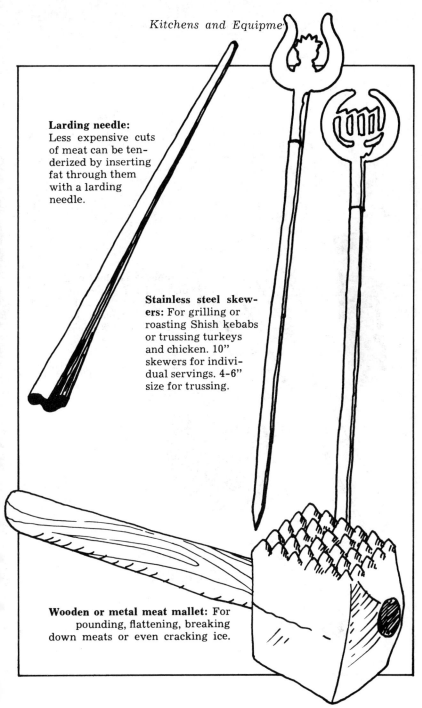

Larding needle:
Less expensive cuts
of meat can be ten-
derized by inserting
fat through them
with a larding
needle.

**Stainless steel skew-
ers:** For grilling or
roasting Shish kebabs
or trussing turkeys
and chicken. 10"
skewers for indivi-
dual servings. 4-6"
size for trussing.

Wooden or metal meat mallet: For
pounding, flattening, breaking
down meats or even cracking ice.

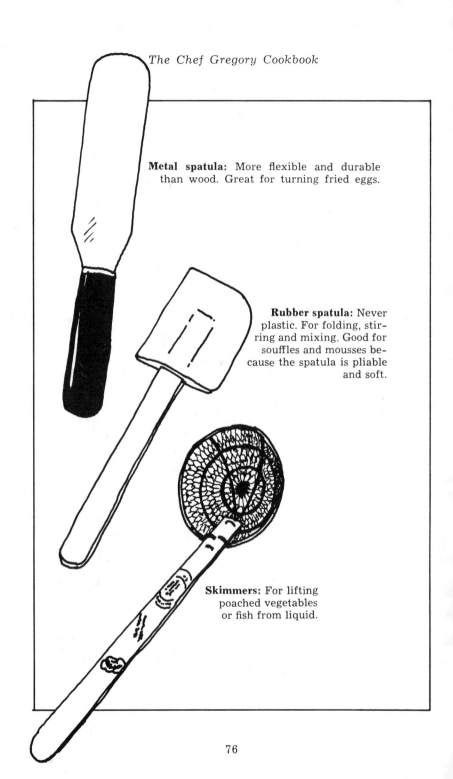

Metal spatula: More flexible and durable than wood. Great for turning fried eggs.

Rubber spatula: Never plastic. For folding, stirring and mixing. Good for souffles and mousses because the spatula is pliable and soft.

Skimmers: For lifting poached vegetables or fish from liquid.

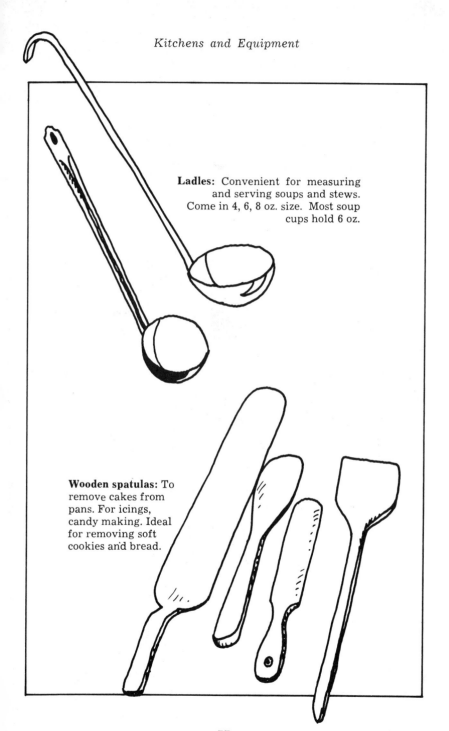

Ladles: Convenient for measuring and serving soups and stews. Come in 4, 6, 8 oz. size. Most soup cups hold 6 oz.

Wooden spatulas: To remove cakes from pans. For icings, candy making. Ideal for removing soft cookies and bread.

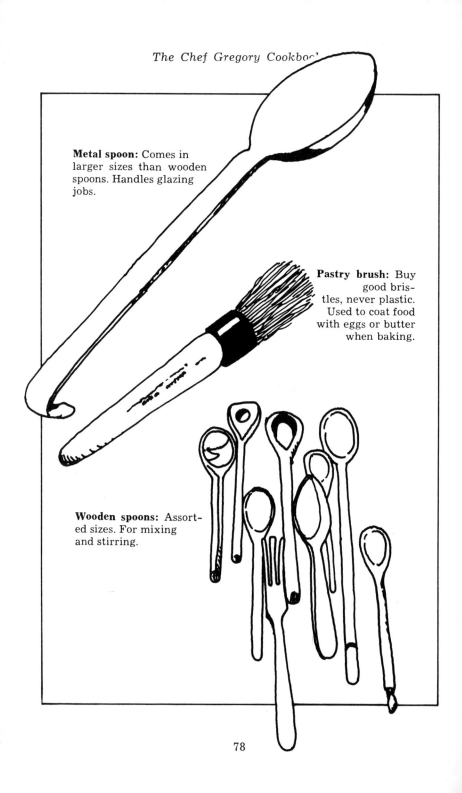

Metal spoon: Comes in larger sizes than wooden spoons. Handles glazing jobs.

Pastry brush: Buy good bristles, never plastic. Used to coat food with eggs or butter when baking.

Wooden spoons: Assorted sizes. For mixing and stirring.

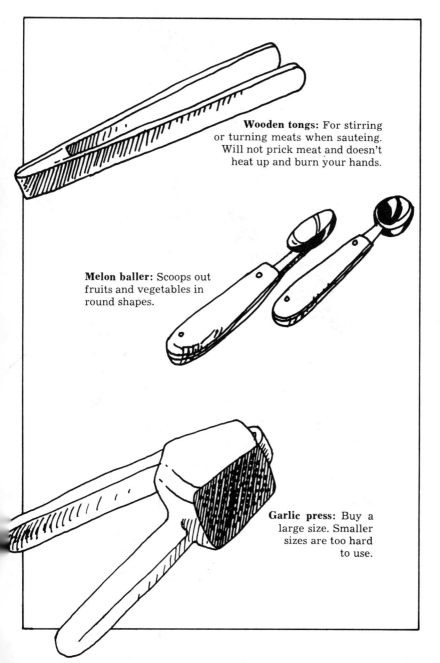

Wooden tongs: For stirring or turning meats when sauteing. Will not prick meat and doesn't heat up and burn your hands.

Melon baller: Scoops out fruits and vegetables in round shapes.

Garlic press: Buy a large size. Smaller sizes are too hard to use.

Apple corer: To remove cores of apples and other fruits.

French peeler: Peels thin skinned fruits and vegetables and can be used to make carrot curls.

Lemon stripper: Easy way to peel fruit.

Pepper grinder: To grind whole peppercorns so that you can enjoy freshly ground pepper at all times. You need one grinder for black and one for white pepper. Don't skimp. Buy a good French grinder.

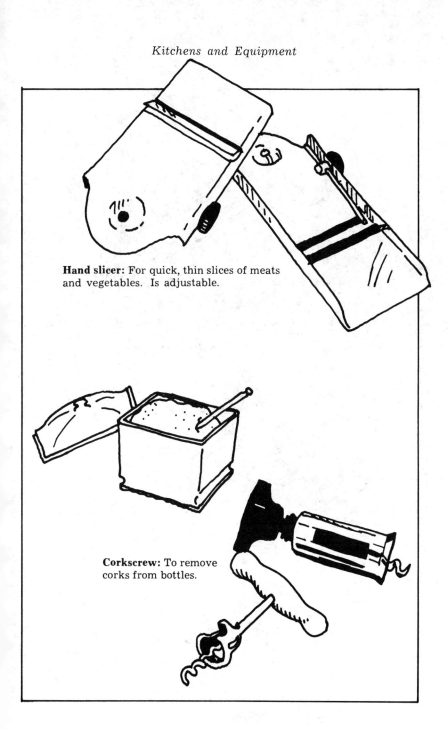

Hand slicer: For quick, thin slices of meats and vegetables. Is adjustable.

Corkscrew: To remove corks from bottles.

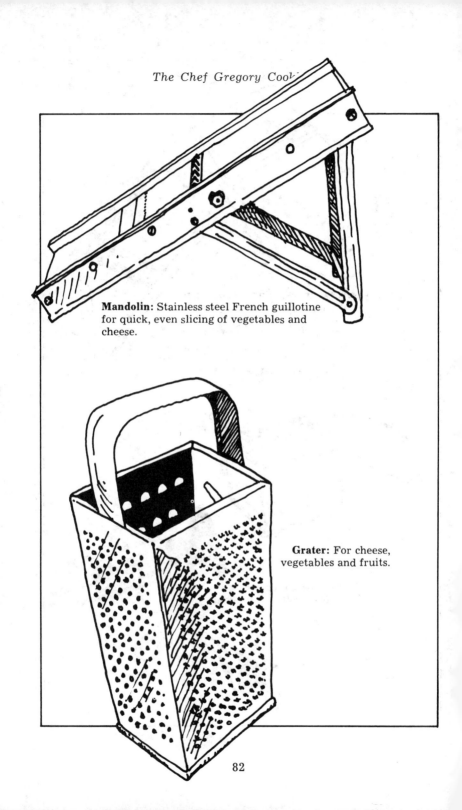

Mandolin: Stainless steel French guillotine for quick, even slicing of vegetables and cheese.

Grater: For cheese, vegetables and fruits.

Blender: Buy at least a 6 cup or 1½ qt. heavy duty blender. It's a great labor and time saver when you are cooking for a large number of people. Chopping by hand takes hours in quantity cooking. Blenders can puree, chop and blend as well as crush ice for drinks.

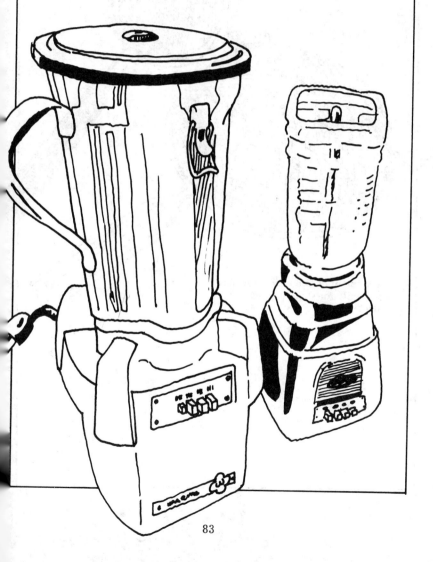

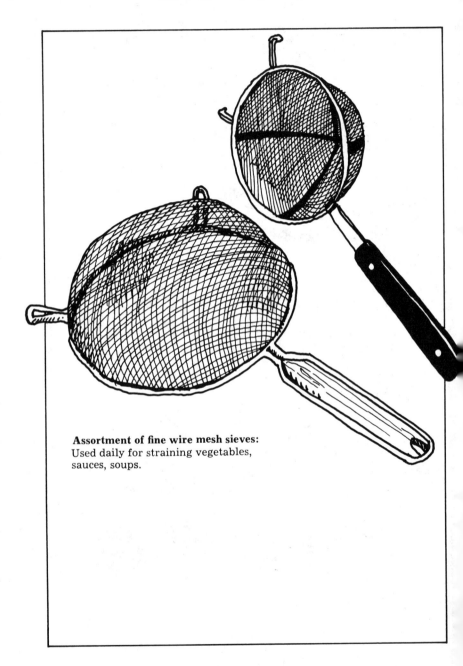

Assortment of fine wire mesh sieves:
Used daily for straining vegetables,
sauces, soups.

Four quart colander: Most popular household size.

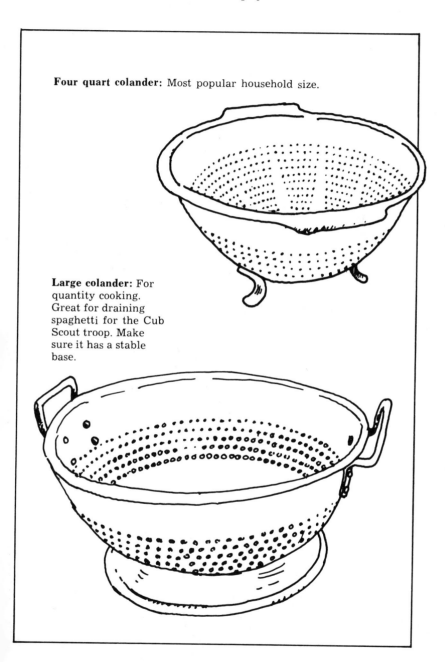

Large colander: For quantity cooking. Great for draining spaghetti for the Cub Scout troop. Make sure it has a stable base.

Mixer: A Kitchen Aid 4-6 qt. heavy duty mixer is the best. Attachments are a dough hook, paddle, wire whisk and grinder.

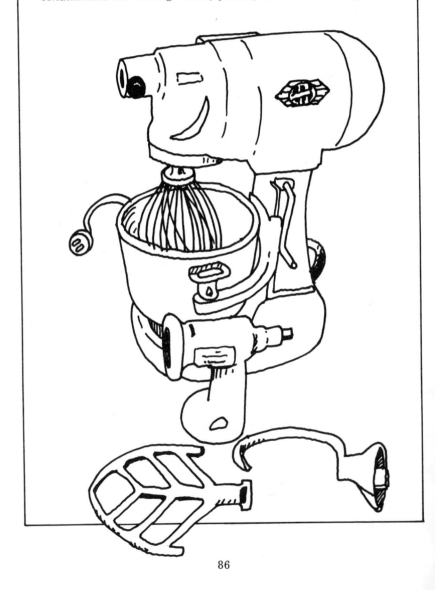

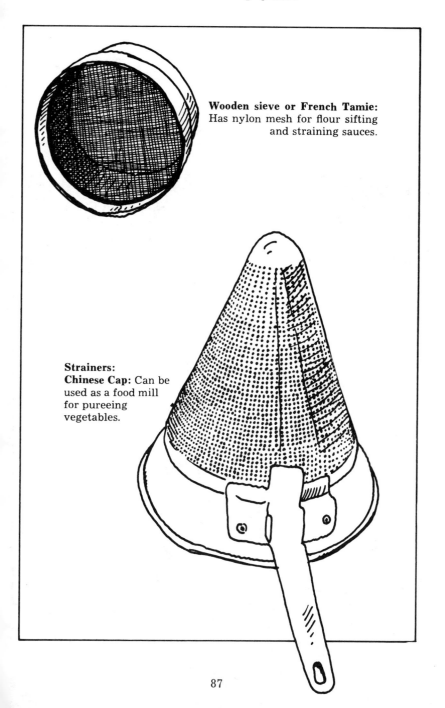

Wooden sieve or French Tamie:
Has nylon mesh for flour sifting
and straining sauces.

Strainers:
Chinese Cap: Can be
used as a food mill
for pureeing
vegetables.

5
How to Entertain

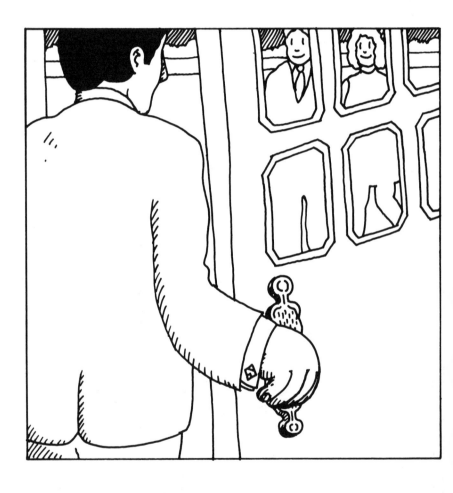

Entertaining takes planning. Here's how to begin. Look around your home and try to picture how many people you can comfortably entertain. How many people can sit in your living room? How many people can mill around and get to a bar area during a cocktail party? The size of your home determines the size of your party as well as the kind of party — formal or informal — you can give. If your house is small, an informal party where people can sit on the floor, on the steps, on cushions is right for you. (Or have smaller groups of people.) If you have more space, you probably have room for tables where people can eat or you can just have more people and be flexible.

But do remember that it is disastrous to have more people than you can comfortably accommodate. Not only will your guests be uncomfortable, but if you have help, it will be impossible for them to serve efficiently.

Even at an informal party, try to have tables scattered around, since it's awfully hard to balance a plate on your lap, handle a knife and fork, and manage a glass of wine, too. At more formal dinners, don't seat more people at tables than is comfortable. Besides being elbowed to death, it becomes almost impossible to squeeze between people to serve and remove dishes from the table.

Now that you're aware of your space, you are ready to take inventory of your cooking equipment, china and silver so that you know what you have to work with. Make sure everything is in good repair and ready to use. Keep an inventory book if you have a variety of equipment so that you will know exactly what you have and where it is.

If you have two or three dozen plates, you can entertain large groups of people easily. It isn't necessary that they match. In fact, it is much more interesting to mix simply designed dinner plates with more ornate salad or dessert size plates or vice versa. The change of pattern on your table can be lovely.

If you aren't equipped? For large parties, good quality plastic plates, forks and glasses are quite acceptable. These can go into the dishwasher and will hold up well for five or six washings. Besides, they're much cheaper than renting china.

Good quality paper napkins are fine, too. The linen napkins that you rent are usually pretty terrible, so if you don't have dozens of linen napkins, pick up some pretty paper ones. The more interestingly designed ones can add to the excitement of your table setting, too.

Check out your wine glasses. An eight to ten ounce wine glass of classic design can be used for a variety of jobs. You don't have to spend a fortune on fancy wine glasses of different varieties. Go to a restaurant supply house. They have a stock of inexpensive glasses and if you buy a classic design, they can be used for fruit compotes, seafood cocktails, cold soups, parfait desserts, and Irish coffee. Need I say more? It's a great investment. Buy a few dozen.

A most important part of your inventory is the capacity of your stove. How many ovens you have and the number of burners you can operate all determine the number of guests you can best serve.

A traumatic experience you should avoid at all costs is to find that all your casseroles can't be heated in the oven, and that you have no place to set things down in your kitchen. Electric hot trays and frying pans come in handy for parties, especially if you only have one oven. Make a blueprint, listing what you will need for serving and how you will serve what. Check off where casseroles will be placed and where food will be heated so you can plan your space efficiently.

Don't forget to measure your refrigerator and freezer space. Make sure the space available is adequate to store the food you will prepare. If you cook in larger quantities than you can store in your refrigerator, what will you do? Plan ahead!

Now that your equipment is checked, and you've noted what you have, what you will need to buy, and you are aware of your space, you're ready to plan your menu.

If you know your guests well, take their likes and dislikes into consideration. If you don't know the people coming, especially older people, ask them if they have any dietary restrictions you should observe to make the party more pleasant for them.

Plan a menu you can handle easily in accordance with your experience and the help you will or will not have. When you are doing all of the work yourself, prepare a menu that is simple in structure — one that can be done ahead of time so that you are free from last minute preparation. I am not a great advocate of freezing finished dishes or casseroles, but there are times when it is necessary.

Almost everything can be prepared the day before the party and refrigerated. This is the most successful way to retain the quality of the food.

My basic rule is to have a few things done beautifully, with imagination, ease, and thorough well-thought-out service.

After you have decided on your menu, make out a shopping list. Divide the list of ingredients into the stores you have to shop to find them and then double check to make sure you haven't forgotten anything.

What amount of food to buy is sometimes a problem. Usually the recipes you are using will tell you what quantities of food to buy, but a few general rules may make your shopping easier.

Well trimmed meat: eight to ten ounces per serving.
Ground beef: eight ounces per person.
All chops: eight to twelve ounces per person.
Sliced cold meat combinations: six to eight ounces per person.
Veal scallops or cutlets: four to six ounces per serving.
Ham: eight to twelve ounces per person.
A 2½ to 3 pound frying chicken: two to three servings.
One duck will serve two people.
Bone in fish: six to eight ounces per person as an entree.
Shellfish and boneless fish: four to six ounces per serving.
Live lobsters: 1½ to 2½ pounds per serving.
Vegetables: separate or in combinations — four to six ounces per person.

Salad greens: one pound will yield four to six servings. *Cheeses*: two or three ounces per person to go with salad or as a dessert.

The kind of party you are having often determines how much food per person you should plan on serving. If you are feeding people after a football game, their appetites may be a lot larger than after a symphony. And who's coming is a deciding factor, too. A pound of spinach will feed two adults or seventy children. Plan accordingly.

When you return with all the goodies you are ready to begin cooking.

You may successfully double recipes in cooking, but do not try more than that at one time. Most household equipment cannot hold larger quantities and the burners on your stove are not usually big enough to heat huge pots. Prepare several smaller batches in quantities easy for you to handle. Most casseroles serve ten to twelve persons, so you can take them from the oven to your table and have hot, appetizing food throughout the party.

As we mentioned earlier, and as Escoffier said best — "People eat as much with their eyes as they do with their palates." Now that you have your menu and your shopping and planning are done, you must next plan how to make your party beautiful.

Some of the most memorable parties I can think of are ones where the host or hostess combined the decorations and the food. The decorations set the mood of the party. They don't have to be elaborate. You can use color, or flowers or some unusual motif to make your party special.

I love fresh flowers and plants and often wonder how people survive without them. I especially like to use wild flowers. Many of these dry beautifully for winter use. Combine some fresh flowers with the dried ones for a delightful table effect.

Use your own sculpture or collections of interesting objects (rocks, shells, candles, ad infinitum) for table centerpieces. They give the party your personal touch. For instance, I made centerpieces for a party for new people who had moved to our neighborhood by arranging antique copper molds, fresh fruit and candles. It stimulated conversation and put everyone at ease.

On a June evening in our garden, I used nothing but German and American flags and hundreds of candles of all sizes for my wife's citizenship party. I asked our guests to come dressed in red, white and blue and the party was spectacular.

Remember that flowers do not show up at night unless they are well lighted. One or two strategically placed arrangements in a well lighted place will do the job.

Pastel colors also fade at night and in artificial light. Remember to use stronger colors under these circumstances.

Put your creative mind to work. Look around your house. You'll be surprised at the ideas that will pop up.

You'll be a smashing success.

Specific dinner details

Below, you'll find descriptions of the four most common ways people entertain at dinners. You may wish to follow them or do variations of them as fits your situation and inclination.

Formal sit-down dinner: A well executed sit-down dinner in strictly formal fashion is a rare treat today. Most households do not have the equipment, the space, and the staff to produce such a fancy event, and besides there are few hardy souls left who have the capacity to endure a five course meal and the wines that accompany it.

On the rare occasion you have a formal dinner, have as much prepared in advance as possible.

Arrange your bar and cocktail area well ahead of time. Have your glasses ready, your liquor out, your mixes made, and your napkins handy.

The china, silver, and serving pieces for each course should be arranged in sequence in the kitchen. If necessary, label each group so that you are super-organized.

Have all garnishes and sauces in the containers in which they will be served arranged and ready for the course they go with.

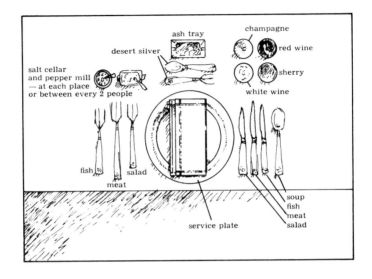

The white and sparkling wines should be chilled at 45-50° (takes about three hours in the refrigerator) with wine openers close by. Red wine should be opened about an hour in advance to give it a chance to breathe. It should be served at room temperature, from 60 to 70°.

The coffee and liqueur trays should be arranged with the necessary china and glasses and silver. Make sure cream and sugar are handy, too.

The table may be set with the silver and glasses for all the courses. Check our diagram for a complete service. When you have set the table, recheck it to make sure everything is there. It's a good idea to have someone else check to see if everything is O.K. It's surprising how you can overlook an item no matter how careful you are.

The courses are usually served in the following order: soup, fish, meat or fowl along with vegetables, salad and cheese, dessert, and coffee. White wine is served with the fish course, red wine with meat, and champagne with dessert. If you have chicken as your main course use the white wine from the first course for the second course, too. Dry sherry may be substituted for the white wine used in first course on occasion.

I am not fond of using bread and butter plates. I prefer hard rolls placed in napkins in the European manner or rolls passed during dinner. The only time I serve butter is with a cheese course. The butter is put on the cheese tray and the guests serve themselves when the cheese is passed. The cheese course usually is combined with the salad course, and served at this time will refresh your palate before dessert.

I do not serve coffee at the table. After the guests have finished their desserts, I like to serve coffee in another room, to provide a break in the evening, to allow guests to regroup and to have a chance to clear the dining table.

Providing both caffinated and decaffinated coffee is a nice touch and after coffee is finished, brandy and liquors are passed. What a beautiful evening!

Modified sit-down dinner: A more moderate dinner is more common and easier on everyone involved. To begin with, the setting is simpler. You use only one wine glass and less silver since you aren't going to serve so many courses. A main course, vegetables, salad, rolls, dessert, wine, good conversation and good friends make a delightful dinner. Enjoy yourself!

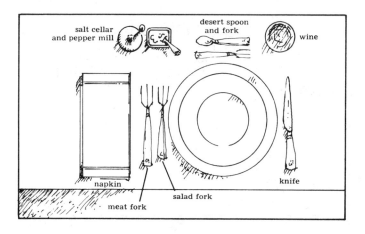

Partial buffet: Partial buffets seem to be the easiest for people to produce today. The first course is on the table when the guests are seated and is removed when they are finished. The main course is laid out on a buffet (have heated plates) and the guests serve themselves. Wine may be placed on coasters on the table so that guests can serve themselves. When the main course is finished, the plates are cleared, the hostess brings dessert to the table, serves it, and passes it around the table to each guest. Coffee is usually served in another room. If one of your guests offers to pour coffee for you, accept, and it will give you time to slip away and clear your dining table. Everyone will be taken care of in the living room, and you can organize the used plates in the kitchen. This is an easy, unpressured, popular way to entertain.

Buffet: For bigger parties, a buffet is fine. The table should be set as shown below. People serve themselves and eat on their laps, trays, tables or wherever they can find a spot. In such a fluid style of entertaining, try to plan a menu that is easy

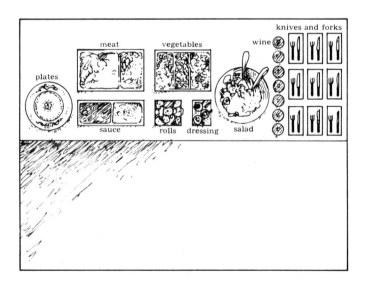

for your guests to eat. It's awfully hard to cut meat on a plate on your lap. How about a chicken casserole with the chicken cut into bite size pieces? Your guests will love you. Wine can be poured ahead of time and placed on the buffet table in glasses so your guests can pick them up as they come through the line or can be placed in carafes and poured by the guests. Put dessert and coffee on another table so your guests can serve themselves when they are ready; or clear your original buffet table and put coffee and dessert there. This is an easy, informal way to entertain lots of people, but don't get carried away and jam too many people together. That makes for a claustrophobic experience! If buffets are done well, they can be lots of fun.

6
Menus

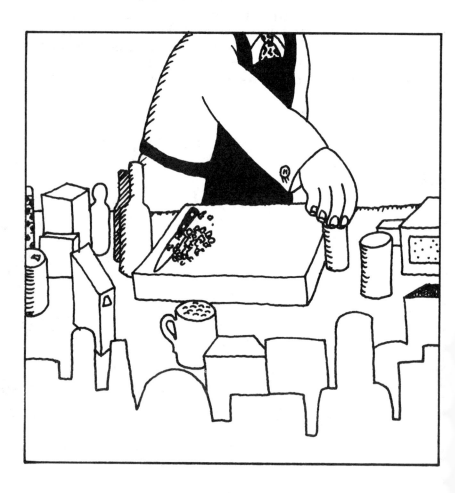

How much salt and pepper?

Salt and pepper are not listed in the recipes in specific quantities. I feel that salt and pepper should be used as a balance, and as such added at the end of a recipe to correct the taste of what you are cooking.

If you add salt first, it may cook down and be too concentrated. And remember, when you cook with wine, you should always use less salt.

So taste what you are cooking, and add salt and pepper according to your own preference. It's much better than adding salt and pepper at the beginning and not liking the taste of what you cooked. Then it's too late to change!

Be French in your thinking and correct the seasoning with salt and pepper at the end.

Using the Index

We have included many recipes with sauces that are interchangeable, many dishes that can be served with a variety of noodles or rice, and lots of desserts with various sauces.

For instance, French fried lamb chops can be served with Bearnaise sauce, snail butter, or Madeira sauce. We have mentioned these along with the recipe for lamb chops. You can find the page on which directions for these recipes are given by looking in the index.

Certain procedures such as poaching fish, peeling tomatoes and applying egg wash to pastry must be followed in many recipes. These may be found in the index, too.

Rather than give the recipes for these sauces and procedures each time they are needed, we have given them only once and mentioned them wherever applicable. The recipes for everything are all there — just look them up!

Wine

I have listed wines with each menu. Some fall into general categories of wines, and with others, I've listed specific vintages or manufacturers. You should substitute as you wish.

(The fun is in the testing.) These listed are some tried and true favorites of mine.

Where you see this mark ⟨🕛⟩ in the margin of a recipe, it means that the recipe may be prepared ahead to that point and then refrigerated. To reheat, bring the dish back to room temperature and heat in a 350° oven for 15 to 20 minutes. This general rule applies to most recipes unless other instructions are given.

If the mark does not appear, it means that this recipe must be prepared and served immediately.

Celestial Salad
Dark Carraway Party Rye Bread
Dutch Orange Parfait
Spanish Rioja White
(Marques de Murrieta)

Celestial Salad   Serves 8

1½ pounds washed, dried salad greens — bibb, head lettuce, Belgian endive, spinach.

Arrange in a salad bowl, then arrange on top in order:

1 pound julienned smoked tongue
1 cup julienned beets
1 cup julienned celery root (cooked or raw)
1 cup finely chopped dill pickle
1 cup crumbled blue cheese (optional)

Just before serving pour over ½ **cup Country French** 🍶 **Dressing** Garnish with **sliced hard-cooked eggs, anchovey fillets** and **chopped parsley.**

Serve with dark carraway party rye bread.

Dutch Orange Parfait   Serves 8

Have ready:

1½ **quarts French vanilla ice cream**
2 **cups stiffly beaten whipped cream,**
   unsweetened
Grated rinds of 2 large oranges
Sections from the oranges
One 6 ounce can defrosted orange juice
Brandy
Grated bitter chocolate

Scoop vanilla ice cream in parfait glasses or dessert bowls. Then, in this order:

Dust with the grated orange rind
Arrange orange sections
1 or 2 Tbl. orange juice concentrate
Splash of brandy
Put on a **swirl of whipped cream.**

Dust the top with the **grated bitter chocolate.** These may be assembled and be kept in the freezer. Remove from freezer about 15 to 20 minutes before serving and let stand at room temperature to soften.

Cream of Watercress Soup
Shish-Kebab
Apricot and Avocado Rice
Kumquat and Ginger Mousse
Bordeaux-Pomerol
(Chateau Gazin, Chateau Nenin
Chateau La Tour-Figeac)

Cream of Watercress Soup   Serves 8

In a sauce pan put:

> **1 bunch watercress, washed, trimmed, and chopped**
> **8 cups chicken stock**
> **Four friends**
> **1 medium-size leek,** chopped and washed
> **1 small onion,** chopped
> **½ cup chopped celery**
> **¼ cup chopped parsley**

Bring to a boil and simmer until the vegetables are tender, about 30 to 40 minutes. Puree this mixture in the blender on medium speed in small batches and return to the sauce pan. Add:

> **2 cups light cream**
> **2 to 3 Tbl. arrowroot**

 Heat and stir until thickened. Taste for seasoning. This soup may be served hot or cold.

Shish-Kebab   Serves 8

Have the butcher bone and trim a **seven pound leg of lamb** and then cut it into 1½ to 2 inch cubes. Put the meat in a bowl and add:

> ¼ **cup olive oil**
> **1 medium-size onion, finely chopped**
> **Four friends**
> **1 Tbl. crushed rosemary**
> **1 Tbl. dill weed**
> **Ground black pepper**
> **Juice of 2 or 3 lemons**
> ¼ **cup red wine vinegar**
> **1 tsp. ground cumin**

Stir, cover, and let marinate, refrigerated, over night or out of the refrigerator for two hours.

> **1 pound mushroom caps, washed, trimmed, and acidulted**
> **2 cups cherry tomatoes, rubbed with oil**
> **2 cups pearl onions**
> **2 cups egg plant cut into one-inch cubes.**
> Acidulate and drizzle with **olive oil.**

Alternate the meat and vegetables on skewers, using about eight ounces of lamb per person.

Broil the skewers on a charcoal grill for about eight to ten minutes about three inches from the source of heat. You may baste them with the remaining marinade.

Apricot and Avocado Rice   Serves 8

In a heavy sauce pan melt ¼ **cup butter** and saute ½ **cup finely chopped onion** until it is transparent. Add:

> **2 cups Uncle Ben's converted rice**
> **2 Tbl. chicken base**

Four friends
1 Tbl. curry powder
1 cup chopped dry apricots
Stir and add **four cups chicken stock.** Bring
to a boil, reduce heat and simmer until the
moisture has been absorbed. When the rice
is cooked add:
2 diced, peeled, seeded avocados
½ cup chopped parsley
½ cup slivered almonds
This is also a good stuffing for game or fowl. Delicious with pork dishes, too.

Kumquat and Ginger Mousse   Serves 8 to 10

Place in a bowl that can be heated:
6 eggs
⅔ cup of sugar
Pinch of salt
Heat over medium heat over hot water until lukewarm, stirring occasionally. Then beat on medium speed
in a mixing bowl 10 to 12 minutes until the eggs are
like mayonnaise.

While the eggs are beating, soften **2 Tbl. gelatin in
½ cup cold water.** When softened, melt over hot water.
Add the melted gelatin to the eggs and beat in **3 ounces
orange juice concentrate and 1 ounce brandy.** Place in
the refrigerator to thicken.
2 cups whipping cream, stiffly beaten
½ cup kumquats, (preserved) chopped fine
¼ cup crystallized ginger
½ cup slivered almonds
When the egg mixture has partially set, fold in the

whipped cream, kumquats, ginger and almonds.

Line a two-quart mold with **lady fingers** and fill with the mousse mixture. Cover and chill several hours.

Unmold and garnish with whipped cream, crystal- lized ginger and kumquats.

Molded Pureed Eggs with Crab Meat
Chicken in Scotch
Spinach Noodles
Grilled Tomatoes
Grand Marnier Frappe
Ohio State Wine
(Meier's Jac Jan)

Molded Pureed Eggs with Crab Meat   Serves 8

This makes a good hors d'oeuvre for cocktails.

Ten to twelve hard-cooked eggs, shelled and rubbed through a fine wire sieve into a bowl. Add:

Four friends
1 Tbl. Dijon mustard
½ cup heavy mayonnaise

Stir until well blended. This should have a thick consistency. Put into a well-oiled, one-quart ring mold, cover with saran wrap and refrigerate several hours or overnight until firm or set.

105

When ready to serve, dip the mold quickly into warm water and run a knife around the edges. Turn out onto a glass plate. Ice the outside of the eggs carefully with **2 cups beaten sour cream.** Fill the center of the iced mold with **2 cups lump crab meat or red caviar or tiny shrimps.** Garnish with **chopped parsley and sprigs of watercress.**

Serve with thin crisp rye bread or rye crackers.

Chicken in Scotch   Serves 8

Eight chicken breasts, skinned, boned, and lightly floured.

In a heavy skillet melt **½ cup butter,** add **1 medium-size chopped onion and saute until transparent.** Add the lightly floured chicken breasts and saute for eight minutes, turning occasionally. Bless with:

> **Four friends**
> **Ground black pepper**
> **Salt**
> **1 pound mushrooms,** trimmed, washed, sliced, and acidulated

Add **½ cup Scotch** and flame. When the flame dies, add **one cup whipping cream.** Deglaze (scrape with spoon) the bottom of the pan and heat for ten minutes.

This recipe is easily prepared in a chafing dish. Serve with green spinach noodles.

Grilled Tomatoes   Serves 8

Eight small ripe tomatoes. Remove the eyes and cut in half. Arrange in a shallow casserole. Sprinkle with:

> **Four friends**
> **Thyme**

Ground black pepper
Drizzle of olive oil
Dust with bread crumbs
Chopped parsley
Place in a 350° oven for 10 to 15 minutes or until
heated through.

Grand Marnier Frappe   Serves 8
    1 pint vanilla ice cream, softened
    2 cups whipping cream, stiffly beaten
    ½ cup orange juice concentrate
    ½ cup Grand Marnier
    Grated rind of two oranges
    Sections from two oranges
Place the ice cream, one cup of the whipped cream,
orange juice concentrate, and the Grand Marnier in a
blender jar. Blend until the mixture has a thin mousse
consistency.

Pour over scoops of **orange ice** or **vanilla ice cream**
in tall crystal cups or goblets. Put a swirl of **whipped
cream on** top and garnish with the orange sections and
sprigs of fresh mint. Serve with a spoon and straw.

**Senegalese Soup
Ham in Puff Pastry
French Tomato Salad
Oranges in Cointreau
California Sauvignon Blanc
(Blanc de Blanc 1969)**

Senegalese Soup   Serves 6 to 8
May be served hot or cold.

Three chicken breasts, baked. When cooked, skin, bone, and dice the chicken.

In a soup pot melt ¼ **cup butter.** Add one **medium-size onion** and saute until transparent. Add and fry for two or three minutes to release the flavor **1 or 2 Tbl. curry powder.** Be careful not to burn the curry powder. Then add:

> ½ **cup flour**
> **1 bay leaf**
> **3 cups chicken stock**
> **1 cup milk**
> **1 cup chopped celery**
> **Four friends**

Stir, bring to the boiling point, reduce the heat and simmer 20 to 30 minutes.

Blend the soup in the blender in small batches on medium speed until pureed.

Return the soup to the fire and add:

> ½ **cup chopped parsley**
> ½ **cup chopped chutney** ("Major Grey's")
> **Diced, cooked chicken breasts**

Bring to the boiling point and garnish with **toasted slivered almonds** or **chopped chives.**

When serving as a cold soup, chill and thin the consistency with **chicken stock or milk.** Remember to slightly over season foods that are to be served cold. The flavors diminish with the cold temperature.

Ham in Puff Pastry   Serves 8

Divide **one pound puff pastry** in half or use **two packages Pepperidge Farm Patty Shells** (frozen) defrosted. Carefully work together and roll out a very thin crust and line the bottom of an 8 to 10 inch quiche pan. Then fill the crust with the following, arranging in layers:

> 1 **cup grated Swiss cheese**
> 2 **Tbl. grated Parmesan cheese**
> 2 **Tbl. chopped parsley**
> ¼ **pound thinly sliced Prosciutto, Kentucky or Virginia Ham**
> In a separate bowl stir:
> 3 **whole eggs**
> **Four friends**
> 3 **Tbl. heavy cream**

Pour this custard over the filling in the crust.

Roll out the second crust and place on top of the quiche. Trim and seal the edges. Make a few holes in the top crust. Brush with **egg wash** for a good brown color.

Use leftover trimmings to make decorations for the top of the pastry. Hearts and flowers is a favorite design.

Bake in 400° oven 25 to 30 minutes or until the pastry is brown and puffed.

This makes a good luncheon or first course dish. Serve hot or cold. Great for picnics!

French Tomato Salad   Serves 8

Dip **eight ripe tomatoes** in boiling water for three or four seconds. Cool under cold water, peel and thinly slice. Arrange the sliced tomatoes on a shallow glass or porcelain tray. Bless with:

> **Four friends**
> **1 bunch chopped green onions**
> **½ cup chopped parsley**
> **Ground black pepper**

Pour over **½ cup Country French Dressing** and let stand 30 minutes. Garnish with **watercress.**

Oranges in Cointreau   Serves 8

Eight navel oranges, peeled and sectioned.

With a sharp paring knife cut down about ½ inch from the top of the orange. Then tilt the orange 90° and slice in a circular direction with the blade of the knife going between the rind of the orange and the fruit. Keep cutting round and round until the rind comes off in one long strip.

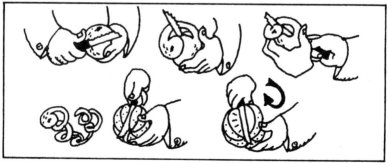

Hold the orange in one hand and cut down the section membrane until you feel the resistance of the center membrane of the orange. Turn the knife and cut up the other side of the membrane and lift the peeled section out.

Place the orange sections in a glass bowl and add **½ cup Cointreau.** Cover and refrigerate.

Serve cold with **whipped cream** and **thin sugar cookies.**

**Oyster and Lettuce Soup
Blue Trout with Steamed Potatoes
Tomatoes Stuffed with Zucchini
Chocolate Pot au Creme
German Moselle
(Moselblumchen 1970 is very good)**

Oyster and Lettuce Soup   Serves 8

In a sauce pan melt **¼ cup butter,** add **one medium-size, diced onion** and saute until transparent. Add:
> **½ cup flour**
> **Four friends**
> **1 tsp. grated nutmeg**
> **3 cups chicken stock**
> **1 cup milk or light cream**
> **1 Tbl. chicken base**
> **2 heads Boston lettuce,** washed, chopped

Stir, bring to the boiling point, reduce the heat and simmer for 30 to 40 minutes.

Blend the soup in small batches on medium speed in your blender.

Return to the fire and add:

½ cup chopped parsley
1 pint chopped oysters with their liquid
½ cup dry sherry

Bring to the boiling point but do not boil.

Blue Trout and Steamed Potatoes   Serves 6 to 8

Six to eight medium-size Idaho potatoes. Peel, cut into quarters and then cut the quarters into oval shapes.

Steam for 18 minutes or until tender. Drain, place in shallow casserole, sprinkle with **melted sweet butter, lemon juice** and **chopped parsley.** Keep warm.

Six to eight small fresh trout, 10 to 12 ounces each.

Fresh frozen trout will work, too. Bone the fish, But Do Not Wash Them. It is the natural coating on the fish that makes them turn blue.

In a fish poacher or a large kettle with a cover put:

4 quarts water
¼ cup kosher salt
1 cup chopped celery
1 medium onion, sliced
1 to 2 bay leaves
Juice and rinds of 2 to 3 lemons
½ cup white wine vinegar
1 bunch parsley stems

Cover and bring to a boil and simmer 20 to 30 minutes.

Have the stock boiling when you are ready to cook

the fish, cover and cook eight minutes. The fish will turn a bright blue. Skim out and serve with **lemon slices, melted butter,** and the steamed potatoes.

Tomatoes Stuffed with Zucchini   Serves 8

In a sauce pan heat:
> **2 Tbl. butter**
> **2 Tbl. oil**

Add **1 small bunch chopped green onions** and saute until transparent. Add:
> **Four friends**
> **1 Tbl. chicken base**
> **3 or 4 small zucchini,** trimmed, washed in warm
>   water and thinly sliced

Cook 6 to 8 minutes.

Slice the tops from **8 small tomatoes** and with a tablespoon scoop out the pulp. Fill the cavities with the zucchini mixture. Dust the tops with **bread crumbs** and **grated Parmesan cheese.**

Bake in 350° oven 20 to 25 minutes.

Chocolate Pot au Creme   Serves 8

In a sauce pan put:
> **8 ounces semi-sweet chocolate**
> **2 cups whipping cream**
> **⅔ cup sugar**
> **Pinch of salt**

Place on a heat-diffuser over medium heat and heat carefully, stirring occasionally until the chocolate has melted. Remove from the heat and beat in:
> **8 egg yolks,** beaten

**½ cup Creme de Cacao or Creme de
Menthe
1 tsp. vanilla**

Strain this custard through a fine sieve and put into pot-au-cream pots, ramekins, custard cups, or demitasse cups. Whatever you decide to use should yield about three to four ounce portions.

Place the filled cups in a hot water bath and bake in a 350° oven 15 minutes. Remove and let cool.

When baking, the cups may or may not be covered with pieces of aluminum foil.

Be careful not to over bake. Bake just until the custard has set, but is still slightly runny in the center.

May be served with **whipped cream** on top.

Chlodnik
Breast of Chicken with Apricots and Prosciutto
Saffron Rice
White Asparagus Salad
Poached Peaches in Champagne
Vouvray

Chlodnik   Serves 8
Cold Russian buttermilk and yogurt soup — very refreshing.

2 to 3 cucumbers, peeled, seeded, finely
chopped

1 bunch green onions, trimmed, finely
   chopped
Four friends
1 Tbl. dill weed
½ cup finely chopped parsley
2 or 3 garlic dill pickles, finely chopped
4 cups buttermilk
2 cups plain yogurt
1 pound lump crab meat or tiny shrimp
Stir and chill for several hours. Serve very cold
with scoops of **sour cream or yogurt.**

Breast of Chicken with Apricots and Prosciutto Serves 8

8 chicken breasts, skinned, boned, halved,
   and pounded thin
16 slices of Prosciutto
32 dried apricots, pounded with a wooden
   mallet until very thin
Flour
Egg wash
Fine bread crumbs
Lay the flattened chicken breasts out, skin side
down, and cover with a slice of the Prosciutto, then two
of the flattened apricots. Roll up the chicken breasts,
tucking in the ends. Dip and dust in the flour, then dip
in the egg wash, then into the bread crumbs until they
are lightly coated. Let the breaded chicken breasts dry
for several minutes. Fry five to eight minutes in deep
fat turning occasionally until they are golden brown.
Drain well and transfer to a heat-proof platter. Keep
warm or reheat in a 350° oven for 15 to 20 minutes.
Serve with bechamel sauce.

Saffron Rice   Serves 8

In a heavy sauce pan melt **¼ cup butter**, add **½ cup finely chopped onion** and saute until the onion is transparent. Add:

>**2 cups Uncle Ben's rice**
>**Four friends**
>**2 Tbl. chicken base**
>**1 to 2 tsp. saffron**

Stir until the rice is coated with the mixture and add **four cups of chicken stock.** Stir, bring to a boil, reduce heat and simmer, uncovered, until the moisture has been absorbed and the rice is dry, light and fluffy.

White Asparagus Salad   Serves 8

Two cans imported white asparagus (2 pound size)

Drain the asparagus well and squeeze **fresh lemon juice** over them. Place them in a shallow glass or porcelain dish. Pour over the asparagus **½ cup Country French Dressing** or **Russian mayonnaise.**

Serve on a bed of **salad greens** and garnish with chopped **parsley** and **watercress.**

Peach in Champagne   Serves 8

Eight large, ripe peaches. Dip them into boiling water for a few seconds, then plunge into cold water to cool. Peel. In a sauce pan put:

>**2 cups water**
>**2 cups sugar**
>**1 inch piece of vanilla bean**
>**Juice of a lemon**

Bring to a boil and simmer for 20 minutes.

Add the peeled peaches and poach them 10 to 12 minutes or until they are just cooked, not over cooked. Remove from the syrup and let cool. Squeeze a little lemon juice over them to keep them white.

When ready to serve, put a chilled poached peach 🍸 into a large wine goblet and then fill it with **dry or sweet champagne.** May use either whole peach with stone or halves with the stone removed.

Gazpacho
Paella Valenciana
Hard Rolls or Crusty Bread
Green Salad with Ripe Spanish Olives
Melon with Port
Sangria

Gazpacho   Serves 8 to 10

Soak **four stale hard rolls** in cold water until they are soft. Squeeze out the moisture, put them in a blender jar and add:

    1 medium-size onion, chopped
    ¼ cup olive oil
    5 or 6 cloves of garlic
    4 large ripe, peeled, seeded,
       chopped tomatoes
    ¼ cup red wine vinegar
    2 peeled, seeded, chopped cucumbers

Four friends
Salt
Pepper
1 Tbl. sweet paprika

Fill the jar with water and blend on medium speed until pureed. Add a **46 ounce can of tomato juice.** Stir together and chill till very cold, for several hours or overnight.

Serve in deep earthenware soup cups and garnish with the following. Or let your guests help themselves to:

Ice cubes
Peeled, chopped tomato
Finely chopped green peppers
Peeled, seeded, diced cucumbers
Chopped parsley
Diced, cooked ham
Croutons

Paella Valenciana   Serves 8 to 10
This recipe is from our friend Juan Piris — the way it's served in his family's restaurant in the North of Spain.

In a large shallow pan or a paella pan heat **½ cup olive oil.** Add:

1 large onion, chopped
1 large green pepper, peeled, seeded and diced
5 or 6 cloves of garlic, chopped

Heat until the onion is transparent and add:

1½ pounds sirloin of beef cut into
½ inch cubes
2 frying chickens boned and cut into
small pieces

Sear for five to ten minutes and add **2 cups Uncle Ben's rice.** Stir until coated. Then add:

> **2 tsp. saffron**
> **2 cups peeled, chopped tomatoes**
> **4 cups chicken stock**

Bring to a boil, reduce heat and simmer until the moisture has been absorbed, about 25 minutes. Then add:

> **Four friends**
> **2 pounds large, peeled, deveined shrimp**
> **1 cup artichoke hearts, drained**
> **1 pound Halibut cut into one inch cubes**
> **1 cup defrosted peas**
> **2 cups mushroom caps, acidulated**
> **1 cup cooked green beans cut into 1½ inch lengths**
> **½ cup diced pimento**
> **½ cup chopped parsley**
> **Salt**
> **Pepper**

Stir the rice mixture and level out. On top of the rice lay in bands:

> **1½ pounds under-cooked asparagus**
> **Strips of red pepper or pimento**
> **2 dozen scrubbed mussels in the shell**
> **1½ dozen scrubbed steamer clams in the shell**
> **1 cup dry white wine or dry sherry**

Cover with a lid and return to the heat or in a 350° oven and cook for 20 to 25 minutes until the fish is cooked and the clams and mussels are open.

Sprinkle with **chopped parsley** and serve immediately.

Mixed Green Salad with Ripe Spanish Olives   Serves 8

>   1 head iceberg lettuce, separated, washed, dried
>   1 head Boston lettuce, separated, washed, dried
>   **Belgian Endive or Romaine lettuce**

Arrange in a wooden salad bowl and add:

>   1 thinly sliced and separated Spanish onion
>   ½ cup chopped parsley
>   ½ cup pitted ripe Spanish olives

Just before serving, sprinkle ½ **cup Country French Dresing** and the **juice of a lemon** over all.

Melon with Port   Serves 8

Two honeydew melons, cut into quarters and seeded. Loosen the fruit from the rind and return to the shell in the natural form. Chill till very cold. Just before serving, pour **light sweet port** over the melon and garnish with wedges of **lemon** or **lime.**

Sangria   Serves 6 to 8

In a tall pitcher add:

>   1 sliced orange with the rind
>   1 sliced lemon with the rind
>   ¼ cup sugar
>   ½ cup Brandy
>   ¼ cup Grand Marnier

Muddle with a wooden spoon and let stand for several hours.

Then add two quarts chilled, **dry red wine.** Stir to blend well. Then add a bit of **plain soda water** and lots of **ice.** You may garnish this with fresh **strawberries** or sliced, fresh, ripe **peaches.**

Grilled Chicken
Almond Rice
Marinated Artichoke Hearts and Avocado
Blueberries with Sour Cream and
Crystallized Ginger
May-Wine

Grilled Chicken   Serves 8

Four 2½ to 3 pound broiling chickens, split in half and
with the back bone removed. Place the chickens in a
shallow pan and bless with:

> **Four friends**
> **Juice of 2 to 3 lemons**
> **2 or 3 bay leaves**
> **Ground black pepper**
> **1 Tbl. crushed rosemary or tarragon**
> **½ cup olive oil**

Rub the inside and outside of the chickens with this
mixture and let them marinate for several hours.

Grill over moderate charcoal heat, turning and
basting frequently about 20 to 25 minutes until cooked.

Serve hot or cold with **lemon wedges.**

Almond Rice   Serves 8

In a heavy sauce pan melt ¼ **cup butter,** add **one medium-size, finely diced onion** and saute until transparent.
Then add:

> **2 cups Uncle Ben's converted rice**
> **Four friends**

½ **cup toasted almonds**
4 cups chicken stock or water

Stir and bring to a boil, reduce heat and simmer for 25 to 30 minutes uncovered, until the moisture has been absorbed and the rice is dry and fluffy.

Stir in ½ **cup toasted, slivered almonds** and **two Tbl. finely chopped parsley** just before serving.

Marinated Artichoke Hearts and Avocados   Serves 8

Two cans artichoke hearts (1 cup drained) Drain, wash carefully in cold water, drain again and acidulate. Place in a bowl with **three to four avocados** that have been cut in half. Also remove the seeds and lift them out of their shells with a kitchen spoon. Add:

½ **cup Country French Dressing**
3 to 4 Tbl. fresh, chopped chives

Let marinate, covered, at room temperature for 30 to 60 minutes. Serve over **bibb lettuce** with a chopped, **hard-cooked egg, diced pimento,** and **chopped, ripe olives.**

Blueberries with Sour Cream and Crystallized Ginger
Serves 8

2 quarts blueberries, washed, picked and drained
2 cups sour cream
½ **cup slivered, crystallized ginger**

Arrange the blueberries in individual goblets or dishes. Put a spoon of sour cream on top and sprinkle with the slivered, crystallized ginger.

Serve with a wedge of **lime** on the side and **thin sugar cookies.**

Cold Sole with Mustard Fruits
Rice Salad
Baba au Rhum with Fruits and Whipped Cream
German Moselle
(Moselblumchen)

Cold Sole with Mustard Fruits   Serves 6 to 8

2½ to 3 pounds lemon or dover sole fillets

Place the fillets in a shallow pan that has been lightly oiled or buttered and add:

2 cups dry white wine
Juice of 2 lemons
Four friends

Cover with a piece of wax paper, place on the heat, bring to a boil, reduce the heat and simmer six to eight minutes or until the fish is white and firm.

Remove from the heat, carefully skim out the fillets, and transfer them to a glass tray or a fish dish and let them cool in the refrigerator. Save the stock for soup.

When the fish is cold, arrange over the fillets:

1 cup lump crab meat
1 pound shrimp
1 cup seedless green grapes
1 cup orange or mandarin orange sections
½ cup kumquats

Mask the fish and fruits with **cold mustard mayonnaise.** Decorate the edges of the tray with peeled, quartered **tomatoes,** cold, **white asparagus** and **lemon slices.**

Garnish the top with **pimento strips, chopped parsley** and **watercress.**

Serve with rice salad.

Baba au Rhum   Serves 8 to 10

Bake a **genoise or a savarin** in a 10 inch ring mold. When baked, unmold, and while still warm pour over and saturate the cake with this hot syrup. In a sauce pan put:

> **2 cups cold water**
> **2 cups granulated sugar**
> **1 cinnamon stick**
> **Juice of 1 lemon**

Stir and bring to a boil and simmer 15 to 20 minutes. Then add **½ cup dark or light rum.**

Let the saturated cake cool in the refrigerator. When cold, pour **one cup rum** over the cake and baste with any of the syrup that is in the bottom of the tray.

Glaze the outside of the cake with **1½ cups apricot preserves** that have been heated in a sauce pan until melted and runny. They will give the cake a nice shiny appearance.

Serve this cake cold with **whipped cream, fresh fruits,** and **candied violets.**

**Shrimp and Asparagus Salad
Gregorian Dressing
Green Crepes and Prosciutto
Almond Custard
Soave-Italian White or
(La Crima Christi del Vesuvio - heavier,
Italian white wine)**

Shrimp and Asparagus Salad   Serves 8

> 2 pounds cooked, fresh asparagus
> 4 ripe tomatoes, peeled and cut into wedges
> 4 chopped, hard-cooked eggs
> 1 pound cooked shrimp
> ¼ cup chopped parsley
> 1 bunch watercress, trimmed

Arrange the asparagus on a flat tray or in a casserole and sprinkle with **Accent.** Sprinkle the chopped egg over the asparagus. Arrange the shrimp over the eggs and sprinkle with the parsley. Garnish with wedges of tomato and watercress. Spoon **Gregorian Dressing** over the shrimp, eggs and asparagus.

Gregorian Dressing

Good with seafoods, cold chicken, raw vegetables or marinated vegetables.

> ½ cup sour cream
> ½ cup cream cheese
> ½ cup mayonnaise
> Four friends
> Juice of a lemon

2 finely chopped green onions
2 Tbl. chopped parsley
1 avocado, peeled and seeded

Place all ingredients in a blender jar and blend on medium speed until smooth.

Store in a covered glass jar in refrigerator. Drop the avocado seed in the dressing to keep it from changing color and darkening.

Green Crepes and Prosciutto   Serves 6 to 8
Crepe Batter   Makes 12 to 18 crepes

> **4 eggs**
> **1 cup milk**
> **1 cup flour**
> **2 Tbl. chopped parsley**
> **5 ounces spinach,** washed, wilted. Squeeze out all moisture.
> **Grated nutmeg**

Put all the ingredients in a blender jar and blend on medium speed until they are pureed. Let this crepe batter rest 30 minutes before using it. Test and thin the batter as needed. See Seafood Crepes recipe for directions to make the crepes. These crepes are not as thin as the plain crepes.

Filling for the Crepes
In a bowl, mix:

> **10 ounces fresh spinach,** trimmed, washed, wilted, drained and finely chopped
> **1 cup grated Swiss cheese**
> **Four friends**
> **Grated nutmeg**

Ground black pepper
4 egg yolks
½ cup chopped parsley
Have ½ pound thinly sliced Proscuitto or
thinly sliced baked ham ready to use.

To assemble:
Spread out the crepes and cover them with the thinly sliced ham. Place about ½ cup of the spinach mixture on the ham and roll up the crepe. Place the filled crepe, seam side down, in a shallow casserole.

Pour **quick tomato sauce** or **bechamel sauce** over the crepes. Bless with **grated Swiss cheese** and **chopped parsley.**

Bake in 350° oven 25 minutes.

Almond Custard   Serves 8

Place the following ingredients in a sauce pan and heat carefully (but do not let boil) until the almond paste melts:

3 cups whipping cream
⅔ cup sugar
Pinch of salt
½ cup almond paste

Remove from the heat and add:

8 egg yolks, beaten
1 tsp. vanilla
½ cup slivered, toasted almonds

Pour into custard cups, place them in a hot water bath and bake in a 350° oven 20 to 25 minutes or until set.

I like this best served at room temperature.

Grilled Tomatoes Stuffed with Crab
French Country Chicken Casserole
Spinach Salad
English Trifle
German Rhine

Grilled Tomatoes Stuffed with Crab   Serves 8 to 10

Four or five medium-size, ripe tomatoes. Remove the eye and cut in half. Squeeze out the seeds carefully. Arrange in a shallow casserole or in individual ramekins.

Filling
In a bowl put:
   ¼ **cup bread crumbs**
   ¼ **cup finely chopped green onion**
   ½ **cup finely chopped celery**
   ½ **cup chopped parsley**
   Juice of a lemon
   ½ **cup grated Swiss cheese**
   Four friends
   1 tsp. dry mustard
   1 tsp. paprika
   1 egg
   1 Tbl. dry sherry or brandy
   2 cups drained crab meat or shrimp, or lobster, or tuna fish

Lightly toss and pile on the tops of the tomato halves. Dust with **Parmesan cheese** and **paprika**.

Bake in 350° oven 15 to 18 minutes.

These may be served with **hollandaise** on top.

French Country Chicken   Serves 8 to 10
Very tasty chicken casserole that can be frozen.

> **Two 4½ pound roasting chickens,** roasted, cooled, boned and cut into 2 inch pieces.
> **1 cup cooked carrots**
> **1 cup cooked peas**
> **1 cup cooked, quartered white turnips**
> **1 pound mushroom caps,** trimmed, washed, acidulated
> **2 cups artichoke hearts**
> **½ pound puff pastry,** rolled out to fit the top of the casserole

Sauce
> **½ cup butter or chicken drippings**
> **½ cup flour**
> **2 cups rich chicken stock**
> **1 cup dry white wine**
> **½ cup dry sherry**
> **1 cup heavy cream**
> **½ cup chopped parsley**
> **Four friends**

In a sauce pan heat the butter or drippings, add the flour and stir. Then add the four friends, chicken stock, dry white wine, dry sherry and stir over medium heat. Bring to a boil, add the heavy cream and simmer for 20 minutes. Then add the chopped parsley.

Arrange the chicken and vegetables in alternating layers in a deep three-quart casserole. Pour the sauce over the chicken and vegetables and shake it down. Let cool and then cover the top with the pastry crust. Brush the top with **egg wash** and bake at 350° for one hour or until the top is well browned.

Spinach Salad   Serves 8

Two pounds fresh spinach, trimmed, washed and dried
    Place the spinach in a salad bowl. Arrange on top
of the spinach:

> **1 medium-size Spanish onion,** thinly sliced
> **1 cup crumbled blue cheese**
> **½ cup crumbled, cooked bacon**
> **1 cup cherry tomatoes,** cut in half
> **¼ cup chopped parsley**

    Just before serving pour **½ cup Country French
Dressing** over the salad.

English Trifle   Serves 8 to 10

> ***1 cup apricot puree**
> **One 8 to 10 inch sponge cake** (from your
>   favorite bakery)
> **½ cup sweet Marsala or cream sherry**
> **3 Tbl. cornstarch**
> **3 Tbl. sugar**
> **¾ cup hot milk**
> **3 egg yolks**
> **1 tsp. vanilla**
> **2 cups stiffly beaten whipped cream**
> **2 to 3 cups fresh and candied fruits: straw-
>   berries, peaches, apricots**
> **½ cup slivered almonds**

Custard

    Combine the sugar and the cornstarch in a sauce
pan and stir in the hot milk. Simmer and stir until

------

    *Either buy canned pureed apricots (can use baby
food) or puree dried, cooked apricots in the blender.

thickened. Remove from the heat and stir in the egg yolks and vanilla. Return to the heat to thicken. Remove and let cool.

Slice the sponge cake in one inch thick slices and line a crystal bowl with the slices. Sprinkle with the Marsala or sherry.

Pour the apricot puree over the cake. Then pour in the cooled custard. Arrange the mixture of fruits and decorate the top with whipped cream. Garnish with the candied fruits and slivered almonds. Cover and place in the refrigerator for at least one hour.

Vichysoisse
Poached Kennebec Salmon
Mousseline Sauce
Russian Vegetable Salad
Oranges Oriental
California Champagne
(Schramsberg, Korbel, Paul Masson)

Vichysoisse   Serves 8

     2 medium-size onions, diced
     5 large leeks, trimmed, chopped, washed
     5 Idaho potatoes, peeled and chopped
     Salt
     Ground white pepper
     2 bay leaves

Four friends
3 quarts chicken stock
2 cups heavy cream or milk
Chopped chives

In a soup pot, melt the butter, add the onions and leeks and heat over medium heat until they are transparent. Then add the potatoes, salt, pepper, bay leaves, four friends and chicken stock. Bring to a boil, reduce the heat and simmer until the vegetables are tender. Blend the soup in small batches on medium speed until pureed.

Thin this base with the cream or milk to the consistency that pleases you. Taste for seasoning.

 Garnish with the chopped chives.

This soup may be served hot or cold.

Fresh Poached Kennebec Salmon Serves 8 to 10

Hot or served cold in aspic

5½ to 6 pound fresh Kennebec salmon
This is light, pink, delicate fish.

Wash the fish well in cold water, inside and out and place on the rack of a fish poacher.

If you do not have a fish poacher, wrap the fish in a terrycloth towel and place on a shallow rack in a deep roasting pan. The towel will circulate the poaching liquid around the fish and cook the whole fish. Also the towel gives you something to lift the fish out of the stock with when it is cooked.

Add enough cold water to cover or almost cover the fish and then add:
Four friends
2 Tbl. kosher salt

Juice and rinds of 4 to 6 lemons
1 bunch parsley stems
2 to 3 bay leaves
1 medium-size onion, sliced
½ cup fresh tarragon or 1 Tbl. dry tarragon
3 or 4 stalks celery

Put on the cover and bring to the boiling point. Reduce the heat and simmer 40 to 45 minutes or until a skewer can pierce the thick part of the fish and the juices come out clear. The fish should also feel firm to the touch when it is done. This same rule applies to any poached fish.

Lift the fish out of the **poaching stock.** Drain and cool. When it cools enough to touch (lukewarm), remove the skin and fins. Use the dull side of a table knife, sliding it down from the head to the tail. The skin will slip off easily. The dark areas just underneath the skin are the fat of the fish. This may be carefully scraped away if desired.

Run the knife parallel to the fins and they will slip out with their bones easily. Just follow the natural contour of these areas.

If you want to remove the inside bones, carefully run the knife down the spinal bone on the top side of the fish until you feel the natural resistance from the inside bone formation. Do this down the entire length of the fish to the tail. Then carefully lift the top side of the fish up, loosening it from the bone structure. This will lift off easily. Set aside. With your finger, pick up the bone structure and pull it up and away from the bottom side of the fish. If the head and tail are still on the fish,

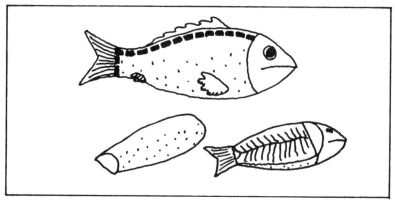

disconnect the spinal bone from the head and tail ends of the fish, then lift it up. There may be a few of the feather bones (rib cage bones) left. If you run the palm of your hand over the exposed part of the fish you will feel the bones and they can be easily extracted with your fingers. When all of the bones have been removed, replace the top side of the fish so it appears as the whole fish.

The boned fish may be placed on a heat-proof fish platter and carefully reheated and served hot with:

> **Hollandaise sauce**
> **Mousseline sauce**
> **Charon sauce**

If you want to serve the fish cold in aspic, strain the stock in which you poached the fish. Let the strained stock stand until it settles and remove about **two quarts of the clear stock.**

Soften **8 Tbl. plain gelatin** in 1½ cups cold fish stock. Let stand until the gelatin blooms (softens and explands). Then add to the rest of the heated fish stock and stir until it has dissolved. Taste for seasoning and place in the refrigerator to chill and set.

This aspic may be poured over the cold fish when in a thickened, syrupy consistency. Do in several layers, repeating the process, until you have a coating of gelatin over the outside of the fish.

The top side of the fish may be decorated with **vegetables** or **leaves** and **stems** cut into patterns and dipped into the softened aspic. These are applied to the cold aspic covering of the fish.

Chop the remaining aspic finely and use this to surround the fish on the platter. Then decorate the edges of the platter with thinly sliced, seeded **lemons** and

halved, **cherry tomatoes.** This does take time to do but can be assembled in stages and done the day before. Usually, I do this over a two-day period. One day is spent cooking, skinning, boning, cooling and making the aspic. The second day is spent decorating the fish and making the tray decorations.

After the aspic and decorations have set, cover with saran wrap and keep very cold in the refrigerator until ready to serve.

The cold salmon may be served with cold:
> **Mousseline sauce**
> **Cucumber sauce**
> **Russian mayonnaise**

Mousseline Sauce

See recipe for hollandaise in Basic Cooking.

Fold **one cup stiffly beaten whipped cream** into cold hollandaise for cold mousseline sauce. Fold the whipped cream into hot hollandaise for hot mousseline sauce.

Russian Vegetable Salad   Serves 8

One cup each:

>**White celery**
>
>**Peas**
>
>**Carrots**
>
>**Green beans**
>
>**Potatoes**

Dice, cook separately, drain, cool and place in a large bowl. Add:

>**6 chopped, hard-cooked eggs**
>
>**1½ cups mayonnaise**
>
>**Juice of a lemon**
>
>**Four friends**
>
>**½ cup chopped parsley**
>
>**Salt**
>
>**Ground white pepper**

Carefully mix together. Taste for seasoning and chill.

To serve, mound on a **bed of lettuce** and garnish with:

>**Peeled, quartered tomatoes**
>
>**Quartered, hard-cooked eggs**
>
>**Chopped parsley or watercress**

Oranges Oriental   Serves 8

Eight navel oranges

With a lemon stripper, starting from the top, carefully peel the skin (in one long string) from the oranges. Then peel the oranges with a sharp knife.

Blanch the orange peels by placing them in a sauce pan and covering them with cold water. Bring to a boil and drain. In another sauce pan make a syrup of:

2 cups water
2 cups granulated sugar

Bring to a boil and simmer for 20 minutes.

Add the blanched orange peels to the syrup and cook for 20 minutes or until they are glazed.

% Arrange the peeled oranges in a shallow tray and pour the remaining syrup over the oranges. Then arrange the candied peels around the oranges. Pour a splash of **Grande Marnier or Cointreau** over each orange.

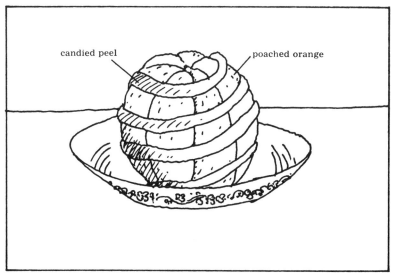

candied peel   poached orange

Sliced Tomatoes and Cucumbers
with Russian Mayonnaise
Rib Eye of Beef
Boullion Potatoes
Spinach Salad with Caesar Salad Dressing
Apricots with Vanilla Ice Cream
French Red Burgundy
(Gevrey-Chambertin, Nuits St. Georges,
Vosnee Romanee)

Sliced Tomatoes and Cucumbers with Russian Dressing
Serves 8

4 to 8 large ripe tomatoes, dipped into
boiling water, then cold water

Peel and slice into ½ inch thick slices **2 to 3 cucumbers,** peeled, seeded and thinly sliced.

Arrange the tomatoes and cucumbers on a **bed of lettuce** on a tray. Sprinkle lightly with **salt** and **Accent.**

Serve with **Russian mayonnaise** on the side.

Rib Eye of Beef (Roasted or Grilled)
Serves 8

Eight pound rib eye of beef

Place the beef in a roasting pan and rub the outside with **oil or butter.**

Bless with the **four friends** and **ground black pepper.** Let stand and come to room temperature.

Roast in 350° oven 2 hours — rare, 2½ hours — medium, 3 hours — well done.

You may put the roast on a spit and grill it over the charcoal about the same length of time.

Serve with Bearnaise sauce, Madeira sauce, Snail butter.

Bouillon Potatoes   Serves 8

Six to eight medium-size, baking potatoes, peeled and thinly sliced.

Place in a sauce pan, cover with cold salted water, and heat to the boiling point. Drain well and place in a two-quart, buttered casserole and add:

    1 large onion, diced and sauteed in **2 Tbl. butter** until transparent
    Four friends
    Two 10½ ounce cans undiluted consomme or bouillon
    ¼ cup finely chopped parsley
    Ground black pepper

Stir and submerge the potatoes. Bake in a 350° oven 45 to 60 minutes or until the bouillon or consomme has been absorbed.

Spinach Salad with Caesar Salad Dressing   Serves 8

Two pounds spinach, trimmed and washed. Dry well and place in a salad bowl.

Pour over the spinach just before serving **½ cup Caesar Dressing.** You may add **one cup seasoned croutons** and **grated Parmesan cheese.**

Apricots with Vanilla Ice Cream   Serves 8

One number 2½ can, peeled, stoned apricots

Drain apricots well and place in a bowl with the **juice of a lemon, ½ cup brandy or Cointreau or Kirsch** and let the fruit marinate covered for several hours.

Pack **two quarts vanilla ice cream** in a two-quart ring mold. Cover with saran wrap and keep in the freezer.

To unmold, quickly rinse in warm water and unmold on a tray. Fill the center with the marinated apricots. Serve with **whipped cream** and **macaroons.**

Tomato Ice
Eggs of the Allies
Grilled Bacon and Ham
Croissants
Crystallized Strawbrries
French Non-Vintage Champagne
(Moet Chandon, Pol Roger, Taittinger)

Tomato Ice Serves 8

In a bowl put:

3 cups tomato juice

two 6 ounce cans of tomato paste

1 cup whipping cream

Four friends

½ cup mayonnaise

Salt

Stir and place in a container or tray in the freezer. Stir occasionally while it is freezing until it is the consistency of sherbet when frozen. May be made in an ice cream freezer.

Serve in goblets with **chopped chives** or **lemon wedges.**

May be used as a frozen soup or served with cold marinated shrimp or other seafoods.

Eggs of the Allies   Serves 8

I created this dish when I was with N.A.T.O. It's a good first course or brunch or luncheon dish.

> **2 pounds mushrooms,** trimmed, washed thinly sliced and acidulated.
> Saute the mushrooms in **two or three Tbl. butter.** Bless with:
> **Four friends**
> **¼ cup dry sherry**
> **2 cups grated Swiss cheese**
> **3 cups Bechamel sauce**
> **1 cup finely chopped parsley**

Beat **16 eggs** together with **one cup whipping cream.** Cook in a heavy pan, stirring constantly until you have a soft custard. Remove from the heat. To assemble:

In the bottom of a buttered, two-quart souffle pot put in this order:

> **⅓ thin layer of Bechamel**
> **½ mushrooms**
> **⅓ parsley**
> **⅓ cheese**
> **½ egg custard**
> **⅓ Bechamel**

½ **mushrooms**
⅓ **parsley**
⅓ **cheese**
½ **egg custard**
⅓ **parsley**
⅓ **Bechamel**
⅓ **cheese**

Dust the top of the casserole with chopped parsley and **paprika.**

Bake in a 350° oven 25 to 30 minutes or until heated through. Serve with grilled tomatoes, bacon, ham, or chicken and croissants for brunch or luncheon.

Crystallized Strawberries   Serves 8

Twenty-four beautiful, ripe strawberries with the stems on. Wash, dry and keep at room temperature on paper towels on a tray until you are ready to dip them.

Glaze for Strawberries

In a heavy enamel sauce pan put:

3 cups corn syrup, light
2 tsp. cream of tartar
1 Tbl. white vinegar

Slowly heat this mixture over moderate heat, stirring occasionally until it is thick and crystal clear. This will take about 45 minutes. Be careful not to splash the syrup on the sides of the pan as it cooks because the syrup will burn and discolor the pan. When you drop the syrup into cold water it should form hard crystal beads.

When the syrup is ready, dip the berries into the syrup one at a time, holding onto the stem until each strawberry is completely coated. Place them on a wire rack or wax paper to cool. The berries should look like glass.

These will hold up two to three hours on a day with little humidity. The berries do best in air conditioning, but do not refrigerate them.

Serve two or three on a silver plate.

Borscht with Sour Cream
Madrid Salad
Hard Rolls
Fresh Fruit Compote in Cantaloupe Shells
Spanish Rose
(Torres, Mondor)

Borscht with Sour Cream   Serves 6 to 8

In a blender jar put:

1 cup beets with the juice (canned)
Four friends
1 medium-size onion, chopped
3 chopped kosher dill pickles
½ cup dill pickle juice
1 Tbl. dill weed
Ground black pepper

Blend on medium speed until finely pureed. Place in a glass jar or bowl and add:

One 46 ounce can heavy tomato juice
1 cup julienne beets
6 sliced hard-cooked eggs

Stir and chill several hours. Serve with scoops of **plain yogurt or sour cream.** Sprinkle with **chopped parsley or dill** and serve with a **thin rye crisp.**

Keeps beautifully in the refrigerator. Good also over the rocks with vodka as a Bloody Russian.

Madrid Salad   Serves 6 to 8

Good summer luncheon.

Line a shallow salad tray or bowl with **salad greens** or **Boston lettuce.** In the center, place in layers:

> **2 cups drained, water-packed tuna fish**
> **1 cup thinly sliced, red Spanish onion**
> **1 cup drained artichoke hearts**
> **1 cup drained garbanzo beans**
> **4 peeled, quartered tomatoes**
> **1 cup provolone cheese,** julienne
> **1 cup drained julienne beets**

Dressing

> **Juice of 2 to 3 lemons**
> **Ground black pepper**
> **2 cloves pressed garlic**
> **1 tsp. dry mustard**
> **¼ cup white wine vinegar**
> **½ to ⅔ cup olive oil**
> **2 to 3 Tbl. drained capers**
> **Salt to taste**

Stir or shake together. Pour over salad and let marinate 30 to 40 minutes.

Fresh Fruit Compote in Cantaloupe Shells   Serves 8

Four ripe cantaloupes, cut in half. Remove the seeds and cut off the bottoms so they will sit flat. You may loosen the fruit in the shell by running a grapefruit knife around the inside edge.

> 1 **quart strawberries,** stemmed and washed..
> 2 **cups seedless green grapes**
> 2 **cups peeled, diced fresh pineapple**
> 1 **cup blueberries or red raspberries**
> 1 **cup apricot preserves**
> ½ **cup light rum**

Stir and let marinate for several hours at room temperature and then fill the cantaloupe with this mixture.

Artichokes Vinaigrette
Chicken with Fennel and Olives
Parsley Rice
Mushroom Salad
Oranges en Suprise
California Johannisberg Riesling
(Louis Martini)

Artichokes Vinaigrette   Serves 8

Eight large green fresh artichokes

Trim stem end so the artichokes will sit flat. Trim the ends of the leaves with a scissors cutting off the thorn at the top end of the leaf.

Wash well in lukewarm water to remove the sand and dirt and place in a deep pot, bottom side down. Cover with cold water and add:

1 medium-size onion, sliced
1 bunch parsley stems
3 or 4 lemons, cut in half
½ cup cider vinegar
8 or 10 peppercorns
¼ cup kosher salt
3 or 4 bay leaves
¼ cup olive oil

Put a smaller cover and weight (a brick) over the artichokes to hold them down in the water. This prevents them from floating to the top. Place on the fire, bring to a boil, reduce the heat and simmer 30 to 90 minutes (depending on the size and age of the artichokes) or until you can easily pull off their bottom leaves. Drain.

The artichokes may be served hot or cold with:

Vinaigrette sauce
Mustard sauce
Hollandaise
Mayonnaise
Melted butter
Country French Dressing

Vinaigrette Sauce
In a bowl add:

Ground black pepper
Juice of one lemon
¼ cup olive oil
1 tsp. dry mustard
1 tsp. garlic salt
1 tsp. salt

146

Stir until well blended and store covered in a glass
jar.

Chicken with Fennel and Olives   Serves 8

Six or eight heads of fennel, trimmed and cut into quarters

Place in cold salted water, bring to a boil and simmer 30 to 40 minutes until tender. Drain and let cool. Set aside.

Three or four frying chickens cut into serving pieces and dusted lightly with **flour.**

In a heavy dutch oven, melt **½ cup butter,** add **one medium-size chopped onion** and saute until transparent. Add the dark pieces of chicken first (the dark pieces take longer to cook than the light pieces) and sear them. Sear the white pieces next and add:

> **Four friends**
> **1 tsp. thyme**
> **2 tsp. fennel seeds**
> **1 tsp. grated nutmeg**
> **1 cup dry white wine**

Bring to the boiling point, reduce the heat and cook 25 minutes. Add:

> **1 cup pitted, green olives**
> **½ cup chopped parsley**
> **The cooked, quartered fennel**

Reheat 20 to 30 minutes on top of the stove or in a 350° oven. Serve with parsley rice.

Parsley Rice   Serves 8

> **¼ cup butter**
> **½ cup diced onion**

Four friends
2 Tbl. chicken base
2 cups Uncle Ben's converted rice
4 cups water or chicken stock
½ cup chopped parsley

In a heavy casserole, melt the butter, add the diced onion and saute until transparent. Add the four friends, chicken base, and the rice. Stir over medium heat until the rice is coated. Add the chicken stock or water, bring to a boil, reduce the heat and simmer uncovered until the moisture has been absorbed and the rice is light and fluffy. Stir in the chopped parsley. When reheating rice that has been cooked the day before, add to the casserole **½ cup water, white wine or chicken stock.**

Mushroom Salad   Serves 8

Place in a mixing bowl:

1 pound fresh mushrooms, washed, trimmed and thinly sliced. Acidulate with fresh **lemon juice.** Add:

¼ cup white wine vinegar
Four friends
Salt
Ground black pepper
½ cup olive oil
½ cup chopped, green onion
2 Tbl. chopped parsley
½ tsp. grated nutmeg

Marinate the mushrooms in a covered bowl for 20 to 30 minutes.

Serve on a bed of crisp **Belgian endive** or **romaine lettuce.**

Oranges en Suprise   Serves 8

Intriguing dessert that may be made several days in advance and kept in the freezer.

Eight large, thick-skinned navel oranges

Drop the oranges in a large pot of boiling water for three to five minutes or enough time to heat the skins. Remove from the boiling water and let cool just enough to handle.

With a sharp knife, slice about one inch down from the top exposing the top of the fruit of the orange. Take a tablespoon, curved side out, and carefully force it between the orange and the skin (pith part) going all around and down to the bottom. When the skin is loosened, carefully push it down so that you can grasp the fruit with your fingers. Twist the orange back and forth and then completely twist it around freeing it from the bottom. Then lift it out of the skin.

Put the skin back into its original shape and replace the top. Put into the refrigerator to chill and firm up.

The removed fruit may be sectioned or sliced for compotes, etc.

Fill the shells of the oranges with **orange water ice or sherbert or vanilla ice cream.** You will need about **two quarts of ice cream** to fill eight oranges. You may put some of the **orange sections** in with the ice. Replace the caps so that the orange has its natural appearance and place in the freezer until ready for use. When serving, place on fresh green leaves* on a dessert plate or tray. You may use leaf shaped cookies to serve with the oranges.

---

*Go to your garden (or to your florist) and get some beautiful green leaves. Grape vine leaves and magnolia leaves are super!

> **French Onion Soup les Halles**
> **French Fried Lamb Chops**
> **Bearnaise Sauce**
> **Spinach Ring Farmiere**
> **Braised Mushrooms**
> **Belgian Endive and Watercress Salad**
> **Sharlotka**
> **Bordeaux-St. Emilion**
> **(Chateau Pavie 1970 is a favorite of mine)**

French Onion Soup les Halles   Serves 8 to 10
"The best onion soup I found in Paris"

> **10 to 12 large, yellow or white cooking
> onions,** thinly sliced
> **¼ cup butter**
> **2 Tbl. olive oil**
> **Four friends**
> **2 Tbl. tomato puree**
> **2 Tbl. beef base**
> **1 Tbl. Dijon mustard**
> **2 quarts beef stock or six 10 ½ ounce
> cans beef consomme**
> **1 cup dry red wine**
> **Juice of 1 lemon**
> **Splash of brandy**
> **Dark rye bread slices**
> **½ cup Parmesan cheese,** grated
> **2 to 3 cups grated Swiss cheese**
> **2 to 3 Tbl. chopped parsley**

Heat the butter and olive oil in a heavy casserole or marmite (clay soup pot) and then add the thinly sliced onions. Cook over medium heat until golden in color. This is very important and will take about 30 minutes to do. Stir occasionally so they do not burn. When the onions are ready, add the four friends, the tomato puree, beef base, mustard, beef stock or consomme, red wine, and lemon juice. Stir and bring to the boiling point, then reduce the heat and simmer, uncovered, for one hour. Taste for seasoning. Add a splash of brandy and chopped parsley. This may be put into individual onion soup crocks or left in a large soup marmite. Cover the top with slices of dark rye bread (float on top) and generously coat with grated Parmesan and the grated Swiss cheese. To reheat, place in 350° oven for 30 to 45 minutes for the large marmite or 12 to 15 minutes for the individual soup crocks. Heat until the crust is golden, melted and bubbly hot.

French Fried Lamb Chops Serves 8

Sixteen lamb chops, cut about 1½ inches thick

Trim off the excess fat and dry well. Dust the chops with **flour,** dip them into **egg wash** and then into **fine bread crumbs.** Put the breaded chops on a screen or rack to dry for a few minutes.

Heat **two inches of cooking oil** in a deep frying pan or dutch oven to about 350°. Fry the chops about three to four minutes on each side until they are nice and brown. Skim them out and drain well on paper towels.

These may be kept in a 350° oven for 20 minutes.

Serve with Bearnaise sauce, snail butter or Madeira sauce.

Sauce Bearnaise

In a casserole place a finely chopped **dry shallot.** If shallots are not available, use small onions but Bearnaise is not as good with onions. Add:

> **Hollandaise sauce** (make amount specified in recipe in Basic Cooking)
>
> **2 Tbl. finely chopped, fresh tarragon or dry tarragon leaf**
>
> **10 black peppercorns,** crushed
>
> **½ cup white wine vinegar**

Place the casserole on the fire and cook until only 1/3 of the original volume is left. Take off the fire, cool for a few minutes then add the reduced sauce to the hollandaise. Then fold in **2 or 3 Tbl. finely chopped parsley.**

Serve with broiled meat, fish, roast beef, tenderloin, sirloin, eggs etc., etc. Can be served hot or cold.

Spinach Ring Farmiere

Fill with braised mushrooms.

> **Two pounds fresh spinach,** washed and cleaned

Wash the spinach in lukewarm water to remove sand and place in a large kettle with a small amount of water. Cover, place on fire and bring to a boil. Turn the spinach over and heat until wilted. This will take five to eight minutes. Drain in a large colander and cool. Squeeze out the water until the spinach is quite dry. Chop finely and place in a bowl. Then add:

> **¼ cup chopped green onion**
>
> **¼ cup chopped parsley**

¼ cup chopped mushrooms
1 tsp. ground nutmeg
¼ cup Parmesan cheese
4 to 5 egg yolks
1 to 2 Tbl. bread crumbs
Salt
Ground black pepper

Stir until well mixed and then place in a well buttered 1½ quart ring mold. Place mold in hot water bath and bake at 350° for 25 to 30 minutes. When ready to unmold, remove from hot water bath, let stand five to ten minutes and run a kitchen knife around the edges. Invert over a large heated platter or tray. Tap the bottom of the mold gently and it will fall out onto the tray. You must let this type of mold cool sufficiently before unmolding so that the cooking action stops. Then it will unmold easily and not fall apart.

The center may be filled with hot braised mushrooms. You may assemble this and keep it in a warm oven until it is ready to be served.

Braised Mushrooms

2½ to 3 pounds mushrooms, trimmed, washed,
    acidulated with the juice of one lemon
¼ cup butter or oil
½ cup chopped onion
Four friends
½ cup dry white wine
2 to 3 Tbl. chopped parsley
Salt
Ground black pepper

Be sure to cook the mushrooms in a stainless steel

or an enameled iron casserole. Place the butter or oil in the casserole and heat over medium heat. Add the chopped onion and saute until transparent. Add the four friends, wine and mushrooms and cook three to five minutes. Add the chopped parsley and season with salt and pepper. May be served separately or used to fill the center of the spinach ring.

Belgian Endive and Watercress Salad   Serves 8 to 10

> 5 to 6 stalks Belgian endive
> 2 bunches watercress
> Juice of 2 to 3 lemons
> Four friends
> Salt
> Ground black pepper
> 1 tsp. dry mustard
> ½ to ⅔ cup olive oil

Wash and trim the endive and watercress and arrange on salad plates or in a salad bowl. Chill.

In a mixing bowl or glass jar, add lemon juice, the four friends, salt, ground black pepper, dry mustard, and the olive oil.

Shake or blend well.

Shake well and pour over salad just before serving.

Sharlotka   Serves 8 to 10

One pound loaf of day old dark rye bread with the crust trimmed off. Break the bread into small pieces in a bowl and add:

> Grated rind of an orange
> Grated rind of a lemon

Juice of a lemon
1 cup dark brown sugar
1 tsp. cinnamon
1 tsp. grated nutmeg
1 cup dry red wine
1 ounce brandy

Stir this mixture until well combined and let stand until the bread is soft.

Peel and thinly slice **6 to 8 tart apples**
1 cup raisins soaked in warm water until plump, then drain
½ cup slivered almonds
1 cup currant or raspberry jelly

Generously butter a two-quart charlotte mold or souffle dish. Put a thin layer of the bread mixture on the bottom and add a layer of apples, some of the currant or raspberry jelly and a sprinkle of almonds.

Repeat these layers until all of the mixtures are used, ending with the bread mixture on top.

Bake in a 350° oven for an hour.

Serve warm or cold, unmolded with whipped cream.

Seafood Crepes
Stuffed Saddle of Lamb
Sauteed Mushrooms
Asparagus Salad
Strawberries with Sauce Nadine
Macaroons
Spanish Claret
(Marques de Riscal, Marques de Murrieta)

Seafood Crepes   Serves 8

Plan 2 crepes per person. This will make 18 to 22 crepes
or 5 or 6 the first try.

Crepe Batter

> **4 eggs**
> **1 cup milk**
> **1 cup flour**
> **1 Tbl. melted butter or oil**

Place the eggs in a bowl and stir until they are well
blended. Stir in the milk, the flour and melted butter.
Let the batter stand at room temperature for 30 minutes. After the batter has rested for 30 minutes, thin it
with milk to the consistency of whipping cream before
it has been whipped. This will assure you that your
crepes will be thin.

To cook the crepes you will need a mixture of ½
cup sweet butter and ½ **cup cooking oil** melted together.
Then skim. The oil keeps the butter from burning.

Use a five inch omelet or crepe pan. Put a quantity

of the oil-butter mixture in the pan and heat the pan and oil over medium heat until the pan is hot. Pour the butter-oil mixture back into the original container. Have only a thin film of the butter-oil mixture on the bottom of the heated pan. Pour one large tablespoon of the crepe batter in the pan. Tilt the pan and let the batter flow over the bottom until there is a thin coating covering the bottom. Circulate the pan over the heat so that the entire bottom of the pan is heated. On most household stoves there is no heat in the center of the burner, so there is a hot spot making things stick in the center of your pans. If you are using an electric stove, the pan must be in contact with the grid of the electric burner. Cook until the crepe is opaque. Shake the pan so that the crepe slides free.

Then with a quick circular jerk, flip the crepe. Remember, to return the pan to the same place so the crepe will fall back into the pan and not on the floor. Heat

it for a minute or so on this side. Then slide the crepe out on a flat kitchen or paper towel that has been spread out on a kitchen counter or table. Let the crepe cool. They may be arranged in stacks.

The cooked crepes should be translucent and almost paper thin and may be cooked with or without color. Without color, they are like parchment and not as well done as when they are light brown and cooked longer. Either taste fine — cook to your liking. The thinner the crepes the better. Do Not Panic if crepes have holes. They will not show when they are filled and rolled.

The crepes may be prepared in advance and kept wrapped in a damp towel in the refrigerator for a week. Or they may be stacked and put into sandwich bags and frozen (they keep six months in the freezer). Do not put crepes in plastic bags in the refrigerator because they will become moldy, especially in self-defrosting refrigerators.

Sauce for filling and to pour over the crepes

½ cup butter
1 medium-size onion, chopped
½ cup flour
1 Tbl. chicken base
Four friends
2 tsp. dry mustard
1 Tbl. sweet Hungarian paprika
2 cups milk or light cream
1 cup dry sherry
3 to 4 egg yolks

Melt the butter in a sauce pan and add the onion and saute until transparent. Remove from heat and stir in the flour, the chicken base, the four friends, dry mustard, paprika, and the milk or cream. Return to the fire, stir and bring to the boiling point. Add the dry sherry, stir, and return to a boil. Reduce heat and simmer 20 to

25 minutes. After the sauce has simmered, remove from the heat and stir the egg yolks into the hot sauce. This should be a fairly thick sauce. Yields three cups sauce.

Filling for the crepes

> **1 pound crab meat**
> **1 pound cooked, sliced shrimp**
> **½ cup finely diced white celery**
> **2 Tbl. chopped parsley**
> **1 cup grated Swiss cheese** (4 ounces)
> **1 cup prepared sauce**
> **1 cup milk or dry sherry or combination**
> **of the two.**

Place all of the ingredients in a bowl and mix. Use one half cup of mixture for each crepe. Place the mixture across the center of the crepe. Roll the crepe into a cigar shape and place the rolled, filled crepe in a shallow casserole, seam side down.

Take the remainder of the sauce and thin down with one cup of milk or dry sherry or combination of the two. Stir into the sauce and pour over the crepes in the casserole. Sprinkle the top with a pinch of **paprika, chopped parsley** and a bit of **grated Swiss cheese.**

Note: This may be made the day before. Take from the refrigerator and let come to room temperature. Heat in 350° oven for 20 to 25 minutes or until hot. Do Not Over Cook. Don't use a metal casserole. The metal reacts badly to the ingredients and you may poison your guests.

Stuffed Saddle of Lamb   Serves 6 to 8

Two boned, full saddles of lamb. Have extra fat trimmed

off. Lay flat. Will weigh 1½ to 2 pounds when prepared.

> **One pound thinly sliced Prosciutto or plain
> boiled ham**
>
> **Two pounds spinach,** washed, wilted, drained
> and finely chopped. Bind together with
> **½ cup heavy cream, 1 tsp. grated nutmeg,**
> and the **four friends.**
>
> **1 cup grated mozarella cheese**
> **½ cup chopped parsley**
> **Garlic salt**

Lay out the saddles of lamb, fat side down and cover
the inside surface with the thinly sliced ham. Then
cover with half of the spinach mixture, sprinkle with
the grated mozarella cheese and then the parsley. Roll
up in a jelly roll shape and place seam side down in
a shallow casserole or roasting pan. Sprinkle the outside
with **garlic salt.**

Roast in pre-heated 400° oven for 25 to 30 minutes.

Lamb Sauce

> **4 cups beef consomme**
> **1 cup tomato puree**
> **Four friends**
> **1 carrot,** peeled and chopped
> **1 cup dry red wine**
> **1 bay leaf**
> **½ cup dry Madeira**
> **Juice from ½ lemon**

Place all ingredients in a sauce pan and bring to a
boil. Reduce the heat and simmer. Reduce sauce until
it thickens and you have about two cups left. Remove

the bay leaf, add the Madeira and lemon juice. Heat but do not boil. Serve over the sliced lamb. (Good over other roasted and grilled meats, too.)

Sauteed Mushrooms

> **1½ pounds mushrooms caps.** Trim and wash quickly in lukewarm water. Dry and squeeze **juice of lemon** over them to keep them white.
> **2 Tbl. butter**
> **2 Tbl. oil**
> **¼ cup finely chopped onion**
> **Four friends**
> **Salt**
> **¼ cup chopped parsley**

Heat the oil and butter in a saute pan. Add the onion and cook until it is transparent. Add the mushrooms, the four friends, and salt and cook over high heat. Shake the pan over the heat, cooking three to four minutes. Garnish with chopped parsley.

Serve along with the lamb.

Asparagus Salad

> **Two pound fresh asparagus,** cut 5 or 6 inches in length. Cook. (See recipe in Basic Cooking.) Drain and cool.
> **Chopped parsley**
> **1 pound salad greens,** washed and cleaned
> **One bunch watercress**
> **2 or 3 Tbl. grated Sap Sago cheese**

Country French Dressing
> **½ cup white wine vinegar**

Juice of 1 lemon
Four friends
Ground black pepper
1 tsp. dry mustard
Kosher salt
½ to ⅔ cup olive oil

Place all in jar, bowl or blender. Beat or blend.

Arrange the lettuce on a salad plate. Place the cold, cooked asparagus spears on top. Garnish with the water-cress. Just before serving, pour ½ to 2/3 cup dressing over the asparagus and sprinkle with chopped parsley and two or three Tbl. grated Sap Sago cheese. Best served at room temperature.

Strawberries with Sauce Nadine   Serves 8

Two quarts strawberries, hulled, washed, drained and at room temperature. Place in crystal compote.

Sauce Nadine

Created for a very special friend and one of my original students and loyal supporters, Nadine Wessendorf.

2 cups granulated sugar
¼ cup sweet butter
Coarsely grated rind of two large navel
    oranges
½ cup slivered almonds
6 ounces defrosted orange juice concentrate
Orange sections from the two navel oranges
½ cup Grand Marnier

Heat a heavy sauce pan or black iron skillet that fits the size of your burner over medium-high heat until you feel the heat penetrate through the bottom of the pan. Pour in the sugar and immediately start stirring with a long handled wooden spoon until it starts to melt. Carefully stir until you have a golden syrup. (If it turns black you have burned the sugar.) Remove from the heat and place on a heat-proof board or tile. Stir in the butter, the coarsely grated orange rind, and the slivered almonds. Carefully add the orange juice concentrate a little at a time. Do not add all at once because the melted sugar will sputter up and cause a very bad burn. When you have stirred in all of the orange juice concentrate, add the orange sections and the Grand Marnier. Let the sauce cool. Don't try to taste during the cooking process. After the sauce is cool, store in a glass jar in the refrigerator. It will thicken when cold. It is best made a day in advance. Good over pancakes, waffles, sponge cakes, ices, ice cream and fresh fruits.

Pour the sauce over the strawberries. May be garnished with lightly sweetened **whipped cream** and served with Mrs. Lippert's **macaroons.**

Mushroom Consomme
Chicken Paprikash
Buttered Noodles
Green Salad
Hot Apple Tart with Brandy and Whipped Cream
Chenin Blanc

Mushroom Consomme   Serves 8

Good diet soup

> **1½ to 2 ounces dried mushrooms**
> **2 quarts beef consomme**
> **½ cup dry sherry or dry Madeira**
> **Juice of one lemon**

Soak the dry mushrooms in cold water for 20 to 30 minutes. When reconstituted, squeeze them out and place them in the consomme. Bring the consomme to the boiling point and simmer 30 to 40 minutes. Add the dry sherry or Madeira and the lemon juice. Return to the boiling point. Serve with thin **slices of lemon.**

Chicken Paprikash   Serves 8

> **¼ cup butter**
> **¼ cup olive oil**
> **4 large onions,** diced
> **8 chicken breasts,** skinned, boned and cut
>   into 2 inch pieces
> **½ cup flour**
> **Four friends**

1 pound mushrooms, washed and trimmed

2 cups dry white wine

1 to 2 bay leaves

1 to 2 Tbl. sweet Hungarian paprika

2 cups sour cream

¼ cup chopped parsley

Splash brandy

Place the butter and oil in a heavy dutch oven or casserole and heat. Add the diced onions and saute until transparent. Add the pieces of chicken and sear them, stirring occasionally. When the chicken is seared, stir in the flour and add the four friends, the mushrooms, bay leaves, wine, and the paprika. Stir and bring to the boiling point. Reduce the heat and simmer 25 to 30 minutes. Season with **salt** and **pepper** when tender. Just before serving, stir in the sour cream, the brandy and the chopped parsley. Serve with buttered noodles.

Buttered Noodles   Serves 8

8 to 12 ounces fine egg noodles

Butter - oil — ¼ cup total

Four friends

Ground black pepper

Add **two or three tablespoons oil** to a large pot of rapidly boiling salted water to keep the pasta from boiling over and from sticking together. Add the noodles and cook 6 to 8 minutes. Drain well. Place in a casserole and season with butter and oil, the four friends and ground black pepper to taste. May be kept warm or reheated in 350° oven 15 to 20 minutes.

Mixed Green Salad

Use a mixture of greens that pleases you — those that are in season when you want to use them. Pour **Country French Dressing** over the greens and your salad is complete.

Hot Apple Tart with Brandy Whipped Cream   Serves 8

10" tart - 8 servings

Pastry

2 cups all-purpose flour
¾ cup butter, softened
2 Tbl. sugar
Pinch of salt
1 whole egg
¼ cup water

Rub flour, butter, sugar and salt together until the consistency is like cornmeal. Add the egg, and gradually add the water until the dough forms. Wrap the dough in a damp towel and refrigerate for 20 to 30 minutes. After the pastry has set, roll out on a lightly floured board and line a ten inch tart pan.

Filling

4 large tart apples. Peel and core the apples. Slice thin. Squeeze **lemon juice** over the slices.

Place **8 ounces dry apricots** in a sauce pan with the **juice and rind of one lemon and one orange.**

Add ½ cup sugar and 1 cup water. Bring

to a boil and simmer 15 to 20 minutes until tender. Then cool.

1 cup apricots preserves
½ cup slivered almonds
Splash of brandy

Fill the bottom of the tart pastry with the cooled apricot mixture and add ½ of the slivered almonds. Then arrange the apple slices in a decorative overlapping pattern on top. Spread the top surface with the apricot preserves and then sprinkle on the remaining slivered almonds. Bake in the 350° oven for 30 to 45 minutes. When done, splash with brandy. I like this served warm.

Brandy Whipped Cream

1 pint cold whipped cream, stiffly beaten
4 Tbl. sugar
Grated rind of a large orange
1 ounce brandy

Beat the whipped cream until stiff and then beat in sugar, grated orange rind and brandy.

Serve with hot apple tart.

> ### Swiss Salad
> ### Choucroute Alsacienne
> ### Dark Rye Broad
> ### Black Forest Plum Cake
> ### Johannisberger Riesling

Swiss Salad   Serves 6 to 8
Good with cold meats and seafoods.

Line a bowl with **one pound Boston or bibb lettuce,** washed and dried. Then, add in layers:

2 cups red or Spanish onion, thinly sliced
8 hard-cooked eggs, quartered
2 cans white asparagus, drained
4 tomatoes, peeled and sliced
1 cup Swiss cheese, shredded

Just before serving, pour **½ cup Country French Dressing** over the salad and sprinkle with chopped parsley.

Choucroute Alsacienne   Serves 10 to 15
Great winter's night dining.

2 pounds fresh sauerkraut (blanched)
½ cup sweet butter
1 large onion, diced
2 tart apples, peeled and diced
2 to 4 cloves garlic
1 cup dry white wine
6 to 8 juniper berries, crushed **or ¼ cup gin**
Three friends
½ cup chopped parsley

Place the fresh sauerkraut in a stainless steel or enamel casserole, cover with cold water, bring to a boil and drain well.

Place the sweet butter in the casserole, and melt over medium heat. Add the onion and saute. Then add the apple, garlic cloves, dry white wine, juniper berries or gin, three friends, chopped parsley, and the blanched, drained sauerkraut. Simmer 30 to 45 minutes.

> **1 bunch carrots,** peeled, cut into equal size pieces. Cook, keeping them underdone. Drain.
>
> **3 to 4 Idaho potatoes,** peeled, cut into equal-size pieces. Cook, keeping them underdone. Drain.
>
> **Sausages,** about one pound each:
>
> **Fresh metts**
>
> **Breakfast sausages** (Blanch three to four minutes to release fat)
>
> **Knockwurst**
>
> **Bratwurst**
>
> **Bockwurst**
>
> **Garlic Franks**
>
> **Smoked pork chops or fresh** (seared) one per person
>
> **½ cup chopped parsley**

Heap the cooked sauerkraut in a large shallow casserole. Arrange the sausages and chops on top of the sauerkraut and the carrots and potatoes on top of the sausages. Sprinkle with chopped parsley.

Bake in 350° oven for 30 to 40 minutes.

Serve with **dark rye bread, dry white wine or steins of cold beer.**

Black Forest Plum Cake   Serves 8

Pastry

Put in mixing bowl and beat until light and creamy:
½ cup butter
⅔ cup sugar
Juice of one lemon
Pinch of allspice
½ tsp. nutmeg
½ tsp. cinnamon
½ tsp. ground cardamon
1 tsp. vanilla
1 whole egg
Stir in:
2 cups flour
2 tsp. baking powder
Should be well blended and have a dry consistency. Let this stand, covered with a towel, for 10 to 15 minutes to let the gluten develop in the flour. Roll this mixture between two pieces of wax paper and then line a ten inch quiche pan with the pastry.

Filling

1 cup apricot preserves
¼ cup slivered almonds
*1 quart fresh blue plums, stoned

Spread the apricot preserves on the bottom of the crust, add the almonds, and then lay the pitted plums in

---

*These plums are in season from October through January. You may substitute peaches or pears or dried fruits, but do not use canned plums.

171

a decorative overlapping pattern on top. Sprinkle the top with **sugar.**

Bake 30 to 40 minutes in a 350° oven. Serve warm with whipped cream.

Creamed Asparagus Soup
Marinated Flank Steak
Country Potatoes
Salad Marguerite
Chocolate Chaliapin
Medoc Bordeaux

Asparagus Soup   Serves 8

¼ cup butter
¼ cup chopped onion
¼ cup flour
Four friends
1 tsp. grated nutmeg
2 cups chicken broth
2 Tbl. chicken base
2 cups half and half
2 cups chopped, cooked asparagus

Melt the butter in a heavy sauce pan, add the onion and saute until transparent. Stir in the four friends, nutmeg, chicken broth, chicken base, half and half and bring to a boil. Reduce heat and add the asparagus. Simmer

25 to 30 minutes. Remove from the heat and blend in small batches in the blender on medium speed until smooth. Return the soup to the heat. Bring up to the boiling point. Taste for seasoning. Garnish with **one of the following:**

> **Asparagus tips**
> **Chopped hard-cooked egg**
> **Parsley**
> **Dot of sour cream**
> **Lemon slices**
> **Croutons**

May be served hot or cold.

Marinated Flank Steak   Serves 6 to 8

Four flank steaks weighing one to one and one half pounds each.

> Place in shallow pan and marinate each with:
> A drizzle of **olive oil**
> **Four friends**
> **Small Tbl. Dijon mustard**
> **Juice of ½ lemon**
> **Ground black pepper**

May marinate overnight, refrigerated or two hours at room temperature.

Grill in pre-heated broiler about three minutes on each side. Keep on the rare or pink side. If they are well-done they will be very tough. Slice in thin slices across the grain. Serve with the **pan juices.**

Country Potatoes   Serves 6 to 8

Three or four Idaho potatoes. Wash and put into sauce pan. Cover with **cold salted water.** Bring to a boil. Reduce heat and simmer until tender, not overcooked. Drain and let cool. Peel and coarsely grate. Place in a bowl and add:

>**3 to 4 eggs**
>**½ cup chopped parsley**
>Lightly toss.

In frying pan heat:

>**¼ cup oil**
>**1 large onion,** chopped
>Saute until transparent.

Add:

>**Four friends**
>**Ground black pepper**
>**1 cup diced, cook ham**

Add the ham and onion mixture to the potatoes and lightly fold together.

In a frying pan heat until very hot, **2 Tbl. oil.** Then add the potato mixture. Shake the pan to keep the potatoes from sticking and heat until crust forms around the edge. Then cover and reduce heat and cook 25 to 30 minutes.

When the potatoes are cooked turn out on a platter or tray. Sprinkle with **chopped parsley.** Cut into wedges.

Salad Marguerite   Serves 8

>**1 pound cooked, green beans**
>**3 or 4 peeled, sliced tomatoes**
>**1 cup julienne beets**
>**1 head cauliflower, cut into flowerettes.**
>Cook.

Arrange these vegetables on a tray in an attractive pattern and coat with the following dressing.

Dressing

In a bowl, mix well:
¼ cup thinly sliced green onion
Four friends
¼ cup capers with juice
3 Tbl. chopped parsley
Juice of one lemon
1 tsp. dry mustard
¼ cup white wine vinegar
½ to ⅔ cup olive oil
Salt to taste

Chocolate Chaliapin   Serves 8

In a heavy sauce pan melt carefully:
8 ounces semi-sweet chocolate
2 cups whipping cream
¼ cup sugar
Pinch of salt
Stir occasionally and do not let boil.
When melted add:
½ cup Creme de Cacao
½ cup vodka
Heat slightly. This mixture should be the consistency of light custard. Serve in small cups with
whipped cream on top and a bit of **grated chocolate.**
Good on a cold day before the fire.

Christmas Eve Dinner Buffet
Oysters on the Half Shell
Iced Shrimp with Russian Mayonnaise
Pâte en Croute
Glögg
Virginia Ham
Cold Tenderloin
Roast Goose
Chestnut Stuffing
Stuffed Apples
Prunes in Port
Claire's Red Cabbage
Potato Dumplings
Boche de Noël
Black Forest Cherry Torte
Miniature Fruit Cakes
Christmas Cookies
Marzipan
Nuts

Oysters on the Half Shell

Serve on beds of crushed ice with **white horseradish** and **lemon wedges.**

Iced Shrimp with Russian Mayonnaise

(See recipes for Marinated Shrimp and Russian Mayonnaise.)

Pâte en Croute
See index for recipe.

Glögg
Serves about 32

"Guaranteed to put all your guests in a carolling mood."

> **1 gallon dry red burgundy**
> **2 oranges,** sliced
> **2 lemons,** sliced
> **½ cup sugar**
> **2 sticks cinnamon**
> **1 Tbl. cardamon seeds**
> **10 whole cloves**
> **1 cup Grand Marnier**

Pour wine into a stainless steel or enamel pot; add sliced fruits and spices tied up in a cheese cloth bag. Bring the mixture to a boil and remove immediately from the heat. When ready to serve, remove the spice bag and reheat the punch. Pour into a silver or enamel bowl placed over a heating unit to keep punch warm.

Add **one quart vodka or Aquavit.** Serve in punch glasses.

Virginia Ham

Already cooked. Can be purchased at Pogue's, Shillito's, Huber's, or wherever you may shop.

Cold Tenderloin

See recipe — Basic Cooking

Roast Goose
Serves 6 to 8

8-10 pound goose

Since fresh goose is a thing of the past, allow two days

for your frozen bird to defrost in the refrigerator. Defrosting poultry at room temperature causes damage to flavor and texture.

Several hours before roasting, bring defrosted **goose** to room temperature. Wash and dry well. Remove excess fat from inside of cavity. **Salt** interior and fill lightly with **stuffing.** (See recipe for stuffing below)

Pierce stuffed goose with kitchen fork around the legs and wings to allow the fat to drain from the bird. Preheat oven to 450°. Place the goose, breast up, on a rack in a shallow open pan. Roast in a moderate 350° oven for 2½ hours, or until the drumstick moves readily. Pour off the fat as it accumulates in the pan.

To insure a crispy brown skin, remove the goose from the oven ten minutes before it is cooked, and, with a pastry brush, brush the bird generously with **ice water.** Turn the oven to 450° for the last ten minutes of roasting.

Chestnut Stuffing   Enough for 8-10 pound goose

Stuffing is a highly perisable item so, to be on the safe side, prepare your stuffing the same day that you roast the goose. To speed up the process, cook gizzards and assemble ingredients ahead of time.

> **Goose gizzards,** chopped
> **3 apples,** cored but not peeled, cut into ½ inch cubes
> **2 hard dinner rolls**
> **1 cup dry white wine**
> **Salt**
> **Pepper**
> **Accent**

1 cup canned French chestnuts, drained, coarsely broken

Soak dinner rolls in wine about five minutes or until soggy. Simmer gizzards in water until tender — about 45 minutes. Combine all the ingredients in a bowl.

Stuffed Apples   Serves 10

"A classic accompaniment for goose — or any kind of game."

> **10 small yellow delicious apples** (one per person)
> **1½ cups white wine**
> **1 Tbl. sugar**
> **Juice of 1 lemon**
> **Jar of Peiselbeeren (lingonberry)**

Peel and core apples and place in shallow heat-proof pan. Add wine, sugar and lemon. Over high heat bring liquid to a boil. Remove pan from heat and set two minutes. (Do not overcook; apples must remain firm.)

Drain apples, fill cavity with Peiselbeeren, a cross between cranberry and current. If this German preserve is not available, substitute raspberry jam.

Prunes in Port   Serves 6 to 8

If you're lucky you'll have some leftovers for breakfast.

> **1 pound box California pitted prunes**
> **Rind and juice of 1 orange and 1 lemon**
> **1 stick cinnamon**
> **2 whole cloves**
> **Pinch sugar**
> **Bottle of sweet port**

In a heavy sauce pan, place fruits, spices and sugar; cover with generous amount of port, and bring mixture to a boil. Reduce heat and simmer 15 minutes. Transfer prunes to ceramic or glass dish.

When cool, remove fruit rinds and spices. Serve in compote dish at room temperature.

Claire's Red Cabbage   Serves 6 to 8
Even calorie-conscious guests can't resist this dish.

> **3 small heads cabbage** (3 pounds)
> **½ pound raw, diced bacon**
> **1 medium onion,** fiinely chopped
> **2 tart red apples,** cored and diced
> **1 Tbl. caraway seeds**
> **2 Tbl. red wine vinegar**
> **3 Tbl. dry red wine**

Remove outer leaves and the core from cabbage. Thinly slice remainder of the cabbage.

In heavy sauce pan, (not aluminum), place bacon, onion and apples. Heat until onion becomes transparent. Add cabbage and cook, uncovered, over medium heat. Stir occasionally until cabbage wilts.

Add caraway seeds, vinegar and wine to mixture. Lower heat and cook until tender, about one-half hour. Add salt and pepper to taste. Flavor should be tart; add more vinegar, if necessary.

Potato Dumplings   Serves 6 to 8

Claire used to fix dumplings the German way which is to poach them in boiling water — until she got tired of being in the kitchen all evening! Using this newer method, dumplings can be prepared the day before, and lose nothing in the translation.

10 medium-size Idaho potatoes
½ pound raw bacon, diced
1 medium onion, chopped
1 cup seasoned croutons
1 large egg
½ cup chopped parsley
1 Tbl. flour
1 cup melted butter
Salt
Pepper

Boil potatoes, uncovered, in their jackets until just tender. Drain and cool. Peel them and grate or rice them. Do not mash. Fry bacon with onion; when onion becomes transparent, pour off excess fat. Add croutons to frying pan, then add this mixture to riced potatoes. Add egg, parsley, flour and salt and pepper to potato mixture and fold ingredients. Form golf ball size dumplings. (Before handling potato mixture, run hands under cold water, dry and dust with flour.) Place dumplings in buttered casserole. Do not stack them and refrigerate.

Several hours before serving time, bring dumplings up to room temperature. Dust with fine **bread crumbs** and drizzle **butter** over dumplings. Bake in 350° oven 30 to 40 minutes, or until heated through.

Boche de Noël
Black Forest Cherry Torte
Miniature Fruit Cakes
Christmas Cookies
Marzipan

These are all traditional Christmas desserts. Servatii's Pastry Shop or Lippert's Bakery or your own favorite baker can supply these beautiful treats for your Christmas gala.

Nuts

Serve plates of assorted nuts that please you.

Artichokes and Shrimp Sauce Charon
Breast of Chicken Cordon Bleu
Buttered Spinach Noodles
Watercress Salad
Lemon Snow
Pouilly Fuisse

Artichokes and Shrimp Sauce Charon   Serves 8

   ½ cup freshly grated Parmesan cheese
   *8 or 16 canned artichoke bottoms, drained
      and acidulated
   Ground black pepper

---

*Use one artichoke per person for first course, two for a main course.

¼ cup chopped parsley
¼ cup chopped onion
¼ cup bread crumbs
1 pound large shrimp, partially cooked
2 to 3 Tbl. olive oil

Place the artichoke bottoms in a shallow, oiled, heat-proof casserole, cavity side up. Mix the cheese, parsley, onion, and bread crumbs together in a bowl and fill the cavities of the artichokes. Place two or three shrimp on top. Drizzle with a little olive oil.

Bake in 350° oven for 10 to 15 minutes. When heated, remove from the oven and coat the tops of the artichokes and shrimp with the Charon Sauce, a sprinkle of **paprika, chopped parsley,** and garnish with **watercress.**

Sauce Charon (tomato flavored hollandaise)
4 to 5 egg yolks
1 Tbl. water
1 cup (2 sticks) melted, skimmed, sweet butter
Salt
Juice of 1 to 2 lemons
1 Tbl. tomato paste

Place egg yolks and water into heat-proof bowl over hot water. Beat with a wire whisk until hot and fluffy. Gradually beat in the melted butter a little at a time until all has been absorbed. Add the salt and lemon juice and stir in the tomato paste. Do not over heat. Remove from the heat and from the hot water. Spoon the sauce (cooled to room temperature) over the hot artichokes and shrimp.

Breast of Chicken Cordon Bleu

> 8 large chicken breasts, skinned, boned, flattened
> 8 slices of Prosciutto or Virginia ham
> 8 slices of imported Swiss cheese
> 1 cup flour
> 3 eggs beaten
> 1 to 2 cups fine bread crumbs
> 2 Tbl. oil
> ½ cup melted butter

Lay the flattened chicken breasts out on a cutting board. Place one slice of ham on each chicken breast and one slice of Swiss cheese on the ham. Then fold the chicken breast over like a sandwich. Dust the chicken breast in the flour and pat between your hands. Dip the chicken breast into the beaten eggs and then coat them with the bread crumbs. Place on tray or wire rack to dry for 10 or 15 minutes.

Heat the butter and oil in a saute pan. When hot, fry the coated, filled chicken breasts until they are golden brown on both sides. Remove, drain, and arrange then in a shallow casserole.

When ready to reheat, place in 350° oven and cook ten to fifteen minutes or until heated through.

Buttered Spinach Noodles   Serves 8

> 8 to 12 ounces spinach noodles (green)
> ¼ cup melted butter
> 1 tsp. ground nutmeg
> Four friends
> Ground black pepper

Drop the noodles in boiling, salted water and

cook 8 to 12 minutes. Drain, place in a shallow casserole and season with the melted butter, nutmeg, four friends, and ground black pepper.

May be done ahead of time. Reheat the casserole in 350° oven 10 to 12 minutes.

Watercress Salad   Serves 8

> **3 large bunches watercress,** trimmed and washed
> **Juice of 2 or 3 lemons**
> **½ cup olive oil**
> **Salt**
> **Ground black pepper**

Place the trimmed, washed watercress in a salad bowl and chill. Just before serving, sprinkle with the lemon juice, olive oil, salt and ground black pepper.

Must be served right away. Will not hold up.

Lemon Snow   Serves 8 to 10
Usually served during the Christmas holidays.

> **2 cups whipping cream,** stiffly beaten
> **8 egg whites,** room temperature
> **1 tsp. cream of tartar**
> **½ cup granulated sugar**
> **3 Tbl. plain gelatin** softened in **½ cup cold water.** Melt over hot water. Cool slightly (warm).
> **Grated rinds of 2 to 3 lemons**
> **Juice of 2 to 3 lemons** (½ cup)

Beat the egg whites with the cream of tartar until they are stiff, but not dry. Gradually beat in the sugar a little at a time until stiff; then beat the warm, melted gelatin into the egg whites. Add the lemon juice and grated lemon rind. Remove the bowl from the mixer and place in the refrigerator and let set for 5 or 10 minutes. It should not be firm. Then, with a wide rubber spatula, fold in the stiffly beaten whipped cream until well blended.

Pour into an oiled, two-quart mold, cover with saran wrap and chill for two hours in the refrigerator.

Unmold by quickly dipping the mold in warm water. Tip the mold to one side and give the side a sharp tap with your hand to break the side of the mold loose and create an air pocket between the mold and the mousse. Turn out onto a platter or tray. Decorate the top with swirls of **whipped cream,** or **strawberries,** or **candied violets** or **fresh raspberries.**

Chestnut Consomme
Danish Loin of Pork
Spaetzle
Danish Red Cabbage
Danish Chocolate Mousse
Dry Rhine Wine

Chestnut Consomme   Serves 8

Five to six cups beef consomme
Four friends

1 pound French chestnuts, drained
Juice of 1 lemon
1 cup dry Madeira

Place all the ingredients in a sauce pan and bring to a boil. Reduce the heat and simmer for 30 minutes.

Just before serving, add **one cup dry Maderia.** Taste for seasoning. Serve with **lemon slices.**

Danish Loin of Pork   Serves 8

Three pound eye of pork loin roast. After boning, cut pocket through the center of the eye.

In a sauce pan put:
8 ounces pitted prunes
1 Tbl. cracked ginger
1 tsp. anise seed
Juice and rind of one lemon

Cover with **water or gin** and bring to a boil. Reduce the heat and simmer until most of the moisture has been absorbed. Let cool.

Stuff the prune mixture into the cavity of the pork and place in a roasting pan, fat side up. Dust the top with **garlic salt** and **ground black pepper.**

Roast in 350° oven 1½ to 2 hours, basting occasionally with **gin** or **orange juice.**

This may be served hot or cold.

Spaetzle   Serves 8

Place in a bowl and mix well:
4 whole eggs
1 cup milk
Pinch of salt

1 tsp. maggi

Add **1½ to 2 cups flour** until you have a heavy batter. Let rest for 30 minutes.

In a shallow sauce pan have **4 or 5 cups of gently boiling, salted water, chicken stock or beef stock.**

Drop the batter into the stock a little at a time through a spaetzle maker or a large hole strainer. Cook until they float to the surface. Skim them out and place in a shallow, buttered casserole. Add more **butter** to keep the spaetzle from sticking together.

 Add **chopped parsley and Parmesan cheese** if desired. Keep warm or reheat in 350° oven for 10 to 15 minutes.

Danish Red Cabbage   Serves 8

> **½ cup butter**
> **½ cup onion**, diced
> **2 tart apples**, cored, peeled, and diced
> **1 Tbl. caraway seed**
> **Four friends**
> **2 pounds red cabbage**, cored, chopped or grated
> **3 Tbl. red wine vinegar**
> **½ cup red wine**
> **1 tsp. sugar**
> **Salt**

Melt the butter in an enamel sauce pan, add the onion, and saute until it is transparent. Add the apple, caraway seed, four friends, and cook a few minutes. Add the cabbage, red wine vinegar, wine, sugar, and salt. Bring to a boil, reduce the heat and simmer uncovered for 30 to 45 minutes.

This dish is better made a few days in advance and then reheated. Store in glass or pottery. Add additional wine when reheating.

Danish Chocolate Mousse   Serves 8 to 10

In a small heat-proof bowl put:
>3 Tbl. plain gelatin
>½ cup Creme de Cacao
>4 ounces semi-sweet chocolate
>¼ cup cold water

Place over hot water and heat until melted. Let cool.

Stiffly beat **2 cups whipping cream.** Set aside.

In a mixing bowl stiffly beat:
>6 egg whites
>Pinch of salt

Gradually add **½ cup sugar.**

Fold the whipped cream and egg whites together. Then fold in the cooled, melted chocolate and blend well. Fold in:
>½ cup toasted, slivered almonds
>1 cup crumbled almond macaroons

Line the sides of a 1½ quart mold with **ladyfingers** and cover the bottom with **grated chocolate.** Fill the center with the chocolate mousse mixture. Cover with saran wrap and refrigerate for at least two hours.

To unmold, dip in warm water and turn out on a plate. Decorate the top with **vanilla flavored whipped cream** and **grated chocolate.**

Chicken Congee
Sweet and Sour Pork
Rice
Oranges, Strawberries and Loquats with Ginger
California Johannisberg

Chicken Congee   Serves 8

In a soup pot place:
> **8 to 10 cups strong chicken stock**
> **¼ cup rice**

Bring to a boil, reduce the heat and simmer 30 to 40 minutes or until the rice is very soft. Add:
> **¼ cup thinly sliced green pepper**
> **½ cup diced, cooked ham**
> **½ cup diced, cooked chicken**
> **½ cup diced celery**
> **¼ cup chopped parsley**
> **4 to 5 dried mushrooms,** sliced. Reconstitute by soaking in cold water 15 to 20 minutes. Then squeeze them out.

Season with:
> **1 drop tabasco**
> **1 Tbl. soy sauce**
> **1 tsp. Accent**

Return to the heat and bring to a boil.
This is a fairly thick soup.

Sweet and Sour Pork   Serves 6 to 8

Prepare and set aside:

2 **medium carrots,** peeled, cut into thin
   strips and then cut into one inch pieces
1 **bunch green onions,** trimmed, cut into
   one inch pieces
1 **small green pepper,** trimmed, seeded, cut
   into thin strips
1 **cup diced, fresh pineapple**
½ **cup water chestnuts,** sliced thinly
1 **cup kumquats,** cut in half, seeded
3 **pork tenderloins,** sliced into ½ inch
   thick slices

In a bowl put:

3 to 4 **egg whites**
½ **cup cornstarch**
2 **Tbl. soy sauce**

Beat together and dip slices of pork in this mixture
to coat.

In a wok or heavy frying pan, heat ½ **cup vegetable
or sesame oil** until very hot. Fry the dipped slices of
pork in the hot oil for three to four minutes or until
crisp and golden. Remove from the fat, drain, and keep
warm.

In the wok or frying pan heat:

¼ **cup cooking or sesame oil** until hot

Add:

Sliced carrots
Green pepper strips
Green onion

Cook about five minutes until they are softened
slightly. Then add the sliced water chestnuts, kumquats,
2 to 3 **Tbl. brown sugar** ¼ **cup red wine vinegar,** ¼ **cup
soy sauce.**

Bring to the boiling point and add the diced pineapple.

In a small bowl stir together:

3 Tbl. cornstarch
½ cup pineapple juice
½ cup dry sherry

Pour this mixture over the ingredients in the wok or skillet. Stir, cover, and heat three to five minutes or until thickened. Pour the hot sauce over the drained, warm, fried pork slices. Serve with boiled white rice.

Oranges, Strawberries, and Loquats with Ginger

Serves 8

In a crystal bowl put:

3 or 4 large navel oranges, peeled and thinly sliced
1 quart strawberries, stemmed and washed
1 cup loquats (if canned, drain well)
¼ cup crystallized ginger, sliced thinly
1 cup apricot preserves

Blend all together. May be chilled or served at room temperature.

Bouillabaisse
Thick Garlic Croutons
Mixed Green Salad
Peaches with Kirsch and Vanilla Ice Cream
Pinot Chardonnay
or Chablis

Bouillabaisse   Serves 10 to 12
Good local translation.

In a large heavy soup pot heat:
> **¼ cup olive oil until hot**

Then add and saute for five minutes:
> **1 large onion,** chopped
> **2 cups diced, white hearts of celery**
> **1 bunch green onions,** chopped
> **1 medium green pepper,** chopped
> **2 to 4 cloves of garlic,** chopped

Then add:
> **Four friends**
> **1 Tbl. curry powder**
> **2 tsp. paprika**
> **2 bay leaves**
> **2 tsp. gumbo file powder**
> **2 tsp. saffron** (strings or powder)
> **2 cups peeled, chopped tomatoes**
> **One 46 ounce can tomato juice**

Bring to a boil and add:
> **2 cups dry white wine** and simmer 25 to
> 30 minutes.

193

Then add:

- 1 **pound sole fillets,** coarsely chopped, fresh or frozen
- 1 **pound red snapper,** fresh or frozen
- 1 **pound lump crabmeat**
- 2 **pounds shrimp,** peeled and deveined
- 2 **cups clams and their juice** (canned)
- 2 **cups mussels in their shells and juice** (canned)

Bring to the boiling point Do not over cook. Garnish with **1 cup chopped parsley.**

Serve with **crusty French bread or thick garlic croutons** in deep soup plates.

Thick Garlic Croutons

In a sauce pan heat **½ cup butter or olive oil** and saute **one medium-size, finely diced onion** until transparent. Add **5 or 6 cloves of pressed garlic.** Heat for one or two minutes. Remove from the heat and add the **four friends** and **¼ cup chopped parsley.** Let cool.

Cut the **French bread** into two-inch thick diagonal slices and coat the surfaces with the mixture.

Arrange the coated slices on a baking tray and dust with **Parmesan cheese** and a sprinkling of **paprika.**

Heat in a 400° oven 15 to 20 minutes or until crispy and brown. Serve hot.

Mixed Green Salad

Your choice of mixed greens with Country French Dressing.

Peaches with Kirsch and Vanilla Ice Cream — Serves 8

Place **16 drained, canned white peach halves** in bowl. Add **¼ cup Kirsch** and let marinate covered for several hours in the refrigerator.

Scoop the **vanilla ice cream** in dessert bowls and place the peach halves on each side of the ice cream. Decorate with **whipped cream swirls** and **shaved chocolate.**

> **Polynesian Ribs**
> **Chinese Chicken**
> **Rice**
> **Ripe Persimmons**
> **Almond Macaroons**
> **California Chenin Blanc**
> **(Beringer, Krug, Mirassou, Sebastiani)**

Polynesian Ribs — Serves 6 to 8

> **6 to 8 pounds lean, well-trimmed, country ribs**
> **⅛ cup dry mustard**
> **Four friends**
> **½ to ⅔ cup soy sauce**

2 to 3 Tbl. grated fresh ginger root. If fresh ginger root is not available, omit it. Do not substitute dried ginger root.

1 to 2 cups dry sherry

Place the ribs in a large pot, cover with cold water, bring to a boil and then drain to remove the excess fat from the meat.

Rub the outside surfaces of the ribs with the dry mustard, four friends, grated ginger root and soy sauce. Place the ribs in a roasting pan and roast in a pre-heated 400° oven 30 to 40 minutes, basting with the dry sherry and turning them as they cook.

Remove from the oven and glaze with the sauce. If needed, add more sherry to the bottom of the pan. Return to the oven for another 15 minutes to finish the surface glazing.

These ribs may be served hot or cold.

Glaze for Ribs

2 cups apricot preserves or orange marmalade
Juice of one lemon
Four friends
2 to 4 Tbl. soy sauce
2 Tbl. horseradish, drained

Place all the ingredients in a sauce pan, bring to a boil, reduce heat and simmer five to ten minutes. Spoon sauce over ribs, then return to oven to glaze.

Chinese Chicken   Serves 8

Slice each of the following and arrange in separate piles or bowls.

1 **large green pepper,** trimmed, seeded, cut into thin, two-inch strips

1 **medium-size onion,** diced

1 **cup white celery,** cut into thin, two-inch strips

1 **bunch trimmed, green onions,** cut into one-inch pieces

1 **pound snow pea pods,** trim and string

1 **cup thinly sliced mushrooms,** acidulated

4 **or 5 whole chicken breasts,** skinned, boned and cut into two-inch strips

1 **cup sliced bamboo shoots**

½ **cup sliced water chestnuts**

1 **cup diced ham in ½-inch cubes**

In a wok or large frying pan, heat **¼ cup sesame or vegetable oil.** When hot, add the celery, green pepper, green onion, and the onion. Stir over the heat until the vegetables are glazed (about three to four minutes). Push the vegetables to the side and add the pieces of chicken. Cook them five to eight minutes or until they are opaque looking. Then squeeze **2 or 3 Tbl. ginger juice** over them (from about ¼ cup grated fresh ginger root — place ginger root in towel and squeeze).

Then add the ham, mushrooms, water chestnuts, bamboo shoots, **1 tsp. Accent, 1 drop tabasco sauce, and ¼ cup soy sauce.** Cover and steam five minutes. Then add:

½ **cup chopped parsley**

½ **cup dry sherry**

2 **to 3 Tbl. arrowroot**

Stir. Place snow pea pods on top, cover, and heat three or four minutes until the sauce has thickened and the pea pods are heated, but still very crisp.

Sprinkle with one cup **Macadamia nuts** just before serving. Serve with boiled white rice.

Ripe Persimmons and Almond Macaroons
Wash and dry the persimmons.

Perfectly ripe persimmons, at room temperature, served with almond macaroons from Mrs. Lippert's bakery add just the right flavor to this menu. What a perfect ending!

> **Quick Cassoulet**
> **Salad for Cassoulet**
> **Fruit and Cheese Tray**
> **White Graves**

Quick Cassoulet Serves 10 to 12

In a heavy sauce pan, heat **2 Tbl. butter.** Add and saute one **medium-size chopped onion** until it is transparent. Add **2 pounds lean pork,** diced into one inch cubes or use **sliced pork tenderloins** and sear them until they are gray, about five to eight minutes. Then add:

> **Four friends**
> **2 or 3 cloves chopped garlic**
> **½ cup diced celery**

1 tsp. thyme
2 bay leaves
2 cups peeled, chopped tomatoes
1 leek, sliced, washed
2 carrots, peeled and diced

Stir and simmer for 30 minutes.

Have ready:

1 five pound duck, roasted, boned, diced
(see recipe Canard Bigarade)
1 pound hard salami, cut into one inch
cubes
Three 15 ounce cans drained flageolets
1 cup chopped parsley
1 cup bread crumbs

In a deep pottery casserole, in layers, in this order,
add:

Chopped parsley
Thin layer of flageolets
Meat mixture: pork, duck, hard salami
Parsley
Thin layer of flageolets
Meat mixture: pork, duck, hard salami
Thin layer of flageolets
Chopped parsley

Add one cup dry white wine and then generously
coat the top with the bread crumbs.

Bake in 350° oven one hour or until the juices have
thickened and the cassoulet is well heated through.

Salad for Cassoulet   Serves 10 to 12

6 or 8 heads Belgian endive, trimmed,
washed, separated

2 bunches watercress, trimmed and cooked
2 cups sliced, pickled beets
3 avocados, peeled and sliced

Arrange the endive and avocados on one side of a tray. Place the beets in the center of the tray and the watercress on the other side.

Pour ½ **cup Country French Dressing** over the endive and avocadoes, NOT on the beets and watercress.

Fruit and Cheese Tray

Arrange a selection of these whole fruits, cheeses and biscuits on a large tray.

Ripe pears
Apples
Seedless grapes
Spanish melon slices
Peaches
Brie cheese
Port-Salut cheese
Danish blue cheese
Hard bread or cheese biscuits
Sweet butter

Tomatoes Stuffed with Crab Meat
Sweetbreads with Ham and Mushrooms
Hominy Grits Souffle
Sabayon with Strawberries
Portuguese Rosé
(Alencia)

Tomatoes Stuffed with Crab Meat   Serves 8

Eight ripe tomatoes, peeled, tops cut off and carefully scooped out

Filling for tomatoes

> **1 cucumber,** peeled, seeded and finely chopped
> **1 tsp. salt**
> **⅔ cup mayonnaise**
> **½ cup sour cream**
> **Four friends**
> **White pepper**
> **1 Tbl. dill weed**
> **2 Tbl. chopped parsley**
> **1 pound crab meat***

Place all the ingredients in a bowl and mix carefully. Stuff the mixture into the tomatoes and arrange on plates. Garnish with **watercress.**

Sweetbreads with Ham and Mushrooms   Serves 8

Four pair veal sweetbreads — should be fresh and very light pink in color.

*In place of the crab meat you may substitute diced shrimp, chicken or lobster.

To clean:

Place in a pan and cover with **cold, salted water.** Add the **juice and rind of a lemon** and let the sweet-breads soak for one hour. Wash well and place in a sauce pan. Cover with **cold, salted water** and add a **slice of onion, juice and rind of a lemon, bay leaf, and celery.** Bring to the boiling point, then reduce the heat and simmer for 10 to 12 minutes. Wash in cold water and let cool. Remove veins and membranes from the outside of the sweetbreads. Store in refrigerator in cold salted water.

Arrange the sweetbreads in a casserole and add **one pound diced cooked ham** and a **one pound can drained, French chestnuts.** Pour sauce over sweetbreads.

Sauce

> ½ **cup butter**
> 1 **medium-size onion,** diced
> ½ **cup flour**
> ½ **cup tomato puree**
> 1 **cup dry red wine**
> 2 **cups beef consomme**
> 1 **pound mushroom caps,** washed, trimmed
> ½ **cup dry Madeira**

Melt the butter in a sauce pan and add the onion and saute until transparent. Stir in the flour, tomato puree, wine, consomme and the mushroom caps. Bring to the boiling point and reduce the heat and simmer for 25 minutes. Add the dry Madeira and a **few drops of lemon juice.** Pour sauce over the sweetbreads. Reheat in 350° oven for 30 minutes.

Hominy Grits Souffle   Serves 8

In a heavy sauce pan saute and drain **½ pound diced bacon.** Add **one medium onion,** finely diced and saute with drained bacon. Then add:

> **Four friends**
> **1 cup grits**
> **1 Tbl. chicken base**
> **4 cups water**

Bring to a boil, then simmer 25 to 30 minutes or until grits are cooked. Let cool.

Stiffly beat **8 egg whites** with a **pinch of salt.**

Add the **eight egg yolks** and **½ cup Parmesan cheese** to the cooked grits.

Fold the hominy mixture into the egg whites. Pour the mixture into a two-quart casserole that has been buttered and dusted with Parmesan cheese. Brush the top with **cream.**

Bake in 350° oven 30 to 40 minutes until brown and puffy. Serve immediately.

This can be mixed one hour ahead. In this case, invert a bowl over the souffle to completely cover it and let it rest at room temperature.

Saybayon with Strawberries   Serves 6 to 8

Place in a large bowl over hot water:

> **8 to 10 egg yolks**
> **2 Tbl. water**
> **⅔ cup sugar**

Beat with wire whisk until light and fluffy. Gradually beat in **2 cups dry white wine** that has been warmed. When the egg yolks have absorbed the wine, add the **juice of 1 or 2 lemons.**

Do not over heat the sauce. It will curdle. If your bowl is too hot, remove it from the heat and place it in cold water to cool.

Serve the sauce warm over **strawberries, poached pears or peaches.** For a cold Sabayon, let the sauce cool and then fold in half the volume of stiffly beaten **whipped cream.**

This sauce may also be frozen as a cold mousse. Good with **shaved chocolate** or **chocolate sauce.**

Marinated Shrimp
Chicken Gregory
Caesar Salad
Zabaglione
Barolo
(Pio Cesare, Borgogno
Pio Cesare 1961 is especially good)

Marinated Shrimp   Serves 8

Two pounds frozen, peeled, deveined shrimp (Mexican Gulf Shrimp are best)

Place the shrimp in a sauce pan, cover with cold, salted water and add:

        Generous amount **kosher salt (¼ cup)**
        2 bay leaves
        Juice and rinds of 2 lemons

Medium-size onion, diced
2 stalks celery
½ cup cider vinegar
Parsley stems (bunch)

Heat and stir occasionally. Bring just up to the point where the water begins to boil and the shrimp have turned pink. Drain immediately, wash and cool in cold water. This will give you tender pink shrimp.

Store in cold water with a **pinch of salt** and **one or two sliced lemons** in the refrigerator. Will keep two or three days only.

Pour the following mixture over the drained shrimp and marinate several hours:

½ cup Country French Dressing
¼ cup drained capers
¼ cup chopped parsley
¼ cup brandy
¼ cup finely diced onions
1 Tbl. dill weed

Put in bowl and stir.

Arrange the marinated shrimp on a **bed of lettuce** and serve with **lemon wedges, parsley** and hard rolls.

Chicken Gregory   Serves 6 to 8

Originally created for Edward M. Condon, President of the H. & S. Pogue Co.

6 to 8 chicken breasts
Four friends
6 to 8 Tbl. butter
1 cup dry white wine

Place chicken breasts in a roasting pan. Sprinkle with the four friends, one Tbl. butter for each chicken breast and pour the dry white wine in the bottom of the pan. Roast in pre-heated 350° oven 30 to 45 minutes or until done. When lukewarm, skin and bone. Set aside.

Green Noodles

12 to 16 ounces green (spinach) noodles cooked in boiling, salted water. Drain. Season with the **four friends, one tsp. grated nutmeg, two to three Tbl. butter or oil.**

Braised Mushrooms

One pound mushroom caps, trimmed, washed and acidulated.

Place in sauce pan with **½ cup dry white wine** and the **four friends.** Heat three to five minutes. Drain, reserving the juices.

Quick Tomato Sauce   Makes 3 to 4 cups

> **¼ cup olive oil**
> **½ cup onion,** chopped
> **2 cups tomato puree**
> **2 cups peeled, chopped tomatoes**
> **1 Tbl. sweet basil**
> **Four friends**
> **2 tsp. sugar**
> **1 tsp. paprika**
> **1 cup chicken stock**

Heat the olive oil in a heavy sauce pan over medium heat, add the chopped onion and saute until transparent. Add the tomato puree, peeled chopped tomatoes, sweet basil, four friends, sugar, paprika and chicken stock.

Bring to the boiling point and reduce the heat and simmer for 30 to 40 minutes.*

    1 cup artichoke hearts (drained)
    1 cup grated Swiss cheese
    ½ cup grated Parmesan cheese
    ½ cup chopped parsley

Assemble:

In a shallow 2½ to 3 quart casserole, place the green noodles in an even layer. Then sprinkle the mushroom caps over all, add half of the grated cheese, arrange the chicken breasts, and add the artichoke hearts. Cover all with the tomato sauce and the remainder of the grated cheese and the chopped parsley.

This may be assembled ahead of time and refrigerated.

Reheat from room temperature in a 350° oven 25 to 35 minutes or until bubbly hot.

This may also be made by substituting cooked shrimp or crab or slices of beef tenderloin in place of the chicken.

Caesar Salad   Serves 8

Two pounds white or light green tender romaine lettuce, washed, separated and cut into two inch pieces. Place in a salad bowl.

Caesar Dressing

    In the blendar jar put:
        Four friends
        2 tsp. dry mustard

---

*You may add the stock from the chicken breasts and mushrooms to this tomato sauce.

3 or 4 cloves garlic
2 ounces oil packed anchovies with the oil
Ground black pepper
Juice of 2 lemons
¼ cup red wine vinegar
2/3 cup olive oil
2 Tbl. chopped parsley
3 coddled eggs (Place eggs in shell in pot of boiling water. Take off heat, cover, and let stand one minute. Remove eggs from water and take out of their shells.)

Blend on medium speed for 25 to 30 seconds until well blended. Pour into glass jar. This can be kept in the refrigerator for three weeks.

Pour about ½ cup of the dressing over the lettuce and then sprinkle with ½ cup Parmesan cheese and 1 cup croutons. (Buy Catherine Clarke brand at your favorite store.)

Zabaglione   Serves 6 to 8

In a bowl that you can heat put:
8 egg yolks
2/3 cup sugar
Pinch of salt

Place over hot water over medium heat and beat with a wire whisk until it is the consistency of hollandaise. Then beat in 1½ cups dry Marsala, a little at a time, until it all has been absorbed and you have a custard consistency. Be careful not to overheat because it will curdle. Remove from the heat and add the juice of a lemon.

Serve warm in champagne glasses or over fresh fruits or sponge cakes. For a cold version, let the sauce cool and fold in half the volume of stiffly beaten whipped cream.

Chicken Egg Drop Soup
Beef Bourguignonne
Noodles
Tomatoes with Sweet Basil
Almond Cream
Bordeaux
(Mouton-Cadet, Marteau Claret, Beau Rivage)

Chicken Egg Drop Soup   Serves 8

> **2 quarts rich chicken stock or consomme**
> (canned or homemade consomme)
> **3 whole eggs beaten**
> **¼ cup chopped parsley**
> **½ cup dry sherry**

Bring the chicken consomme to a boil, then reduce the heat and simmer. When simmering, slowly pour in the beaten eggs in a fine stream from above. The eggs will cook almost immediately. Stir gently. Heat briefly, then garnish with the chopped parsley and sherry. Heat to the boiling point.

Beef Bourguignonne   Serves 8

The classic French beef stew. It makes a great party dish. Especially good for buffets and quantity cooking.

- ½ **pound diced, salt pork or bacon**
- 1 **medium-size onion**, diced
- 4 **pounds stewing beef,** cut into one inch cubes
- ½ **cup flour**
- 4 **cups dry red wine** (burgundy type)
- **Four friends**
- **Ground black pepper**
- 2 **bay leaves**
- 1 **cup tomato puree**
- 1 **pound mushroom caps,** washed and trimmed
- 2 **cups pearl onions**
- **Splash of brandy**
- ½ **cup chopped parsley**

In a heavy dutch oven or stewing pot, cook the salt pork or bacon over medium heat until half done. Drain and return to the fire. Add the diced onion and saute with the bacon until transparent. Then add the cubes of beef and sear over high heat. Stir while searing. When the cubes of meat are seared, sprinkle the flour over them and stir. Add the four friends, pepper, bay leaves, tomato puree, mushroom caps, the wine, and stir, bringing them to a boil. Reduce the heat and simmer uncovered 60 to 90 minutes, or until the beef is tender, stirring occasionally. Then add the pearl onions, parsley and a splash of brandy.

Remove the bay leaves and cook 10 to 15 minutes.

Best made in advance and then reheated. Serve with buttered noodles or rice.

Tomatoes with Sweet Basil   Serves 6 to 8
Four or five ripe tomatoes

Dip the tomatoes into boiling water for four or five seconds, then plunge into cold water. With a paring knife, remove the skins. Slice into medium slices and arrange on a glass or pottery tray.

Sweet Basil Dressing

> **¼ cup chopped fresh sweet basil or 2 Tbl. dry basil**
> **Ground black pepper**
> **Four friends**
> **¼ cup white wine vinegar**
> **½ cup olive oil**
> **Salt**
> **½ cup chopped red, Spanish sweet onion**
> **¼ cup chopped parsley**
> **Juice of one lemon**

Mix all ingredients together in a jar or bowl. Taste for seasoning. Pour over room temperature tomatoes. Garnish with salad greens.

For better tasting winter tomatoes, leave them out of the refrigerator and keep at room temperature. (They look pretty in a wicker basket on your counter.) The tomatoes will ripen and take on a more garden fresh flavor and will last just as long outside the refrigerator as in.

Almond Cream   Serves 6 to 8

> **3 cups whipping cream**
> **Pinch of salt**
> **⅔ cup sugar**
> **½ cup almond paste**
> **1 tsp. vanilla**
> **6 to 8 egg yolks,** beaten
> **2 Tbl. butter,** melted
> **½ cup slivered almonds,** toasted in hot
>   butter

In an enamel sauce pan, combine the cream, salt, sugar, almond paste, and vanilla. Put on the fire, stir, and bring to the boiling point, but do not let boil. Heat until the almond paste has melted. Remove from the heat and beat in the egg yolks. Return to the fire and stir with a wooden spoon until it has thickened to a custard consistency. Remove from the heat and pour into individual custard cups or a one-quart mold. Sprinkle the top with the toasted slivered almonds. Bake 10 to 15 minutes at 350° or until the custard is set. Remove from the oven and let cool. Best at room temperature. This may be served with fresh or canned fruits, peaches, pears, and strawberries.

> **Crab Meat Bisque**
> **Lamb Shanks Neopolitan**
> **Green Rice**
> **Romaine, Artichoke Hearts, Anchovy Salad**
> **Pears with Gorgonzola and Brandy**
> **Bardolino**

Crab Meat Bisque   Serves 8 to 10
                              6 to 8 ounces per serving

  ½ cup butter
  1 medium-size onion, diced fine
  ½ cup flour
  Four friends
  1 tsp. dry mustard
  1 Tbl. paprika
  1 Tbl. chicken base
  White pepper
  5 cups milks or light cream
  1 cup dry white wine
  2 cups crab meat (one pound lump or
    diced King crab meat)
  Splash brandy or dry sherry
  ¼ cup chopped parsley

Melt the butter in a heavy casserole and add the
diced onion. Saute until transparent. Stir in the flour,
four friends, dry mustard, paprika, chicken base, pinch
of white pepper, and the light cream or milk. Bring to
a boil and add the dry white wine. Return to the fire,
bring to a boil, reduce the heat, and simmer 20 to 30
minutes. Taste to correct seasoning. Add the crab meat

and splash of brandy. Bring up to the boiling point, but do not boil and add the parsley just before serving.

Lamb Shanks Neopolitan Serves 8

> **8 lamb shanks** — about 1¼ pound each
> **¼ cup olive oil**
> **1 medium-size onion,** diced
> **2 to 3 cloves garlic,** chopped
> **Four friends**
> **2 bay leaves**
> **1 cup dry white wine**
> **1 cup tomato puree**
> **1 tsp. thyme**
> **1 pound mushrooms**
> **½ cup chopped parsley**

Heat the olive oil in a heavy dutch oven, add the diced onion and saute until transparent. Add the lamb shanks and sear them. (You may have to do this a few at a time.) Place all the lamb shanks back in the pot and add the chopped garlic, four friends, bay leaves, dry white wine, tomato puree, thyme, and the mushrooms. Bring to a boil and put the casserole into a pre-heated 350° oven. Bake, basting occasionally, 45 to 60 minutes or until the lamb shanks are tender and the sauce has thickened. Skim off any excess fat and garnish with the chopped parsley.

Green Rice Serves 8

> **½ stick butter**
> **1 medium-size onion,** diced
> **1½ cups Uncle Ben's converted rice**
> **Four friends**

1 Tbl. chicken base
3 cups chicken stock or water
1 cup finely chopped parsley

Melt the butter in a heavy casserole and add the diced onion and saute until transparent. Stir in the rice and mix until it is coated with the butter-onion mixture. Add the four friends, chicken base, and chicken stock and bring to a boil. Reduce the heat and simmer until the moisture has been absorbed and the rice is fluffy.

Stir in the chopped parsley with a fork.

Also good served with sea foods, chicken, and veal.

Romaine, Artichoke Hearts, and Anchovy Salad Serves 8

2 pounds light green, romaine lettuce hearts, washed and dried
1 cup small, canned artichoke hearts, drained
One 2 to 3 ounce tin of anchovy fillets, packed in oil
4 ounce jar pimentoes, sliced into thin strips
¼ cup chopped parsley
¼ cup grated Parmesan cheese

Arrange the romaine which has been cut into two inch pieces in a salad bowl. Add the artichoke hearts, the anchovy fillets with the oil, and the pimento strips. Garnish with the chopped parsley, sprinkle on the Parmesan and a bit of ground black pepper.

Pour ½ cup Country French Dressing over this just before serving.

Pears with Gorgonzola and Brandy Serves 8

8 ripe pears, cored and peeled. Cut slice from bottom so they will sit up and

squeeze **lemon juice** over them to keep from changing color.

4 to 6 ounces gorgonzola cheese at room temperature

4 to 6 ounces cream cheese at room temperature

¼ cup brandy

Place the softened cheeses in a mixing bowl and beat until they are light and fluffy. Beat in the brandy until the mixture is the consistency of whipped cream. Put the cheese mixture into a pastry bag with a star tube tip and fill the centers of the pears with the cheese, ending with a rosette at the top. May be placed on a fresh green leaf* on a dessert plate. Best served at room temperature.

---

*Be imaginative. Go into your yard or take a walk down the street and see what looks good. Grape leaves are great. Magnolia leaves, too. If nothing looks good when you need it or it happens to be winter, better visit your favorite florist.

> **Crab Meat Quiche**
> **Spanish Chicken**
> **Red Onion and Orange Salad**
> **Chocolate Mousse**
> **Chianti Classico**
> **(Olivieri, Frescobaldi, Villa Antinori)**

Crab Meat Quiche   Serves 8

> **Eight ounces puff pastry.** Roll out thinly
> (¼ inch) and line an eight to ten inch
> quiche pan.
> **2 Tbl. butter**
> **3 Tbl. finely chopped onion**

Melt the butter in a sauce pan and saute the onions
until transparent. Season with **four friends** and cool.

Custard

In a bowl add and mix together well:
> **4 whole eggs**
> **1 tsp. dry mustard**
> **Four friends**
> **½ cup tomato puree**
> **½ cup light cream**
> **2 to 3 Tbl. chopped parsley**

Place in layers in this order on the pastry. Sprinkle
the bottom of the crust with **2 to 3 Tbl. Parmesan cheese,
2 to 3 Tbl. chopped parsley, ½ cup grated Swiss cheese.**
Arrange the cooked onions over all.
Then add:

3 or 4 chopped anchovy fillets
1 cup crab meat
½ cup grated Swiss cheese
2 to 3 Tbl. chopped parsley

Pour the custard mixture over the ingredients and bake in 350° oven — 30 to 40 minutes — or until the custard is set.

Quiches may be assembled the day before except for adding the custard mixture. Cover the quiche with saran or plastic wrap and put the custard in a separate jar or bowl in the refrigerator. Stir and add the custard just before you put the quiche in the oven to bake.

To freeze

Bake, keeping slightly under done. Reheat the defrosted quiche in a 350° oven for 15 to 20 minutes or enough to heat through and finish the cooking.

These general rules apply to all quiches.

Spanish Chicken Serves 6 to 8

½ pound bacon, diced. Cook until half done and drain well.
Two 3 pound frying chickens cut into serving pieces. Discard the heavy bones.
1 medium onion, chopped
1 small green pepper, trimmed, seeded, diced
1 medium-size leek, chopped and washed
2 carrots, peeled and chopped
3 cloves garlic, chopped
Three friends

2 bay leaves
1 tsp. saffron
2 tsp. paprika
1 cup brown rice
1 cup drained, chopped tomatoes (canned)
1 pound mushroom caps, trimmed and
washed
One 10 ounce can baby clams and juice
1 cup beef or chicken consomme
1 cup dry sherry

Place the diced, cooked bacon in a heavy casserole. Add the chopped onion, green pepper, leek and carrots and saute until onion is transparent. Add the chicken and sear over medium high heat. Add garlic, the three friends, bay leaves, saffron, paprika, brown rice, tomatoes, mushrooms, clams and juice, consomme and the dry sherry. Bring to the boiling point and then place in 350° oven and bake 40 to 60 minutes or until the moisture has been absorbed. Remove from the oven and add **1 cup drained artichoke hearts, 1 cup defrosted tiny peas, ½ cup chopped parsley and ¼ cup diced pimento.** There should be enough heat in the casserole to cook the peas.

Red Onion and Orange Salad   Serves 8

2 heads romaine lettuce, trimmed and
washed
2 Spanish red onions, peeled and thinly
sliced
2 large navel oranges, peeled and thinly
sliced
¼ cup finely chopped parsley

Arrange the above ingredients in layers in a salad bowl or on a platter. Add the dressing just before serving.

Dressing

Can be made in a bowl or jar and shaken up or made in the blender.

> **¼ cup white wine vinegar**
> **Juice of 1 lemon**
> **Four friends**
> **½ cup olive oil**
> **Salt**
> **Ground black pepper**

Mix well and pour over the salad.

Chocolate Mousse   Serves 8

This is an Italian meringue-type mousse.

> **2 cups whipping cream,** stiffly beaten
> **6 egg whites** at room temperature
> **1 tsp. cream of tartar**
> **⅔ cup sugar**
> **1 tsp. vanilla**

Add the cream of tartar to the egg whites and beat the egg whites until they are stiff. Gradually beat in the sugar a little at a time and add the vanilla. Continue to beat the egg whites stiffly as for meringue.

Fold the whipped cream and egg whites together with a wide rubber spatula. Refrigerate.

In a sauce pan carefully melt, then cool:

> **4 ounces semi-sweet chocolate**
> **½ cup dark or light rum**

Fold the cooled chocolate into the meringue and whipped cream mixture until well blended. If the chocolate is too warm it will make the meringue mixture collapse.

Place the mousse in a bowl or individual serving dishes. Decorate with **whipped cream** and **grated chocolate.** Refrigerate.

This mousse is like the one served at the Maisonette, created by Chef Pierre Adrian.

French Oyster Stew
Grilled Lamb with Puree of Cauliflower
Tomatoes Provencale
French Pear Tart
Chateauneuf-du-Pape

French Oyster Stew   Serves 6

¼ **cup butter**
½ **cup diced onion**
½ **cup finely diced celery**
Four friends
1 tsp. paprika
Pinch of white pepper
1 tsp. grated nutmeg
1 cup dry white wine
1 quart oysters with their liquid

Melt the butter in a heavy casserole, add the onion, and saute until transparent. Add the celery, four friends, paprika, white pepper, nutmeg, dry white wine, and the oysters. Heat over medium heat until the oysters curl, about three to five minutes. Remove from the heat and strain, saving the stock, oysters, celery and onion.

Finely chop the oysters, celery, and onion and set aside.

To the stock add **2 cups milk or light cream** and bring to a boil. Return the chopped oysters, onion, and celery.

Stir in **2 Tbl. arrowroot** to thicken the soup. Heat until thickened. Add **3 Tbl. chopped parsley** and **½ cup dry sherry.**

Heat but do not boil.

Can be frozen.

Grilled Lamb with Puree of Cauliflower   Serves 8

4½ pound leg of lamb. Bone, trim off excess fat and gristle, cut into inch thick steaks across the leg. Place the steaks in a flat covered shallow pan and marinate with the following for 2 to 3 hours in the refrigerator.

> **¼ cup olive oil**
> **Juice of 2 to 3 lemons**
> **Four friends**
> **1 to 2 Tbl. crushed rosemary**
> **Ground black pepper**

After the lamb has marinated, return to room temperature and grill under a hot broiler or over charcoal.

2 to 3 minutes per side for rare

5 to 7 minutes per side for medium

8 to 12 minutes per side for well done

Remove the lamb and place on a heat-proof platter and spread a generous coating of **pureed cauliflower** over the top. Dust with **Parmesan cheese** and **paprika**. Run under a hot broiler to lightly brown.

Puree of Cauliflower

One large head of cauliflower, trimmed and cut into flowerettes. Place in sauce pan, cover with **cold, salted water** and add **½ cup milk.** Bring to a boil and cook 12 to 18 minutes or until tender. Drain well.

    Mash the cauliflower and add:

> **Four friends**
> **½ cup Parmesan cheese**
> **Pinch of grated nutmeg**
> **1 to 2 Tbl. butter**

Tomatoes Provencale   Serves 8

Eight small tomatoes, washed, cored and cut in half.

    In a small bowl, add and mix together and sprinkle over the tops of the tomatoes:

> **4 Tbl. bread crumbs**
> **2 Tbl. finely chopped onion**
> **2 to 3 Tbl. chopped garlic**
> **2 to 3 Tbl. chopped parsley**
> **2 to 3 Tbl. olive oil**
> **1 to 2 Tbl. sweet basil**
> **Ground black pepper**

    The tomatoes may be placed around the prepared lamb steaks and grilled along with the lamb or baked in a 350° oven for 10 to 12 minutes.

French Pear Tart   Serves 8

Line an 8 to 10 inch quiche pan with **½ pound puff pastry** rolled ¼ inch thick.

Spread **one cup orange marmalade or apricot pre-serves** on the bottom of the crust.

Core, peel and cut into wedges **3 or 4 large pears.** Use a stainless steel knife to prevent them from turning dark. Squeeze **lemon juice** over them. Then arrange in a decorative pattern over the marmalade. Sprinkle with ¼ **cup brown sugar** and ½ **cup slivered almonds.**

Bake in 425° oven for 25 to 30 minutes.

Serve hot with **whipped cream.**

This may be made with apricots, apples, or peaches.

Steak Tartar
Salmon Baked In Puff Pastry with Cucumber Sauce
Saurkraut Schwartzkopf
Broccoli Salad
Mustard Mayonnaise
Peaches with Raspberry Sauce
French Sauterne
(Chateau Rieussec 1947:
very rare wine for special occasions)
(others: Chateau Rieussec, Chateau Suduirat
good, but not rare)

Steak Tartar   Serves 8

Great for buffet and cocktail parties.

Two pounds lean, freshly ground fillet, sirloin, or round steak. Make sure there is no fat in the beef. Put into a bowl. In the blender jar put:

> **1 medium-size onion,** chopped
> **Four friends**
> **1 Tbl. Dijon mustard**
> **2 Tbl. olive oil**
> **Salt**
> **Ground black pepper**
> **2 ounces oil packed anchovies**
> **2-3 eggs**
> **¼ cup brandy or cognac**

Blend on medium speed until all is combined and add to the beef. Then add:

> **¼ cup drained capers**
> **½ cup finely chopped parsley**

Carefully blend all the ingredients together as if you are making meat loaf. DO NOT OVER WORK.

This may be put into an oiled glass or ceramic mold, covered securely, and refrigerated, or served immediately.

Serve with sour rye or dark rye bread.

Salmon Baked In Puff Pastry   Serves 8 to 10

Beautiful for buffets. Fun for children to help make. Other fish may also be used.

> **2 pounds puff pastry**
> **3½ to 4 pounds fresh salmon fillets or other boned fish fillets.** Skin and dry well.
> **1½ pounds mushrooms,** trimmed, washed, acidulated, and thinly sliced. Saute in
> **two or three Tbl. butter.** Season with the

four friends and cook 3 to 5
minutes. Drain and cool.

Divide the pastry in half and roll out into rectangles, about 6 inches by 18 inches, ¼ inch thick.

Place the fish fillets on the pastry in the form of a fish shape. Add the drained, cooled mushrooms and **¼ cup finely chopped parsley.** Then cover with the second piece of pastry. Brush all the edges with **egg wash** and seal. With a sharp knife, cut around the edges, removing the excess pastry, making the form of a fish with head, tail and fins. Use the dull side of the knife to make the lines in the fins and tail.

With a melon scoop, starting at the tail end of the fish, make indentations in the top surface of the pastry for the scales.

With the cut-off scraps of pastry make the eye and mouth, gluing them on with the egg wash.

When the fish is decorated, make sure the edges are well sealed. Press with the tines of a fork if necessary and turn under. Brush the entire cut side with egg wash.

With a large spatula carefully transfer the fish to a very shallow cookie sheet. Be sure that the cookie sheet has an edge around it so the fat from the pastry will not run into your oven when it bakes.

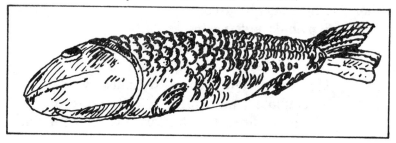

Bake in a 425° oven 45 to 60 minutes until well puffed and brown.

When baked, remove from the oven and run a long, thin spatula underneath the fish to loosen it from the pan. When loose and free, use two heavier spatulas to lift and place it on a fish plate or tray which should be very near by.

Serve with Hollandaise, Mousseline, Aurora or Cucumber Sauce.

This may be served hot or cold.

Cold Cucumber Sauce   Serves 8

Peel, seed, and thinly slice **two to three firm cucumbers.** Place the cucumbers in a bowl with **two Tbl. salt.** Mix well and let the cucumbers stand for 30 to 60 minutes. Wash them well with cold water, drain and squeeze dry in a towel. Place the pressed cucumbers in a bowl and add:

1 cup mayonnaise
1 cup sour cream
Four friends
Juice of a lemon
2 Tbl. olive oil
2 Tbl. chopped parsley
1 Tbl. dill weed

Stir until well blender, cover and refrigerate. The sauce should marinate for several hours for the best flavor.

Good with cold meats, fish, and vegetables.

Hot Cucumber Sauce   Serves 8

Two to three large firm cucumbers, peeled, seeded and

diced. Place the cucumbers in a bowl and add **two Tbl. salt.** Blend well. Let marinate for 30-60 minutes. Then wash the cucumbers well in cold water, drain and squeeze out dry in a towel. Place the pressed cucumbers in a sauce pan and add:

> **2½ to 3 cups strained Bechamel Sauce**
> **2 tsp. dry mustard**
> **2 Tbl. finely chopped parsley**
> **1 Tbl. dill weed**
> **Juice of one lemon**

Stir and blend well. Place on the fire and bring to a boil.

Serve over hot fish, chicken, veal and vegetables.

Sauerkraut Schwartzkopf   Serves 8

Two pounds fresh saurkraut put in an enamel pot and covered with cold water. Bring to a boil and simmer for 15 minutes. Drain well. In the enamel pot melt **½ cup butter** and add **½ cup finely chopped onion.** Saute until transparent. Then add:

> **The drained, blanched saurkraut**
> **Four friends**
> **1 or 2 bay leaves**
> **One 10½ can cream of tomato soup**
> **1 cup vodka**

Stir and bring to a boil. Reduce heat and simmer for 30 to 45 minutes, stirring occasionally until the moisture has been absorbed.

At the end of the cooking time, stir in **one to two cups sour cream.** Heat briefly and add the **juice of a lemon.**

Broccoli Salad   Serves 8

Two bunches cooked broccoli — see vegetable chart.
Drain well and cool. Arrange the broccoli on a bed of
salad greens and sprinkle **three to four chopped, hard-
cooked eggs** over them.

Serve with mustard mayonnaise.

Mustard Mayonnaise

To serve with cold meats, fish or vegetables
>   **2 cups mayonnaise**
>   **Four friends**
>   **2 to 3 Tbl. finely chopped onion**
>   **Ground black pepper**
>   **2 to 3 Tbl. Dijon mustard**
>   **Juice of one lemon**
>   **2 to 3 Tbl. finely chopped parsley**

Stir together and refrigerate.

Peaches with Raspberry Sauce   Serves 8

Eight poached peaches or well-drained, **canned peaches**

Raspberry Sauce

In a sauce pan put **one quart fresh raspberries or
two cups frozen raspberries with the juice and one cup
sugar.**

Put on the fire and bring to a boil. Reduce heat and
simmer for 20 minutes, stirring occasionally. When the
raspberries are cooked, push them through a fine sieve.
Be careful not to push the seeds through. You should
have about 1½ cups of puree. Cool and add to the puree
¼ cup Kirsch.

To serve:

Pour the raspberry sauce into a flat crystal bowl and

carefully arrange the poached, drained peaches in the sauce.

This may be served with or without scoops of strawberry or vanilla ice cream and whipped cream.

> **Cold Lobster with Aioli Sauce**
> **Tondouri Chicken**
> **Cold Rice Salad**
> **Brussels Sprout and Tomato Salad**
> **Fresh Red Raspberries with Lemon Ice**
> **New York State Champagne**
> **(Great Western)**

Cold Lobster with Aioli Sauce

Four live lobsters, two pounds each.

Put the live lobsters into a deep pot, cover them with cold water, and add:

> **Generous amount salt**
> **1 medium-size onion,** chopped
> **2 bay leaves**
> **3 lemons, rinds and juice**
> **1 small bunch celery,** chopped
> **1 bunch parsley**
> **Seaweed,** if available

Cover the pot, put on the fire, bring to a boil, reduce heat and simmer for 8 to 12 minutes. Remove lobsters from the water, let drain, and cool.

When cold, cut in half length-wise and remove the intestine. Crack the shell and claws. Garnish with **lemon** on a bed of **lettuce** and serve with **Aioli Sauce.**

Always cook live lobsters in cold water rather than dropping them in boiling hot water. Cold water, heated gradually on the fire, lulls the lobster as opposed to the shock of being dropped into boiling water. The result is much more tender meat. Try it!

Aioli Sauce (garlic mayonnaise)
Good for shell fish, meats, and vegetables.

In a blender jar put:

> **8 or 10 cloves garlic**
> **2 tsp. dry mustard**
> **Juice of 2 lemons**
> **Salt**
> **Ground black pepper**
> **6 egg yolks**

Blend on medium speed until pureed and then slowly, in a thin stream, pour in **1½ cups olive oil.** Blend on medium speed until all the oil has been added, then change to high speed for two or three seconds. This should have the consistency of mayonnaise.

If the sauce breaks (separates) in the blender, it is usually because the motor of the blender heats the egg and oil emulsion too much.

To remedy this, place the jar in the refrigerator for a few minutes to chill, then return to the motor and re-blend for a few seconds until the sauce goes back together. This same rule applies to blender mayonnaise. Store in a covered glass jar in the refrigerator.

Tondouri Chicken   Serves 8

Four 2½ - 3 pound frying chickens cut into quarters. Remove the back bone and wing tips and place the pieces into a large bowl and add:

>**Four friends**
>**1 large onion,** thinly sliced
>**4 or 5 limes, juice and rinds**
>**Ground black pepper**
>**2 to 3 Tbl. curry powder**
>**2 cups plain yogurt**
>**4 cups buttermilk**

Mix this until well blended and the pieces of chicken are coated. Cover and let marinate, refrigerated, for 24 to 36 hours, turning the pieces occasionally.

Place the drained pieces of chicken in a shallow roasting pan and roast in a 400° oven for 45 to 60 minutes, basting occasionally with the marinade until the chicken is quite dry and crispy.

You may cook the chicken over a low charcoal fire on a grill. Cook slowly, turning and basting with the marinade until the chicken is well cooked and crispy. This should take about 45 minutes.

Serve with **wedges of fresh lime** and **chutney.**
May be served hot or cold.

Brussels Sprout and Tomato Salad   Serves 8

>**Boston lettuce**
>**Endive**
>**Cooked Brussels sprouts**

Cherry tomatoes, cut in half
Chopped Spanish onion
Chopped parsley
Watercress for garnish

Line a bowl with the salad greens. Arrange the Brussels sprouts and tomatoes on the lettuce and sprinkle them with the onion and parsley. Garnish with watercress. Add **French dressing.**

French Dressing

1 Tbl. Dijon mustard
Four friends
½ cup red wine vinegar
Juice of 1 lemon
½ cup olive oil
Pinch salt
2 to 3 Tbl. chopped parsley

Blend the ingredients in a bowl with a whisk and taste for seasoning.

Rice Salad   Serves 8

Place **2 cups cooked, cold white rice** in a bowl Add:
½ cup finely diced celery
1 medium-size onion, chopped fine
½ cup chopped parsley
½ cup chopped green pepper
¼ cup chopped green pimento olive
½ cup slivered almonds
½ cup Country French Dressing

Toss together and place in a 1½ quart oiled mold, ring mold, or on a **bed of lettuce.**

Good with cold sliced meats or shellfish, too.

Raspberries with Lemon Ice   Serves 8

> **1 quart fresh red raspberries,** washed and
> drained
> **1 quart lemon water ice**

Put scoops of **lemon water ice in** tall crystal goblets
or champagne flutes. Cover with the raspberries.

Grilled Trout
Roast Rack of Lamb Celestial with Snail Butter
Braised Belgian Endive
Profiteroles with Chocolate Sauce
California Sauvignon Blanc
(Wente Bros., Beaulieu Vineyard)

Grilled Trout   Serves 8

Eight 10 to 12 ounce Rainbow trout, boned or one 4½ to
5 pound boned Lake or Brown Trout

Wash and dry well and oil the outside with **butter
or cooking oil.** You may stuff the inside with any of the
following.

> **Soubise**
> **Spinach Farmiere**
> **Duxelles**

Skewer the opening.

Place on an oiled baking tray or in a wire fish grilling container.

Place about three to four inches from the moderate source of heat and grill eight to ten minutes on each side for the larger trout. Baste occasionally with **melted butter** or **oil** or **dry white wine.**

The fish may also be cooked in a shallow, buttered casserole. Add enough **dry white wine** to cover the bottom of the casserole and bake in a 350° oven 20 to 30 minutes for the small trout or 30 to 40 minutes for the larger trout.

> **Serve with Hollandaise sauce**
> **Veronique sauce**
> **Newburg sauce**

Roast Rack of Lamb Celestial   Serves 8

Four 2½ pound, trimmed racks of lamb. Have the butcher cut through the back bone where the ribs join the back bone to make the lamb much easier to carve at the table.

Put the racks into the roasting pan rib side down to form a natural roasting rack and bless the outside with:

> **Four friends**
> **Rosemary**
> **Ground black pepper**
> **Juice of one or two lemons**

Roast the racks in a 400° oven 25 to 35 minutes or until pink. Remove from the oven, drain, and coat the outside of the racks with a layer of the following mixture.

Stir together in a bowl until a crumbly consistency:

> **3 cups bread crumbs**

1 cup Parmesan cheese
Four friends
½ cup finely chopped parsley
Ground black pepper
¼ cup olive oil or 2 eggs
1 Tbl. crushed rosemary or thyme

Press on the outside of the lamb, return to the oven, and roast for 10 to 15 minutes or until browned. Serve immediately with snail butter.

Snail Butter

The butter for stuffing snail shells or to serve with grilled meats and fish or vegetables.

May be made up and kept in the refrigerator or frozen rolled in lengths in waxed paper to slice off when needed.

In a mixing bowl put:

1 pound semi-soft butter
1 cup finely chopped parsley
5 or 6 pressed cloves of garlic
Ground black pepper
Three friends
Juice of 2 or 3 lemons
Pinch of grated nutmeg
3 or 4 chopped shallots

Beat on a low speed until the ingredients are softened and start to combine. Gradually increase the speed and whip until the ingredients are all combined and are light and fluffy like whipped cream.

Scrape out on wax paper and roll up in 1½ inch diameter rolls. Put in the refrigerator to chill and set until ready for use.

Best made in advance to let the flavor age.

To serve: slice into ¾ inch thick slices and place on the hot meats, vegetables, or fish. Even good spread on crusty bread and hard rolls.

Braised Belgian Endive   Serves 8

Eight or ten stalks of Belgian endive, trimmed and cut in half length-wise.

Place in a stainless steel or an enamel shallow pan. Squeeze the **juice of one or two lemons** over the endive and add:

> **1 sliced onion**
> **Four friends**
> **¼ cup butter or olive oil**
> **1 to 2 cups chicken stock**

Cover with a piece of wax paper to fit the diameter of the pan.

Put on the fire, and bring to the boiling point. Reduce heat and simmer for 20 to 25 minutes or until the endive is tender and most of the stock has evaporated.

Put the cooked endive into a shallow casserole. Dust with **bread crumbs, Parmesan cheese, chopped parsley** and a **dash of paprika.**

Run under a hot broiler until glazed or in a 350° oven for 15 to 20 minutes.

Profiteroles with Chocolate Sauce   Serves 8

Choux paste will make three dozen two inch diameter shells.

In a heavy sauce pan put:

> **2 cups water**
> **½ cup butter**

Pinch of salt

Put on the fire, bring to a boil, and boil until the butter has melted. Quickly dump in **1½ cups of flour** and stir with a wooden spoon. Continue to cook over high heat, stirring the flour until you have a heavy, clay-like paste that leaves the sides of the pan in a mass. Remove from the heat and cool slightly. Beat in **6 to 8 eggs** one at a time.

This will take a good arm and a bit of doing. The resulting paste should be thick and creamy.

Drop the paste by the teaspoonful on an ungreased cookie sheet or tray. You may also put the paste through a pastry bag with a plain round tube making dots the size of a quarter and about two inches apart in each direction on the baking sheet.

Bake in a 375 to 400° oven 20 minutes or until puffed and dry to the touch. The paste will expand three times its original size. If the choux shells have not been sufficiently baked and dried, they will collapse when cool. Keep in a dry, warm place.

Filling

Coffee flavored whipped cream

Stiffly beat **2 cups whipping cream sweetened** with **¼ cup sugar** and **1 to 2 Tbl. instant powdered coffee.**

Put into pastry bag with small round tip, press into the bottom side of the choux shell, and fill.

You may leave the whipping cream plain if you wish or add **¼ cup cocoa** to the cream in place of the coffee. The choux shells may also be filled with **a flavored ice cream** and stored in the freezer until ready to use.

Pile the filled choux shells into a pyramid on a tray or four each on individual dessert dishes. Pour **warm chocolate sauce** over them and sprinkle the tops with **chopped pistachio nuts or toasted, slivered almonds or chopped pecans.**

> **Cream of Spinach Soup**
> **Blanquette de Veau**
> **Rice or Noodles**
> **Asparagus and White Grape Salad**
> **Hot Curried Fruit Compote**
> **Pouilly Fume Blanc**

Cream of Spinach Soup   Serves 8

In a large soup pot put:
> **2 pounds washed, trimmed spinach**
> **8 cups chicken stock**
> **1 medium-size onion**, chopped
> **Four friends**

Bring to a boil and simmer for 30 to 40 minutes until the vegetables are tender. Puree the soup in small batches in the blender on medium speed.

Return to the soup pot and add:
> **1 to 2 cups heavy cream**
> **Salt**

Ground black pepper
1 tsp. ground nutmeg
2 to 3 Tbl. arrowroot

Return to the fire and stir. Bring to a boil and heat until thickened. Taste for seasoning. Serve with **croutons.**

To serve cold, thin the chilled soup with **milk or chicken stock.**

Blanquette de Veau   Serves 8

Place **three pounds of veal cut into one-inch cubes** in a sauce pan, cover with **water,** and bring to a boil. Drain immediately and wash in cold water. Set aside.

In a dutch oven, stainless steel, magnalite or enamel pot, melt **½ cup butter** and add **one medium-size, chopped onion.** Saute until transparent. Then braise the blanched pieces of veal in the butter and onion about five minutes, keeping them very white. Then add:

Four friends
½ **cup flour** - sprinkled over
2 **Tbl. chicken base**
2 **bay leaves**
1 **cup finely chopped parsley**
1 **tsp. thyme**
1 **tsp. grated nutmeg**
3 **cups light cream**

Stir and bring to the boiling point. Then add **one cup dry white wine.** Stir, reduce the heat, and simmer uncovered for 40 to 60 minutes or until the veal is tender. Add:

1 pound mushroom caps, washed and trimmed. Cut the larger caps into quarters. Remove the bay leaves and simmer for 15 minutes. Remove from the heat and stir in:

4 egg yolks
¼ cup finely chopped parsley

Return to the heat but do not let boil. Serve with ⬯ rice or buttered noodles.

Asparagus and White Grape Salad　　Serves 8

Two pounds white or green asparagus, cooked, drained and chilled. Arrange the asparagus on a bed of **Belgian endive.**

Dressing

In a bowl put:

2 cups stemmed, seedless grapes, cut in half
2/3 cup mayonnaise or yogurt
½ cup sour cream
Juice of a lemon
Four friends

Stir to combine. Pour this over the asparagus just ⬯ before serving.

Hot Curried Compote　　Serves 8

In a sauce pan, melt:

2 Tbl. butter and add
1 Tbl. curry powder. Fry one to two minutes.

Add **½ cup dark brown sugar** and **½ cup chopped chutney.** Bring to a boil, add, and stir in **½ cup rum.**

To this sauce add:

8 white peach or pear halves, well drained
8 figs

1 **cup seedless white raisins**
1 **cup mandarin orange sections,** drained

Put on the fire and bring to the boiling point or bake in a casserole in a 350° oven 20 to 25 minutes.

May be garnished with **slivered almonds** and served with **whipped cream.**

Marinated Shrimp and Wild Rice Ring
Russian Mayonnaise
Orange and Onion Salad
Cold Coffee Parfait
California Rose
(Almaden, Krug, Beaulieu Vineyard, Mirassou)

Marinated Shrimp and Wild Rice Ring   Serves 8

Prepare **marinated shrimp.** Chill.

Cook **wild rice.** When the rice is cooked, let it cool. Add to the rice:

½ **cup finely chopped green onions**
½ **cup finely chopped celery**
½ **cup finely chopped parsley**
½ **cup finely chopped raw carrots**
½ **cup Country French Dressing**

Toss this mixture together and put into a two-quart ring mold. Cover the bottom with a circle of wax paper. Let this stand covered, refrigerated, several hours to marinate.

To unmold, quickly rinse the outside with hot water. Run a knife around the outside edge and turn out on a glass tray.

Fill the center with the marinated shrimp. You may garnish this with peeled, sliced **tomatoes** and **watercress**.

Serve **Russian mayonnaise** on the side.

Russian Mayonnaise

Great sauce to have in the refrigerator. Good on fish, vegetables, cold meats, and salads or can be used as a dip.

In a bowl put:
> **6 hard-cooked eggs,** sieved
> **1½ cup mayonnaise**
> **½ cup yogurt or sour cream**
> **Four friends**
> **¼ cup finely chopped parsley**
> **2 tsp. dry mustard**
> **2 Tbl. olive oil**
> **1 Tbl. dill weed**
> **Juice of a lemon**

Stir until well combined. Put in a covered glass jar and refrigerate. Best made the day before it is to be used.

Orange and Onion Salad   Serves 8

Four navel oranges, peeled. Slice the oranges thin crosswise and arrange them on a bed of trimmed, dried **spinach (about a pound).**

Peel and thinly slice **two medium-size red Spanish onions.** Separate the slices and arrange over the orange slices.

Pour **½ cup Country French Dressing** over the oranges and onions just before serving.

Cold Coffee Parfait   Serves 8

In a blender jar put:

> **1½ cups of very strong cold coffee**
> **2 cups coffee ice cream**
> **5 or 6 ice cubes**

Blend on medium speed until the ice is crushed.

Pour this mixture into tall cups or goblets containing a scoop of **coffee ice cream** and **one ounce Kalua or Creme de Cacao.** Decorate the top with **unsweetened whipped cream** and a **sprig of fresh mint.**

May be done ahead and kept in the freezer for about one hour. Do not garnish with mint until just before serving.

Serve with a straw and spoon.

Mushrooms Sous Clouche
Grilled Double Sirloin
Beer and Vermouth Sauce
Potatoes Chenonceaux
Green Beans with Sour Cream Sauce
Fried Camembert
French Bordeaux
(Chateau Raymond)
or
California Cabernet Sauvignon
(Christian Bros., Martini, Inglenook,
Beaulieu Vineyard)

Mushrooms Sous Clouche   Serves 8

40 same-size, perfect mushrooms, trimmed washed, dried, and acidulated

8 slices of white toast. Remove crust and trim to fit under clouche or dome.

8 slices of bacon, chopped and sauteed until done. Drain well.

8 Tbl. each finely chopped parsley and onion

8 Tbl. butter

To prepare this recipe successfully, make sure the au gratin dishes have flat bottoms so that you will get the proper seal between the dish and the glass clouche.

Place the croutons on the bottom of the au gratin dish and put a tablespoon of chopped onion and parsley on top. Next add the drained cooked bacon and a tablespoon of butter.

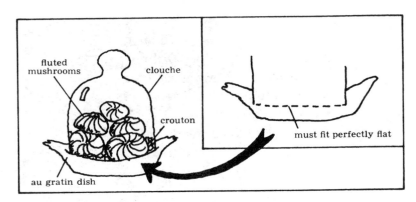

fluted mushrooms
clouche
crouton
au gratin dish
must fit perfectly flat

Pile five mushrooms into a pyramid. Place the domes over all so that they are sitting flush with the bottom of the au gratin dish.

Bake in a 400° oven 30 minutes. You will need a napkin and a knife to break the seal of the dome when serving. The dome should be clear, not steamy or cloudy when properly done.

Grilled Double Sirloin   Serve 8 to 12
To me this is the only steak.

Have the butcher cut a **3-inch-thick sirloin which will weigh seven to eight pounds.** Trim off the extra heavy fat leaving just a thin covering on the outside. Pin the "tail" down with wooden skewers unless you have some-one who will like his steak on the well-done side.

Coat the outside of the steak with **cooking oil or olive oil** and rub with:
> **Four friends**
> **Coarsely ground black pepper**
> **1 Tbl. Dijon mustard**

Let the steak stand at room temperature and mar-inate for one or two hours.

This steak may be cooked in the broiler or oven about 3 inches from the source of heat. For rare meat, I cook mine about 12 to 14 minutes on each side, 15 to 20 minutes on each side for medium.

For accurate grill cooking, there is a great meat grilling therometer. Magic Arrow was developed by David Trott and takes the guess work out of cooking this formidable steak and other grilled meats.

When the steak has cooked, remove it from the heat and transfer it to a cutting plank and let it rest 10 to 15 minutes, covered with a towel. Then thinly slice crosswise. Serve with:

> Halves of fresh lemons
> Bearnaise sauce
> Dijon mustard
> Beer and Vermouth Sauce

Beer and Vermouth Sauce

In a sauce pan put:

> **1 cup butter**
> **1 can stale beer, light or dark**
> **½ cup dry vermouth**
> **¼ cup Worcestershire sauce**
> **Ground black pepper**
> **Juice of 2 lemons**
> **3 to 4 Tbl. dry mustard**

Stir and place on heat. Bring to a boil, reduce the heat, and simmer 15 to 20 minutes.

Good over fish as well as grilled meats.

Potatoes Chenonceaux   Serves 8

Four to six Idaho potatoes, peeled and julienned. Put the potatoes in cold salted water, bring to a boil, and cook

three to five minutes. Drain and wash in cold water. Do
not over cook.

2 cups grated Swiss cheese
½ cup chopped parsley
1 large onion, thinly sliced and sauteed in
butter until transparent

Arrange in alternating layers in a two-quart souffle
pot or casserole and pour the following custard recipe
over the potatoes.

Stir together in a bowl:

4 to 5 eggs
1½ cups cream
Four friends
Grated nutmeg

Bake in a 350° oven 34 to 40 minutes or until set.
Good with roasts as well as grilled meats.

Green Beans with Sour Cream Sauce   Serves 8

Two pounds trimmed, washed and cooked green beans —
see vegetable chart

Put in a casserole, pour over sour cream sauce, and
heat.

Sour Cream Sauce

In a sauce pan melt **two Tbl. butter,** add **two Tbl.
finely minced onions** and saute until transparent.

Add, off the heat:

2 Tbl. flour or arrowroot
Four friends
2 tsp. dry mustard
1 cup cream
Salt
White pepper

Stir. Return to the heat and bring to a boil. Reduce heat and simmer for 10 to 12 minutes. Remove from the heat and stir in **one cup sour cream** and **juice of one or two lemons,** according to taste. Return to the heat, but do not let boil. Add **one to two Tbl. finely chopped parsley.**

Pour over the hot green beans.

Good over other vegetables or on sauteed veal, chicken or fish.

Fried Camembert Serves 8

Eight 2½ to 3 ounce wedges of cold ripe Camembert cheese

Dip each of the pieces into **flour,** then into a bowl with **three well-beaten eggs.** Then coat with **one cup fine bread crumbs.**

Put the breaded wedges of cheese on a wire screen to dry. Then keep chilled in the refrigerator.

When ready to cook, fry in hot deep fat (350°) for four to five minutes or until the crust is golden brown. Skim out carefully and drain on paper towels.

Serve hot with **plain cheese biscuits** and **Bar-le-Duc red currant jam** or **raspberry** or **strawberry jam.**

Clam Consomme with Sherry
Veal Orloff
Gruyere Cheese Salad
Crepes Diane
German Rhine
(Liebfraumilch, Johannisberger,
Niersteiner)

Clam Consomme with Sherry   Serves 8

In a large sauce pan put:

4 cups clam juice, fresh or canned
4 cups chicken consomme
Four friends
Juice of 1 or 2 lemons

Put on the fire, bring to a boil, reduce heat, and simmer for 10 to 15 minutes. Add **½ cup dry sherry.** Heat, but do not boil.

Serve in bouillon cups with a dollop of **unsweetened whipped cream** and **chopped chives.**

This may also be jellied and served cold. To do this, add to the soup: **3 to 4 Tbl. plain gelatin softened in ⅔ cup chicken consomme.** When softened, stir this mixture into the heated soup and dissolve.

Place in the refrigerator to chill and set. Serve as above.

Veal Orloff   Serves 8

A very good "do-ahead" party dish.

Eight veal chops about ¾ to 1-inch thick.

Saute the veal chops in a heavy skillet or saute pan with a **Tbl. of butter for each chop.** Season with **four friends** and cook about three to four minutes on each side. Remove, drain and cool.

Arrange the chops on a flat shallow casserole and place one slice of **pate de foie (canned from France or Denmark)** on the top of each chop. Then cover the pate and the top of the chop with **Soubise** and mold it to the shape of the chop.

Dust with **grated Parmesan or Swiss cheese, paprika** and **finely chopped parsley.**

When ready to bake, sprinkle the chops with **brandy** and put in enough **dry white wine** to cover the bottom of the pan or casserole with a thin film.

Bake in a 350° oven 30 to 40 minutes.

This may also be done with lamb chops or sauteed scallops of veal.

Soubise

Rice and onion sauce or stuffing.

Two large onions peeled, chopped and sauteed in ¼ cup butter, keeping the onion light in color, not brown.

Two cups of rice boiled in 4 cups of chicken stock until tender and dry. Grind the rice and onions together through the medium blade of a food chopper and add:

> ½ **cup Parmesan cheese**
> **Four friends**
> **2 or 3 egg yolks**
> **Salt**
> **Ground white pepper to taste**
> **1 to 2 Tbl. heavy cream**
> **Pinch of grated nutmeg**

Stir until well combined. This should have a thick consistency.

Can be used as a stuffing for poultry, fish or veal, or stuffed into vegetable cases (tomato, zucchini, eggplant, mushrooms) as a filling.

Gruyere Cheese Salad   Serves 8

> **1-1½ pounds slivered Gruyere cheese**
> **Salad greens** — bibb lettuce, spinach, endive
> **Bunches of watercress** for garnish
> **Chopped parsley**

Dressing

> **Four friends**
> **Ground black pepper**
> **1 Tbl. Dijon mustard**
> **½ cup chopped parsley**
> **¼ cup red wine vinegar**
> **½ cup olive oil**
> **Salt to taste**

Line a bowl with the salad greens. Toss the cheese with the dressing and arrange the cheese mixture in the center of the greens. Garnish with watercress and chopped parsley.

Crepes Diane   Serves 8

A good show at the table.

Make **16 crepes.** Fold into fourths.

> **¼ cup butter**
> **½ cup sugar**
> **½ cup Creme de Cacao**
> **½ cup slivered, toasted almonds**
> **¼ cup brandy**

**1 quart coffee, vanilla or chocolate ice
cream in scoops**
Warmed chocolate sauce
Whipped cream, lightly sweetened
In a flambe pan or a shallow skillet, melt the butter and
then add the sugar and carmelize. Add the Creme de
Cacao and dissolve the carmelized sugar into a syrup.
Add the crepes folded into fourths; coat and heat them in
the sauce in the pan. When heated, add the toasted, slivered almonds, and pour on the brandy. Ignite and
flambe. Serve immediately with the scoops of ice cream,
warmed chocolate sauce and a **spoonful of whipped
cream.**

Quick Black Bean Soup
Chicken with Morels
Cucumber Stuffed Tomatoes
Kafka
White Loire Valley
(Saumur, Muscadet, Pouilly Fume)

Quick Black Bean Soup   Serves 8

In a heavy soup pot melt ¼ **cup butter**, add **one medium-
size, chopped onion** and saute until transparent. Add:
Four friends
Two 1 pound cans black beans
Five 10½ ounce cans beef consomme

Juice and rind of a lemon
1 cup dry sherry

Stir, and bring to a boil, reduce heat, and simmer for 25 to 30 minutes.

Puree the soup or run through the blender. Flavor with dry sherry and serve with **thin lemon slices** and **chopped hard-cooked eggs.**

Chicken with Morels   Serves 8
It is a special spring treat when these mushrooms are in season.

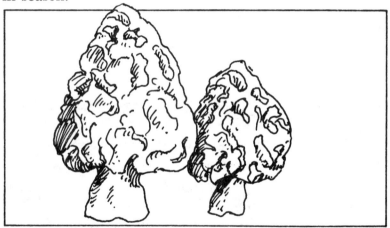

Soak **two cups morels** in heavily salted water 30 to 40 minutes to remove the sand, dirt, and any insects that may be hiding inside their ruffled caps. Rinse again in cold water, trim the stems and dry well. Cut in half length-wise.

Since morels grow wild and you have to hunt to find, you may not have access to them. Don't substitute mushrooms for morels, use canned, wild mushrooms from Germany called pfifferlinge.

Eight chicken breasts, skinned, boned and halved. Slightly flatten the half-breast and dredge in **flour.**

In a heavy saute pan melt **½ cup butter,** add **one medium-size onion,** chopped fine and saute until transparent. Then add the chicken breasts and saute on each side four to six minutes until they are lightly browned. Add:

> **Four friends**
> **1 tsp. thyme**
> **½ cup tomato puree**
> **2 Tbl. beef base**
> **Cleaned, sliced mushrooms**
> **2 cups chicken or beef stock or consomme**
> **1 cup dry sherry**

Bring to the boiling point, reduce the heat and simmer for 25 to 30 minutes, stirring occasionally. Seasou with **ground black pepper, the juice of a lemon, ½ cup chopped parsley,** and a **splash of brandy** or **dry Madeira.** Return to the boiling point and serve with rice or noodles.

Stuffed Tomatoes — Serves 8

> **8 tomatoes,** one per person
> **2 cucumbers,** peeled, seeded and chopped
> **Juice of 1 lemon**
> **¼ cup chopped parsley**
> **2 cloves garlic,** pressed
> **Ground black pepper**
> **Accent**
> **2 to 3 Tbl. olive oil**

Peel and scoop out the tomatoes. Marinate cucumbers in seasoning. Stuff cucumber mixture in tomatoes.

Kafka   Serves 8 to 10

In a mixing bowl put:

1 pound creamed cottage cheese
2 cups sour cream
1 cup confectioners sugar
One 6 ounce can of frozen orange juice concentrate, defrosted
Grated rind and juice of a lemon
1 ounce brandy or Grand Marnier

Beat on medium speed for 10 to 14 minutes until well combined.

In the meantime, soften **3 Tbl. plain gelatin** in ½ **cup cold water.** When softened, melt over hot water. Then fold into the cottage cheese mixture. Put into the refrigerator to set.

Stiffly beat **2 cups whipping cream** and fold into the set cottage cheese mixture.

Rinse a two-quart mold with cold water and fill the wet mold with the Kafka mixture. Cover and refrigerate for two to three hours.

Unmold and serve with **fresh or candied fruits.**

Eggplant Stuffed with Crab Meat
Leg of Lamb Florentine
Flageolets
Gnocchi Romano
Mixed Green Salad
Strawberries in Chocolate with Strega
California Pinot Chardonnay

Eggplant Stuffed with Crab Meat   Serves 8

Four small-size egg plants, halved with a stainless steel knife to keep them from turning dark. Scoop out and reserve the pulp from the egg plants, leaving shells that are about ½ inch thick. Poach the shells in boiling salted water for five minutes. Drain well and dry with paper towels. Place them cavity side up in a shallow baking pan.

Filling for Egg Plants

> **Chopped eggplant pulp**
> **½ cup olive oil**
> **Small bunch green onions,** chopped
> **1 cup diced celery**
> **1 small green pepper,** trimmed, seeded, chopped
> **Four friends**
> **1 Tbl. sweet basil**
> **2 tsp. paprika**
> **¼ cup red wine vinegar**
> **1 pound can peeled, chopped tomatoes** (2 cups)

Ground black pepper
Salt
½ cup bread crumbs
½ cup chopped parsley
1 pound crab meat, or shrimp, or lobster,
    or chicken or lamb, cooked, diced

Heat the olive oil in a sauce pan and saute the green onions for three to five minutes. Add the celery, eggplant, green pepper, four friends, basil, paprika, vinegar, salt, pepper, and tomatoes. Stir over medium heat for five minutes. Remove from the heat, add the bread crumbs, parsley and crab meat or other meats. Blend and stuff this mixture into the shells.

Sprinkle the tops with **Parmesan cheese.**

Bake in 350° oven 25 to 30 minutes or until heated through.

Stuffed Leg of Lamb Florentine   Serves 8 to 10

Have the butcher bone and remove the heavy fat and gristle from a **four to four and a half pound leg of lamb.** Put the lamb in a shallow baking dish and marinate for several hours or over night in the refrigerator.

Marinade

    Juice of 2 or 3 lemons
    Ground black pepper
    Four friends
    2 Tbl. olive oil
    1 Tbl. crushed rosemary

Filling for the Leg of Lamb

Place in a bowl and mix well:

2 pounds spinach, trimmed, washed and wilted. Drain well, squeeze out excess moisture and chop fine.

1 medium-size onion, chopped fine
Four friends
Ground black pepper
½ cup Parmesan cheese
2 Tbl. olive oil
3 whole eggs
1 cup chopped, raw mushrooms

Fill the cavity of the leg of lamb with the spinach mixture. Sew or skewer the lamb back into its natural shape and place it seam side down in the roasting pan.

Roast in pre-heated 400° oven for 15 minutes.

Then turn the oven to 350° for 30 to 40 more minutes for pink lamb.

Sauce for Lamb

In sauce pan place:

4 cups beef consomme
½ cup tomato puree
1 bay leaf
Four friends
1 cup dry red wine

Bring to a boil, reduce the heat and simmer. Reduce the sauce to about two cups. Then just before serving add:

Splash of brandy or dry Madeira
Juice of 1 lemon
2 to 3 Tbl. chopped parsley

Carve the leg of lamb into thin slices and arrange the slices on a tray. Pour some of the hot sauce over them and sprinkle with chopped parsley and garnish with **watercress.**

Serve the extra sauce on the side in gravy boat.
Serve with flageolets and Gnocchi Romana

Flageolets (small kidney beans)   Serves 8

In a sauce pan heat:

    2 Tbl. olive oil

    2 Tbl. butter

    1 medium-size chopped onion, sauteed for
    five minutes

Then add:

    Four friends

    1 small Tbl. crushed rosemary

    2 Tbl. chopped parsley

    Ground black pepper

    2 cups drained, washed flageolets

    1 Tbl. chicken base

    1 cup dry white wine

    Juice of one lemon

Bring to a boil and simmer for 25 to 30 minutes until the moisture has been absorbed. Just before serving, add **2 or 3 Tbl. finely chopped parsley.**

Gnocchi Romana   Serves 8

In a heavy sauce pan, melt **¼ cup butter,** add **one medium-size, diced onion** and saute until transparent. Add:

    Four friends

    1 Tbl. chicken base

    1 cup white or yellow corn meal

    4 cups water

Stir, bring to the boiling point, reduce the heat and simmer until very thick. Remove from the heat and add:

    1 cup grated Paresan cheese

    3 whole eggs

Stir and spread mixture in an oiled flat pan and let

cool. When cold, cut into squares or triangles and arrange in a shallow buttered casserole. Dust with **grated** **Parmesan cheese** and drizzle with a little **olive oil.**

Bake in hot 450° oven for 20 to 25 minutes until the cheese has melted and is bubbly. Serve immediately.

Mixed Green Salad
Your choice of mixed greens with **Country French Dressing.**

Strawberries in Chocolate with Strega   Serves 8

Two quarts strawberries, hulled and washed in warm water. Drain and dry. Place in a bowl and add **½ cup Strega.** Cover and let marinate several hours.

  1 pint stiffly beaten, whipped cream
  8 ounces semi-sweet, grated chocolate

Fold the grated chocolate into the whipped cream.

Serve the strawberries in dessert bowls with a spoon of the chocolate whipped cream on top.

Small chocolate rum-filled macaroons are good with this.

Crabmeat and Avocado Ravigote
Tournedos Archiduc
Pommes de terre Lorette
Salad Dubarry
Strawberries Bourbonnais
Bordeaux - St. Emilion
(Chateau Pavie 1966 is especially good)

Crabmeat and Avocado Ravigote   Serves 8

Four ripe avocados, cut in half. Remove the seed and lift the avocado from the shell with a kitchen spoon by sliding it between the skin and the peel. This is much quicker and easier than trying to peel an avocado with a knife. Squeeze **lemon juice** over the avocado shell to keep it from turning dark.

Filling

 One pound cooked crabmeat, shrimp, or lobster added to the following sauce.
 In a bowl, stir until well blended:
    ¼ cup drained, chopped capers
    Ground black pepper
    Salt
    Juice of a lemon
    Four friends
    2 Tbl. chopped parsley
    ½ cup finely chopped celery
    1 cup mayonnaise
    3 hard-cooked, chopped eggs

Fill the shells with crabmeat mixture and sprinkle the tops with **chopped parsley, paprika,** and **pureed egg yolk** (Memosa). Place on beds of **Boston lettuce** and garnish with **watercress, cherry tomatoes,** and **cantaloupe balls.**

Ways to Ripen Avocados Faster

1. Bake in 350° oven 10 to 15 minutes, remove and let cool (outside will turn black).
2. Bury in flour in a canister overnight.

Tournedos Archiduc Serves 6 to 8

Two tournedos per person for dinner.
One tournedo per person for luncheon.

In a shallow oval casserole that is well oiled or buttered, place:

16 artichoke bottoms that have been rinsed and drained

16 small grilling tomato halves, one for each artichoke bottom

Squeeze the tomato halves gently to remove the seeds. Bless with the **four friends** and sprinkle the top with **bread crumbs.**

Cut **small beef tenderloins** into 1½ to 2 inch thick steaks. (You may have your butcher do this.) Place on a baking tray and bless with the **four friends,** a little **olive oil** and the **juice of one or two lemons.** Dust with **ground black pepper.** Let the tournedos marinate in this mixture. May be done the night before if refrigerated, or at room temperature for one or two hours.

When ready, quickly sear each side in hot oil or butter keeping them underdone. Place the tournedo on top of the tomato.

Wash, trim, and acidulate **one large mushroom cap for each tournedo.** Quickly saute the caps in a little **oil or butter,** drain and place on top of the tournedo.

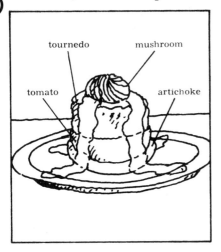

tournedo

mushroom

tomato

artichoke

This may be assembled in advance. When ready to serve, reheat the room temperature tournedos in a pre-heated 425° oven for 10 to 15 minutes.

Pour heated **Madeira sauce** over each and sprinkle with **chopped parsley.**

May be served with Pommes de terres Lorette or noodles.

Pommes de terres Lorette   Serves 8

Four or five medium-size baking potatoes, peeled and cut into equal-size pieces. Place in a sauce pan and cover with cold salted water. Bring to a boil, reduce the heat and simmer until the potatoes are tender. Remove from the heat, drain, and mash. You should have about three cups of mashed potatoes. Add **Choux paste** to the mashed potatoes and mix until well blended. **Salt** to taste. You may add to this mixture about **one cup chopped parsley, one cup diced, cooked ham, one cup grated cheese. (Parmesan, Swiss or Cheddar)**

To cook:

Have about **two inches hot cooking fat** at 350° in a deep, heavy pot or iron frying pan.

You will need a skimmer to remove the fried potatoes from the fat and a tray lined with paper towels to drain them. Shape the potatoes using two kitchen spoons (dessert or tablespoon size). First, dip the spoons into the hot fat. Then scoop out the potato mixture with one spoon and place the other spoon on top to form a walnut shape. Then, carefully drop the potato into the hot fat. Fry three to four minutes until they are golden

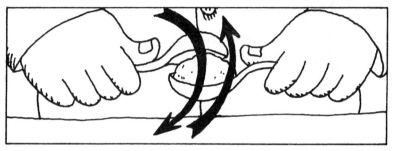

brown and are floating on the surface of the fat. Skim out and drain. Do not pile on top of each other. These may be done ahead of time and reheated in a 350° oven for 10 to 15 minutes.

Salad Dubarry   Serves 8
Madame Dubarry loved Louis XIV and cauliflower.

One large head cauliflower, cooked. (See Basic Cooking) Drain and let cool.

      2 cans small, white asparagus, drained
      1 cup small, cooked carrots
      ½ cup chopped parsley
      Belgian endive, trimmed, washed, separated

Place the cooked cauliflower in the center of a large salad plate or tray. Arrange the leaves of Belgian endive radiating out from the cauliflower. Lay the asparagus in the leaves of the endive. Arrange the cooked

carrots around the cauliflower and then sprinkle chopped
parsley over all.

Pour on dressing.

Dressing

In a bowl or blender jar add:
Juice of 2 to 3 lemons
Four friends
2 tsp. dry mustard
Ground white pepper
⅔ cup olive oil
2 egg yolks
2 Tbl. white wine vinegar
1 Tbl. anchovy paste

Stir or blend well and pour over salad. This dressing must be kept refrigerated in a covered glass jar.

Strawberries Bourbonnais   Serves 8

The Bourbonnais sauce is good over fresh or canned
fruits, ices, ice cream, puddings, cakes, pancakes or
waffles.

One to two quarts stemmed, washed strawberries
placed in a crystal bowl. Pour sauce over the strawberries. May be served with **whipped cream and macaroons.**

Bourbonnais Sauce

Use a heavy cast aluminum or black iron skillet and
make sure the bottom of the pan fits the size burner
you are going to use. Place on medium heat until you
can feel the heat penetrate through the bottom of the

pan to the palm of your hand when it is held over the pan. When the pan is hot, immediately add **two cups granulated sugar.** Stir with a long handled, wooden spoon. As the sugar starts to melt, stir gently until you have a golden-colored syrup. Remove from the heat and place on a heavy heat-proof board or tile, not on your Formica counter.

Add **¼ cup sweet butter to the melted sugar.** Stir. When the butter has melted, add **one half cup whipping cream** very carefully, a little at a time. Then stir **½ to 1 cup bourbon** into the sauce.

Let the sauce cool down, pour into a glass container, cover and refrigerate. When cooled, the sauce has the consistency of carmel sauce.

Can be kept in the refrigerator for several weeks.

Coquille of Scallops and Shrimp
Swiss Crown Roast of Lamb
Brussels Sprout Salad
Gregorian Chocolate Cake
Bordeaux
(Chateau Cissac is good)

Coquille of Scallops and Shrimp   Serves 8

Place **one pint bay scallops** in a sauce pan with **one cup dry white wine** and the **juice of a lemon.** Bring to the boiling point, drain immediately and reserve the **stock.**

1 pound tiny, cooked shrimp (defrosted)
½ cup finely diced celery
8 Tbl. fine bread crumbs
8 coquille shells, 4 inch size
¼ cup chopped parsley

In each of the coquille shells, put a Tbl. of the bread crumbs then some chopped celery, and fill with the poached scallops and the tiny shrimp. Sprinkle with chopped parsley and cover the top with the following sauce.

Sauce

In a sauce pan melt **¼ cup butter**, add **½ cup finely diced onion** and saute until transparent. Add off the heat:

3 Tbl. flour or arrowroot
Four friends
2 tsp. dry mustard
The stock from the poached scallops
1 cup cream

Stir and bring to a boil, reduce the heat and simmer until thickened. Remove from the heat and stir in **three or four egg yolks.**

Spoon the sauce over the filled shells, dust with **paprika, chopped parsley** and **grated Swiss Cheese.**

Bake in a 350° oven 15 to 20 minutes.

Swiss Crown Roast of Lamb   Serves 8

Have the butcher make a **three or four rib rack of lamb into a crown roast.** Have him trim off the excess fat.

Rub the outside of the lamb with **lemon juice, garlic** and **crushed rosemary.**

Roast the lamb in a 350° oven about 30 minutes. Remove from the oven, drain and cool. Put the crown roast in a shallow round casserole and fill the center with Swiss potatoes.

Swiss potatoes

Peel and coarsely grate **six to eight medium-size baking potatoes.** Soak them in a bowl of cold water for about 30 minutes to remove the heavy surface starch. Drain well.

Fry **one pound diced bacon** until it is half done in a black iron skillet.

Drain and add **one large diced onion** and saute until transparent. Then add:

> **The drained, grated potatoes**
> **Four friends**
> **Ground black pepper**

Stir and fry 25 to 30 minutes until the potatoes are cooked. Add:

> **½ cup chopped parsley**
> **1 cup grated Swiss cheese**
> **Salt to taste**

Fill the center of the crown roast with the potatoes and bake in a 350° oven 25 to 30 minutes. Serve with **thinned brown or Madeira sauce.**

Brussels Sprout Salad   Serves 8

> **Salad greens**
> **1 bunch watercress**
> **1 quart fresh Brussels sprouts,** trimmed, washed, and poached in cold salted water 8 to 12 minutes.

Line a bowl with the salad greens. Arrange the

Brussels sprouts in the bowl, pour the dressing over them and garnish with **watercress.**

Dressing

> **1 Tbl. Dijon mustard**
> **Four friends**
> **½ cup red wine vinegar**
> **Juice of 1 lemon**
> **½ cup olive oil**
> **Pinch salt**
> **2 to 3 Tbl. chopped parsley**

Blend ingredients with a whisk and taste for seasoning.

 Dressing may be prepared ahead.

Gregorian Chocolate Cake Serves 8 to 10
A dessert for chocoholics.

Crush or pound a **10 ounce package of Nabisco's Famous Chocolate Wafers** very fine with a rolling pin.

Place the fine cookie crumbs in a bowl and add **¼ cup melted butter** to make a crumb mixture. Press this mixture into a ten inch spring form pan to make a thin crust part of the way up the side of the pan.

In a sauce pan put:

> **1 pound semi-sweet chocolate (Mailliard)**
> **1 cup whipping cream**

Place over gentle heat and melt the chocolate. Remove from the heat, stir and cool.

Separate **8 eggs.** Put the yolks in a bowl and add **1 tsp. vanilla** and **½ cup flour.** Stir until well blended and then fold into the chocolate mixture.

Beat the 8 egg whites with a **pinch of salt** until stiff.

Fold the egg whites into the chocolate mixture until well blended.

Pour the chocolate mixture into the lined spring form pan and bake in a 350° oven for 30 minutes.

This cake must be kept on the underdone side, like a soft custard. Remove from the oven and let cool. Serve in small wedges at room temperature with **whipped cream.**

Pate Maison in Aspic
Breast of Chicken Veronique
A Walk In The Woods Salad
Sour Cream Mousse
German Moselle
(Piesporter, Bernkasetler)
(Wehlener Sonnenhur)

Pate Maison   Serves 10 to 12

In a bowl put:
- **1 pound finely ground raw veal**
- **1 pound boned, skinned, ground raw chicken breasts**
- **1 pound ground raw chicken livers**

Four friends
2 cups whipping cream
8 egg whites
½ cup dry Madeira, sherry or Cognac
1 tsp. paprika
1 tsp. grated nutmeg
Salt
1 tsp. thyme

Stir all of these ingredients together and run through the blender in small batches. Blend the batches together and then put the pate mixture in a two-quart souffle pot or pate mold. Bake in a 350° oven 1½ hours or until the juices are clear. Remove from the oven, weigh down the top with a heavy plate and let cool. Serve with **crackers** and **lemon wedges.**

This may also be baked in puff pastry or served cold in aspic.

Beef or Chicken Aspic   Serves 8

8 cups beef or chicken consomme or
clarified stock
Four friends
½ cup dry sherry or Madeira
Juice of a lemon
8 Tbl. plain gelatin, softened in 1½ cups of
the cold consomme

Heat 1½ cups of the consomme and stir in the softened gelatin until it is dissolved. Add the remainder of the consomme, the four friends, sherry or Madeira and lemon juice. Pour into vegetable or meat molds and place in the refrigerator to chill and set. You may also finely chop the aspic when it is set to garnish cold platters, molds, and pate.

Breast of Chicken Veronique   Serves 8

Eight chicken breasts, roasted, cooled, skinned, boned,
and left in their natural shape. Arrange side by side in
a shallow casserole. In a sauce pan put:

2 cups seedless green grapes
1 cup dry white wine

Cover, place on the fire, bring to a boil, drain, and
save the stock from the grapes.

Put the grapes over and around the chicken breasts
in the casserole and sprinkle with:

¼ cup chopped parsley
½ cup grated Swiss cheese

Then coat with **Veronique sauce.**

Veronique Sauce

In a sauce pan melt **¼ cup butter,** add **½ cup finely
chopped onion** and saute until transparent.

Add off the heat:

3 Tbl. arrowroot or flour
2 Tbl. chicken base
Four friends
2 tsp. dry mustard
The drained stock from the grapes
1½ cups heavy cream

Stir and return to the heat, bring to a boil, and cook
until thickened, about 10 to 15 minutes. Remove from
the heat and stir in **3 or 4 egg yolks** and **¼ cup dry
sherry.** Pour the sauce over the chicken and grapes.
Bless the top with **grated Swiss cheese** and **chopped
parsley.**

Heat from room temperature in a 350° oven 25 to 30
minutes or until bubbly hot and heated through. Serve
with green rice or rice pilaf.

A Walk In The Woods Salad   Serves 8 to 10

Dressing

> **1 pound mushroom caps,** trimmed, washed
>   and acidulated
> **Four friends**
> **¼ cup vinegar**
> **¼ cup dry white wine**
> **¼ cup olive oil**
> **Salt**

Heat ingredients for five minutes. Taste for seasoning. It may need additional vinegar and salt.

Salad

> **Fiddlehead ferns, dandelion greens, lettuce,**
>   **watercress and parsley,** 1 pound in all
> **Tomatoes,** peeled and thinly sliced
> **Canned hearts of celery or fresh celery,**
>   braised
> **Canned dilled green beans**
> **Canned small beets**

Arrange greens on flat dish. Marinate celery hearts in dressing, when cool. Drain canned vegetables and arrange them in piles on the bed of greens. Sprinkle with **chopped parsley** and garnish with **watercress.** Pour dressing over the salad.

Sour Cream Mousse   Serves 8

In a mixing bowl put:
> **6 egg whites**
> **Pinch of salt**

Beat until stiff but not dry. In the meantime, soften **2 Tbl. plain gelatin in ½ cup cold water** in a small bowl. When the gelatin is softened, melt it over hot water. Add the melted and slightly cooled gelatin to the egg whites along with the finely grated **rind of a lemon,** an **orange,** and **⅔ cup sugar.** Beat stiffly as for a meringue.

In another mixing bowl put:

> **8 ounces cream cheese**
> **2 cups sour cream**
> **Juice of a lemon**
> **Juice of an orange**

Beat on medium speed until the consistency of whipping cream.

Then fold the egg white and sour cream mixture together with a wide rubber spatula. Put this mixture in a two-quart oiled mold and chill two to three hours. Unmold. Serve with **fresh raspberries** and a **splash of Grand Marnier.**

Salmon with Cucumber and Mustard Sauce
English Spiced Beef
Curried Raisin Rice
Heart of Palm Salad
Peaches Jean
Moulin-a-Vent 1967

Salmon with Cucumber and Mustard Sauce   Serves 8

Three to four pounds fresh salmon fillets (other fish fillets may be used), skinned and boned

Lay fillets in a shallow, heat-proof casserole. Add:

1 cup dry white wine

Juice of 1 lemon

Poach fish 10 to 12 minutes in 350° oven. Remove and drain, saving the stock.

In a sauce pan melt **¼ cup butter.** Trim, split, chop, wash in warm water the **white part of two medium-size leeks.** Saute them in the butter. Add:

Four friends

1 Tbl. chicken base

2 Tbl. Dijon mustard

Cook about three to five minutes. Then add:

stock from the fish

2 Tbl. arrowroot

½ cup heavy cream

Stir and bring to a boil. Remove from the heat and stir in **three to four egg yolks.** Set aside.

Peel, seed and thinly slice **two cucumbers.** Place in cold, salted water, bring to the boiling point and drain well. Arrange over the poached salmon. Sprinkle with **chopped parsley** and **½ cup grated Swiss cheese.** Then pour the mustard sauce over all. Bless with **parsley.**

Reheat in 350° oven 20 to 25 minutes or until heated through.

English Spiced Beef   Serves 8

> **1 pound bacon,** diced
> **1 medium-size onion,** chopped
> **3 pound stewing beef,** cut into one-inch pieces
> **½ cup tomato puree**
> **Four friends**
> **Ground black pepper**
> **1 tsp. ground cumin seed**
> **½ tsp. ground cloves**
> **1 tsp. cinnamon**
> **1 tsp. nutmeg**
> **8 juniper berries,** crushed or **¼ cup gin**
> **½ cup chutney**
> **½ cup walnut sauce**
> **½ cup red wine vinegar**
> **2 cups dry sherry**
> **1 cup pickled walnuts**
> **Splash of brandy**

In a heavy casserole, fry the diced bacon until half done. Drain off excess fat. Add the onion and saute with the bacon until transparent. Then add the diced stewing beef and sear with the bacon and onion. When the pieces of beef are seared, add the tomato puree, four friends, pepper, cumin, cloves, cinnamon, nutmeg, crushed juniper berries, chutney, walnut sauce, vinegar, and sherry.

Stir, bring to the boiling point, reduce the heat and simmer 40 to 60 minutes, uncovered, until the sauce thickens. Stir occasionally. Add pickled walnuts and splash of brandy. Serve with curried raisin rice.

Curried Raisin Rice   Serves 8

> ½ stick butter
> 1 medium-size onion, chopped (½ cup)
> 1 Tbl. mild curry powder
> 1½ cup Uncle Ben's converted rice
> Four friends
> 1 Tbl. chicken base
> 3 cups water or chicken stock
> 1 cup white raisins

In a heavy casserole, melt the butter, add the chopped onion and saute until transparent. Then add the curry powder and fry two or three minutes to release the curry flavor. Stir in the rice and mix until coated with the curry mixture. Stir in the four friends, chicken base, and raisins. Add the water or chicken stock, bring to a boil, reduce the heat and simmer, uncovered, until the liquid has been absorbed and the rice is dry and fluffy.

Hearts of Palm Salad   Serves 8

> Boston lettuce
> 6 to 8 medium tomatoes
> Chopped parsley
> Chopped eggs (optional)

Line a bowl with lettuce. Peel tomatoes, slice the tops off and remove the seeds gently. (Scoop out with a spoon.) Place in the bowl with the lettuce. Add the chopped eggs.

Dressing

> **Small, diced red onion**
> **Juice of 1 lemon**
> **2 Tbl. chopped parsley**
> **Four friends**
> **¼ cup red wine vinegar**
> **¼ cup olive oil**
> **1 large tsp. Dijon mustard**
> **Salt and pepper to taste**

Dice **one can hearts of palm** and toss in the dressing. Blend ingredients and taste for seasoning.

Spoon dressing over the lettuce and stuff the hearts of palm and onion mixture in the tomato cavities.

Sprinkle with chopped parsley.

Peaches Jean

16 drained white peach halves, canned

Place the peaches in a shallow, oven-proof casserole, cavity side up. Fill the cavity with a spoonful of the following mixture:

> **16 crumbled (day old) almond macaroons,** 3 to 4 inches in diameter (small rather than the large cookies)
> **1 cup apricot preserves**
> **½ cup slivered almonds**
> **½ cup Grand Marnier**

Bake the assembled peaches 10 to 15 minutes in a 350° oven. Serve hot. This may also be done with pears.

> **Tomato Quiche**
> **Veal Kidneys with Madeira Sauce**
> **Sauteed Mushrooms**
> **Rice Pilaf**
> **Fresh Pineapple and Strawberries in Kirsch**
> **Beaujolais**

Tomato Quiche   Serves 8

Line a ten inch deep quiche pan with a **pound of puff pastry** rolled out ¼ inch thick.

Sprinkle the bottom of the crust with:

    ½ cup grated Swiss cheese
    ½ cup chopped green onion
    2 Tbl. chopped parsley
    3 or 4 tomatoes, peeled and cut into 1 inch thick slices to fill the pan

Cover the tops of the tomatoes with **½ cup grated Swiss cheese** and chop a **two ounce can of oil-packed anchovies** and sprinkle over the top.

Fill the quiche with the following custard

In a bowl put:

    4 to 5 eggs
    Four friends
    2 tsp. paprika
    1 Tbl. sweet basil
    1½ cups milk

Stir well and pour this mixture over the quiche. Bake in a 350° oven 45 to 55 minutes until set.

You may serve with hollandaise on top.

Veal Kidneys with Madeira Sauce   Serves 8

Eight fresh veal kidneys. Place the kidneys in a bowl or a pan and cover them with cold salted water. Let the kidneys soak for two to three hours or over night in the refrigerator. Drain, wash well, place in a sauce pan and cover with cold salted water. Add:

1 to 2 bay leaves
1 sliced onion
Juice and rind of 1 lemon
2 stalks of celery, chopped

Bring to a boil and simmer 15 to 18 minutes. Drain, wash in cold water and cool.

Slice each kidney in half length-wise. Remove the central vein and tissue and the thin membrane from the outside of the kidney and any white fat with a paring knife.

Keep covered in cold water in the refrigerator until ready to use.

You clean lamb and beef kidneys or veal sweet breads in this same manner.

Drain and dry the cleaned veal kidneys well and dredge lightly in **flour.**

Saute the kidneys in ¼ **cup melted butter** for eight to ten minutes. **Add ¼ cup finely diced onion** and a **splash of brandy,** heat for two to three minutes and serve with Madeira Sauce. Rice pilaf goes well with this dish.

Madeira Sauce
Make **basic brown sauce.** Strain the brown sauce, put into a sauce pan and place on the fire. To 2½ to 3 cups of brown sauce add:

½ to ⅔ cup of dry Madeira
Juice of ½ lemon
Ground black pepper

Heat to the boiling point, but do not let boil. Serve immediately. Good over roasted meats, fowl, game and poached eggs. Also can be used as a sauce for casseroles with these ingredients.

Sauteed Mushrooms   Serves 8

Two pounds mushrooms, washed, trimmed and acidulated
In a large saute pan heat ½ **cup oil** or **butter** until hot and add the mushrooms, **four friends** and **ground black pepper.**

Saute over high heat for three to five minutes. Add **two to three Tbl. finely chopped parsley.**

Fresh Strawberries and Pineapple in Kirsch   Serves 8

1 large ripe pineapple, peeled and cut into cubes
2 quarts ripe strawberries, stemmed
Place in a large bowl and sprinkle over them:
½ cup finely granulated sugar or
½ cup Kirsch
1 cup apricot preserves
Cover and refrigerate and let marinate several hours. Serve in compotes or melon halves with **slivered almonds** sprinkled on top.

Shrimp Ravigote
Breast of Chicken with Tarragon
Rice
Tomatoes and Mushrooms a la Grecque
Strawberries, Powdered Sugar and Cognac
French dry Chablis
(Chateau La Coste Blanc de Blanc)

Shrimp Ravigote   Serves 8

1 pound cooked shrimp, crabmeat, or lobster
6 to 8 avocado halves
Boston lettuce
Watercress
Cherry tomatoes
Cantaloupe balls

Sauce

¼ cup capers
Ground black pepper
Juice of 1 lemon
Four friends
2 Tbl. chopped parsley
½ cup small diced celery
1 cup mayonnaise
Salt
3 cooked, chopped eggs

Place sauce ingredients except eggs in a dish and
stir. Add shrimp and eggs and stir. This may be prepared a day ahead and refrigerated in a loosely covered dish. Line serving dish with Boston lettuce. Place

avocado shells in the dish and brush with lemon juice. (Cut small slice off back of each avocado half to prevent them from sliding.) Fill shells with shrimp.

Garnish with watercress, tomatoes, and cantaloupe balls.

Breast of Chicken with Tarragon   Serves 8

Eight roasted chicken breasts. When you roast the chicken, add **1 Tbl. dried tarragon or ½ cup chopped fresh "French" tarragon** and cook with the chicken. Remove from the oven, drain and reserve the **stock.** Cool, skin, and bone the chicken and arrange in a shallow casserole.

Tarragon Sauce

In a sauce pan heat **¼ cup butter or the fat drippings** from the roasted chicken and add:

    3 Tbl. arrowroot or ¼ cup flour
    Four friends
    2 cups chicken stock or stock from the chicken
    1 cup heavy cream
    ¼ cup French tarragon leaves, coarsely chopped

Stir, bring to a boil, reduce heat and simmer until the sauce has thickened. Add the **juice of a lemon** and beat **3 or 4 egg yolks** off the heat. Return to the fire to heat and thicken for three to five minutes, but do not let boil.

Pour the sauce over the chicken breasts. Reheat in a 350° oven 20 to 25 minutes. Serve with rice.

Tomatoes and Mushrooms a la Grecque   Serves 6 to 8

    6 to 8 tomatoes, peeled, halved and

scooped out
2 pound mushroom caps, acidulated
Brussels sprouts, hot or cold
(1 quart fresh or 2 boxes, frozen)
¼ cup olive oil
Small bunch green onions, chopped
Four friends
Garlic, generous amount
¼ cup vinegar
Ground black pepper
Pinch salt
½ cup chopped parsley
Accent

Blend oil, onions, four friends, garlic, vinegar, pepper, and salt in sauce pan. Bring to the boiling point, add mushroom caps and Brussels sprouts and heat 3 to 4 minutes. Add chopped parsley. This mixture can be prepared ahead and kept in glass jars. Does not need refrigeration.

Arrange tomatoes on a platter and sprinkle with Accent. Arrange the mushroom mixture in tomato shells. Spoon sauce over the top and sprinkle with chopped parsley. Surround with **watercress. lettuce and endive.**

Strawberries, Powdered Sugar and Cognac   Serves 8
A Swiss do-it-yourself dessert.

Two quarts ripe, perfect strawberries, washed with the stems left on. Dry, have at room temperature, and arrange in a crystal or silver compote.

Give each person a small bowl or Chinese teacup filled with **powdered sugar** and one filled with **Cognac.**

Place the compote filled with strawberries in the center of the table and everyone will take a strawberry, dip it into the Cognac, then into the powdered sugar. It's like a fondue. What a happy dessert!

Minestrone
Leg of Lamb Provencal
Stuffed Zucchini
Olive Rice
Savarin au Cognac
Medoc
(St. Emilion - fine wine)
(Chateau Gloria, Chateau Lanessan,
Chateau Meyney - less expensive)
(Chateau Phelan - Segur)

Minestrone   Serves 8 to 10

¼ cup olive oil
1½ **medium-size onions,** chopped not diced
1 **cup white celery,** diced
1 **cup carrots,** diced
1 **cup zucchini,** diced
1 **cup curly endive,** cut up
1 **cup cabbage,** shredded

Four friends
2 tsp. oregano
1 Tbl. basil
1 tsp. paprika
1 cup tomato puree
1 can diced tomatoes
1½ cups canned garbanzo beans with juice
4 to 6 cups beef or chicken stock
1 cup elbow macaroni or seashells

Place all ingredients in soup pot except macaroni
and bring to the boiling point. When boiling, add
macaroni or seashells. Simmer 45 minutes. Can be
served as a main dish with green salad, crusty bread
and cheese.

Leg of Lamb Provencal   Serves 8 to 10

6½ to 7 pound leg of lamb. Trim off
excess fat and skin and rub these seasonings over the outside surfaces of the
leg of lamb.
Four friends
Lemon juice
1 Tbl. anchovy paste
1 Tbl. Dijon mustard

Place the following in the bottom of the roasting
pan.

1 cup chopped onion
1 cup dry red wine
1 Tbl. Rosemary
2 bay leaves
2 cups peeled, chopped tomatoes

Place the leg of lamb on top. Roast in pre-heated

350° oven one and one-half hours. Keep leg of lamb warm.

Garnish and Sauce for Lamb

> **3 Tbl. olive oil**
> **1 pound mushroom caps**, wash, trim and acidulate
> **2 cups pearl onions**
> **2 cups artichoke hearts** (drained)
> **½ cup chopped parsley**
> **Stock and vegetables from the roasting pan,** but remove the bay leaves

Heat olive oil in saute pan, add mushroom caps and saute two to three minutes. Add onions, stock, and vegetables. Heat quickly to reduce and thicken. Then add artichokes and parsley.

Serve with the sliced lamb and olive rice.

Stuffed Zucchini   Serves 8

Eight small zucchini. Trim, wash in warm water and slice in half length-wise. Place in cold, salted water, bring to a boil, and cook about two minutes. Drain, cool and scrape out seeds.

Stuffing

Place in bowl and mix:

> **1 pound mushrooms** that have been trimmed, washed, finely chopped, and acidulated
> **Four friends**
> **Ground black pepper**
> **2 to 3 Tbl. chopped parsley**
> **½ cup Parmesan cheese**
> **½ cup bread crumbs**
> **2 eggs**

Arrange the zucchini shells in a shallow, buttered baking dish. Fill the cavities with the stuffing mixture and dust the tops with grated Parmesan.

Bake in 350° oven 20 to 25 minutes.

Olive Rice
Serves 8 to 10

In a heavy sauce pan heat:

¼ **cup olive oil,** add one **medium-size, finely chopped onion** and saute until transparent.

Add:

Four friends

14 ounces Uncle Ben's converted rice

2 Tbl. chicken base

½ cup tomato puree

3½ cups water or chicken stock

1 cup chopped Greek olives, green or ripe

½ cup chopped parsley

Stir and bring to a boil, reduce the heat and simmer uncovered 25 to 30 minutes or until the moisture has been absorbed and the rice is dry and fluffy.

Savarin au Cognac
Serves 8 to 10

1 cake yeast

⅔ cup warm milk

1 Tbl. sugar

2 cups flour

4 eggs, beaten

Salt

⅔ cup butter, softened

Grated rind of a lemon

Dissolve the yeast cake in the warm milk and add the sugar.

289

In a bowl, combine the flour, salt, eggs, lemon rind, add the yeast mixture and beat until well blended. It should have a soft, sticky consistency. Cover the bowl and let it rise in a warm place for about 45 minutes.

Punch the dough down and stir in the softened butter. Then beat by hand using a wooden spoon until the butter has been absorbed. Pour the dough into a buttered, two-quart ring mold, cover with a towel and let rise until double in bulk.

Bake in 350° oven 35 to 45 minutes.

Unmold on a rack or cake plate and soak with cognac syrup.

Cognac Syrup

1½ cups water

1 cup sugar

Bring to a boil and cook 15 minutes. Remove from the heat and add **½ cup cognac.**

Fill the center with **fresh or canned fruits** and serve with **whipped cream.**

> **Persian Leg of Lamb with Prunes**
> **Kasha with Currants and Lentils**
> **Zucchini and Cucumbers with Yogurt Sauce**
> **Flat Bread**
> **Baklava**
> **California Chablis**
> **(Almaden, Beaulieu Vinegard, Wente Bros.)**

Persian Leg of Lamb with Prunes   Serves 8 to 10

Have the butcher bone and trim a **6½ to 7 pound leg of lamb.** Remove the heavy fat and place in a roasting pan and rub inside and out with:

> **1 Tbl. ground cumin**
> **1 tsp. ground cinnamon**
> **1 tsp. ground cloves**
> **1 Tbl. dill weed**
> **1 Tbl. crushed rosemary**
> **Juice of 2 or 3 lemons**
> **¼ cup olive oil**
> **Ground black pepper**

Let marinate over night or for several hours. Push the leg of lamb back into shape and roast in a 350° oven 45 to 60 minutes for rare lamb.

While the lamb is roasting, cook in a sauce pan:

> **1 pound pitted prunes**
> **Juice and rind of a lemon and orange**
> **1 stick of cinnamon**
> **3 or 4 cardamon seeds**
> **Water to cover**

Bring to a boil and simmer until the moisture has been absorbed.

Place the cooked prunes over the outside of the cooked lamb, sprinkle with **dark brown sugar** and return to a hot 425° oven for 15 to 20 minutes to glaze.

Kasha with Currants and Lentils   Serves 8 to 10

In a heavy sauce pan melt **½ cup butter**, add **one medium-size, chopped onion,** and saute until transparent. Then add:

> **1½ cups washed lentils**
> **Four friends**
> **4 cups chicken stock**

Bring to a boil, reduce heat and simmer until the lentils are tender.

Add:

> **1 cup currants that have been plumped***
> **1 cup kasha**

If needed, add:

> **1 to 2 cups chicken stock**

Stir, cover, and steam for 20 to 30 minutes or until the kasha is fluffy. Add **½ cup chopped parsley** just before serving.

Zucchini and Cucumber with Yogurt Sauce   Serves 8

Wash, trim, and slice thin with skins left on:

> **4 to 6 tender cucumbers**
> **4 to 6 tender zucchini**

Place the sliced cucumbers and zucchini in a bowl and add:

_____

*Reconstitute by soaking in water.

1 medium-size onion, thinly sliced
1 Tbl. dill weed
Four friends
2 cups plain yogurt

Stir together, cover, and let marinate several hours.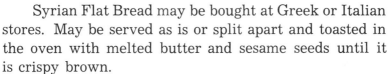
May be garnished with **cherry tomatoes.**

Syrian Flat Bread may be bought at Greek or Italian stores. May be served as is or split apart and toasted in the oven with melted butter and sesame seeds until it is crispy brown.

The Bakalava may be purchased frozen at these same stores. Defrost and warm it in the oven for a few minutes before serving.

Stuffed Mushrooms
Broiled Quail with Currant Sauce
Baked Stuffed Avocados with Cauliflower
Frozen Strawberry Mousse
California Burgundy
(Inglenook, Martini, Almaden, Beringer Bros.)

Stuffed Mushrooms   Serves 8

32 large mushrooms — trim, remove the stems, and chop fine.

In a saute pan melt **¼ cup butter,** add **one medium-size finely chopped onion** and saute until transparent. Then add:

> **Chopped mushroom stems**
> **Four friends**
> **½ cup finely chopped walnuts**
> **¼ cup chopped parsley**

Saute for three to five minutes and add **½ cup bread crumbs** and stir in **1 or 2 eggs** off the heat.

Stuff the mushrooms with this mixture. Place in a buttered, shallow casserole and sprinkle with **dry sherry or Madeira.** Bake in a 400° oven 20 minutes. Serve as a first course or as a vegetable.

Broiled Quail with Currant Sauce   Serves 8

> **16 quail**
> **16 Tbl. butter**
> **Four friends**
> **1 medium onion,** finely chopped
> **Splash of brandy**
> **Juice of a lemon**
> **1 cup currant jelly**

Place the quail in a broiling pan and coat each with one Tbl. butter. Bless with the four friends and put the chopped onion around the quail.

Place about three inches from the heat and broil 10 to 15 minutes turning occasionally. When done, place in a heat-proof casserole in a warm oven.

Pour the juices into a sauce pan. Add the lemon juice, currant jelly, bring to a boil and reduce quickly until it thickens slightly. Add the brandy and pour the sauce over the quail.

Serve immediately on **large croutons.**

Baked Stuffed Avocados with Cauliflower   Serves 8

> 1 head cauliflower
> Four friends
> 2 Tbl. chopped parsley
> 2 eggs
> ½ pound grated Swiss cheese
> 2 Tbl. cream
> Grated nutmeg
> 4 under-ripe avocados

Cut the cauliflower into flowerettes and cook in salt water and ½ cup milk until tender, but still crisp. Drain and allow cauliflower to dry. Coarsely chop the cauliflower and season with four friends, parsley, eggs, Swiss cheese, cream and nutmeg. Stir. Peel and cut avocados in half. Scoop out the seeds. Gently stuff the cauliflower mixture into the avocado halves using generous portions. Sprinkle with **chopped parsley, paprika,** and **Parmesan cheese.** Bake in glass or enamel pan in 350° oven for 15 to 20 minutes.

If you prepare this ahead of time, squeeze **lemon juice** on the avocado and refrigerate in a glass or enamel pan securely covered with saran wrap.

Frozen Strawberry Mousse   Serves 10 to 12

In a sauce pan stir well and bring up to the boiling point:

> 8 whole eggs
> 1 cup sugar
> 1 tsp. salt
> 4 cups whipping cream

Remove from the heat and cool. Place this cooled custard in the freezing container of an ice cream freezer and add:

4 cups fresh, drained strawberries
1 ounce Creme de Almond
½ cup slivered almonds
1 cup broken macaroons

Put the paddle in and the cover on and pack the freezing chamber to the top with crushed ice and rock salt. Turn on the freezer or crank for 30 to 40 minutes until frozen or ice cream freezer turns off or stops. Remove the paddle and scrape off the frozen mousse. Pack the mousse in ice or put into a three-quart mold. Cover and put in the freezer to ripen. Serve with **fresh strawberries.**

May be made with any fresh, canned, or frozen fruits.

Ice cream freezers are fun, and are making a comeback in popularity. Buy the five quart size. An electric freezer is easiest to use, but if you find an old one in your basement, it will do fine — you just need strong arms and a sense of humor.

Cream of Mushroom Soup
Baked Halibut with Spanish Sauce
Rice Pilaf
Asparagus and Avocado Vinaigrette
Genoise with Chocolate Sauce
Premium California Chablis
(Wente Bros., Almaden, Beaulieu Vineyard)

Cream of Mushroom Soup   Serves 8

In a sauce pan melt **¼ cup butter** and saute **one medium-size, chopped onion** until transparent. Then add:

     1½ pounds mushrooms, washed and trimmed
     One cup dry white wine
     Juice of a lemon
     Four friends

Bring to a boil and add:

     2 cups light cream
     2 Tbl. chicken base
     Pinch of grated nutmeg

Simmer for 20 minutes. Blend in small batches on medium speed. Then add:

     1 or 2 Tbl. arrowroot
     ½ cup dry sherry
     ½ cup chopped parsley

Return to the heat until thickened and taste for seasoning. This may also be done using all chicken stock.

Baked Halibut with Spanish Sauce   Serves 6 to 8

Place **two to three pounds boned halibut fillets** in a shallow casserole.

Sauce
In a sauce pan heat until the onion is transparent:
>   2 Tbl. olive oil
>   ½ cup chopped onion
>   ½ cup chopped green pepper
>   1 or 2 cloves chopped garlic

Add:
>   Three friends
>   2 tsp. paprika
>   Ground black pepper
>   Salt
>   2 cups peeled, chopped tomatoes
>   2 Tbl. capers
>   2 Tbl. chopped pimento
>   Pinch sugar
>   2 Tbl. chopped parsley

Cook for 15 to 20 minutes over medium heat.
Pour sauce over the fish fillets and bake in 350° oven 30 to 40 minutes.

Rice Pilaf   Serves 8

>   ½ cup butter
>   1½ cups Uncle Ben's converted rice
>   ½ cup chopped onion
>   3 cups chicken stock
>   Four friends

Melt the butter in a sauce pan, add the onion and saute until transparent. Add the rice and the four friends. Stir until the rice is coated with the mixture and add the chicken stock. Bring to a boil, reduce the heat and simmer until the moisture has been absorbed and the rice is light and fluffy.

Asparagus and Avocado Vinaigrette   Serves 8

Two pounds asparagus, washed, trimmed, and cooked. Cool and arrange on a bed of lettuce.

In a blender jar put:

Three peeled, seeded ripe avocados
½ cup Country French Dressing
Juice of one lemon

Blend until pureed.

Spoon the sauce over the cold asparagus and garnish with **chopped green onion** and **parsley.**

Genoise   Serves 8 to 10

Basic pastry for cakes, jellyrolls, savarins, etc.

In a bowl that you can heat put:

5 large eggs
Pinch of salt
⅔ cup sugar

Heat over hot water until lukewarm, stirring occasionally. When warm, beat in the mixing bowl on medium speed until the mixture is the consistency of mayonnaise. Add **1 tsp. vanilla.**

Remove from the mixer and carefully fold in **2 cups sifted cake flour** or **all purpose flour** and **¼ cup melted, cooled butter** with a wide rubber spatula.

Pour the batter into a buttered and floured 8 or 10 inch spring form pan.

Bake in a 350° oven 30 to 40 minutes or until the cake springs back to the touch.

To make a Chocolate Genoise use 1½ cups cake or all purpose flour and **½ cup cocoa.** Sift together and fold into the egg mixture. Then add the melted butter. Pour the chocolate sauce over the cooled cake and garnish with whipped cream.

Chocolate Sauce

In a heavy sauce pan melt the following ingredients but do not let boil. Stir with a wooden spoon.

8 ounces semi-sweet chocolate
1 cup confectioners sugar
2 Tbl. butter
Pinch of salt
½ cup whipping cream

When melted, remove from the heat and beat with a wooden spoon until cooled. It should be thick and shiny. Then add **¼ cup Creme de Cacao or one tsp. vanilla.**

Store in a covered glass jar in the refrigerator.

Good over ice cream, cakes or as an icing.

Fried Vegetables
Delhi Chicken Curry
Puree of Yellow Lentils
Cucumber and Yogurt Salad
Silver Carrot Pudding

It is traditional to serve non-alcoholic beverages with these recipes since they originate from Delhi where alcohol is forbidden.

Fried Vegetables Serves 8

Good first course or hors d'oeuvre for cocktails

1 small head cauliflower, trimmed and cut into flowerettes
1 bunch broccoli, cut into flowerettes
1 small egg plant, cut into one-inch squares
1 pound mushroom caps, washed and trimmed
2 inches frying oil, heated in a deep iron skillet or dutch oven to the smoking point, 350°

Batter for the Vegetables
In a bowl put:

4 cups Buttermilk Bisquick or pancake mix
1 large Tbl. curry powder
4 cups buttermilk

Stir until it is well combined and has a thick batter consistency.

Dip the vegetables into the batter and fry them in the deep fat for five to eight minutes or until they are crispy brown. Skim out and drain on paper towels and keep warm.

Good dipped in Indian Tap Sauce or Chutney either of which can be purchased at the grocery.

Delhi Chicken Curry   Serves 6 to 8

From my friend Nitty Singh

In a heavy dutch oven heat **¼ cup cooking oil**, add **three large chopped onions** and saute until they are transparent. Add:

> **1 tsp. turmeric**
> **1 Tbl. freshly grated ginger**
> **4 or 5 cloves garlic,** crushed
> **Ground black pepper**
> **Salt**
> **½ tsp. ground cloves**
> **½ tsp. cinnamon**
> **1 tsp. ground coriander**
> **½ tsp. nutmeg**
> **2 cups peeled, chopped tomatoes**
> **½ tsp. cayenne pepper**

Heat for two or three minutes until the aroma develops. Then add two or three **2½ to 3 pound cut-up frying chickens.** The heavy bones, wing tips, and skin should be removed. Stir until the chicken is coated with the mixture for about five to ten minutes. Then add **three cups yogurt or buttermilk** and bring to a boil. Cover the pan and let simmer, stirring occasionally, for 45 minutes to an hour or until tender. Serve hot with **rice** or **pureed yellow lentils.**

Puree of Yellow Lentils   Serves 8 to 10

In a heavy sauce pan heat **¼ cup oil,** add **one medium-size, finely chopped onion** and saute until trasparent. Then add:

> **1 pound washed yellow lentils**
> **1 Tbl. curry powder**
> **Four friends**
> **2 Tbl. chicken base**
> **8 cups chicken stock**

Stir and bring to a boil, reduce heat and simmer until the lentils are soft and the moisture has been absorbed. This will take 60 to 90 minutes.

Cucumber and Yogurt Salad   Serves 8

Place **four large cucumbers** that have been peeled, seeded and sliced in a bowl and add:

> **1 medium-size onion,** thinly sliced
> **Ground black pepper**
> **Salt**
> **Juice of 1 lemon or lime**
> **1 to 2 cups plain yogurt**

Stir, cover and, marinate, refrigerated, for several hours. Serve with **crisp lettuce** and **peeled, quartered tomatoes.**

Carrot Pudding   Serves 8

In a heavy sauce pan heat **½ cup oil** and **eight crushed cardamon seeds** for two or three minutes. Then add **two pounds peeled, raw carrots,** finely grated. Cook for five minutes and then add:

> **4 cups milk**

1½ cups sugar
1 ounce slivered almonds
1 ounce pistachio nuts

Bring to a boil, reduce heat and simmer, stirring occasionally, to prevent burning. Cook slowly until the milk has evaporated.

Serve this pudding warm, decorated with *Indian Silver leaves.

——————————

*Actual sterling silver, tissue-paper-thin leaves of gold or silver that are edible. Most likely you'll have to go to New York to find them.

Turban of Sole with Hollandaise
Roast Duckling Bigarade
Wild Rice or Pilaf
Brussels Sprouts and Chestnuts
Crepes Filled with Lemon Souffle
Classified Growth - Medoc
(Chateau Latour, Chateau Lascombes,
Chateau Cos d'Estournel)

Turban of Sole with Hollandaise   Serves 8

Eight inch ring mold generously buttered.
2½ pounds fresh sole fillets.

Line the ring mold with the sole fillets putting the white side down and the wider end to the outside of the ring mold. Overlap them all the way around. Let the ends hang out over the edges.

Filling

In the blender put:

> 2 **pounds raw shrimp**
> 8 **egg whites**
> 1 **cup whipping cream**
> **Four friends**
> 1 **Tbl. paprika**
> 2 **tsp. dry mustard**
> ½ **tsp. grated nutmeg**

Blend on medium speed until the consistency of whipping cream. Spoon this mixture into the mold and fill. Turn the overhanging ends of the fish back on top of the shrimp, filling all the way around. Cover the top with wax paper and bake in a hot water bath in a 350° oven 45 to 60 minutes.

Turn the mold out on a round platter and absorb any excess moisture with paper towels. Fill the center with **hollandaise sauce.** Garnish with **cooked shrimp, chopped parsley,** and a **bouquet of watercress.**

Roast Duckling Bigarade   Serves 8

Three or four 4½ to 5 pound Long Island Ducklings. There are really only two servings per duck.

Place the ducks in a roasting pan and bless the outside with the **four friends. Onions or apples** should be stuffed in the cavities.

Roast in a pre-heated 400° oven 25 to 30 minutes. Remove from the oven, and let cool. When cool, split the

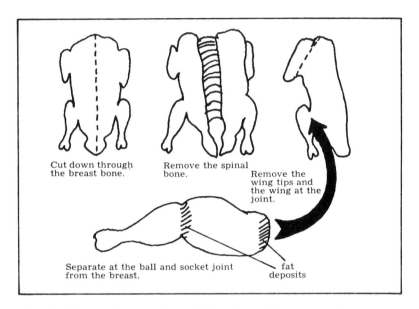

Cut down through the breast bone.

Remove the spinal bone.

Remove the wing tips and the wing at the joint.

Separate at the ball and socket joint from the breast.

fat deposits

ducks down the center of the breast bone and open up. With your cleaver, chop out the back spinal bone. The ducks will be split exactly in half.

Separate the half between the hip and ball and socket joint and the backbone joint.

At the top of the wing ball and socket joint and the hip joint are the heavy deposits of fat. With your fingers or paring knife remove these deposits.

You may also remove the breast and rib bones from the breast meat of the ducks.

Return the pieces of duck to the roasting pan and heat in a 350° oven for 15 or 20 minutes to get rid of the surface fat. Remove from the oven and drain well.

This is the best and most successful way to get rid of the excess fat from the ducks. It is a messy job, but well worth the effort in the end.

Bigarade Sauce

Make **brown sauce** and strain it.

Place the strained brown sauce in a sauce pan and add:

1 cup bitter orange marmalade (Dundee)
One 6 ounce can defrosted orange juice concentrate
½ cup brandy
Juice of a lemon

Bring to a boil and simmer for 20 to 30 minutes.

In the meantime, coarsely grate the rinds of **three or four large navel oranges.** *Blanch the rinds, drain well, and add them to the sauce. Then add **½ cup Grand Marnier or Cointreau** and the **orange sections.**

Arrange the roasted, drained pieces of duck in a deep casserole and pour the sauce over them.

Bake in a 350° oven for 35 to 45 minutes.

Serve with wild rice, polenta, or a pilaf.

Brussels Sprouts and Chestnuts   Serves 8

Two pounds tiny Brussels sprouts. Trim and remove any yellowed leaves and make a cut into the bottom of each stem.

Put the Brussels sprouts in a sauce pan and cover with cold, salted water. Cover with paper towels and bring to a boil and simmer 12 to 18 minutes or until tender. Drain and place in a casserole with:

---

*Place in cold water in a covered pot on the fire. Bring to a rapid boil, drain and wash in cold water. Blanching removes the strong flavors (of the orange) or excess fats from meat.

1 pound can drained, French chestnuts
Juice of a lemon
Four friends
Grated nutmeg
3 or 4 Tbl. melted butter
Reheat in a 350° oven 20 to 25 minutes.

Crepes Filled with Lemon Souffle   Serves 8

Make **16 crepes.** See crepe recipe.

Lemon Souffle
In a sauce pan melt **¼ cup butter** and add:
⅔ cup sugar
Pinch of salt
3 Tbl. arrowroot
1½ cups water
**Grated rinds of 3 or 4 lemons and their
   juice**
Stir and bring to a boil and cook until thickened. Remove from the heat and add **5 egg yolks.** Stir and return to the fire and heat for two or three minutes. Remove and let cool.

Beat the **5 egg whites** until very stiff and then fold the cooled lemon mixture into the egg whites with a wide rubber spatula.

Have a large, shallow, well-buttered casserole ready. Fill ½ of each crepe with a large spoonful of the souffle mixture and fold the other half over. Carefully place in the casserole.

When all are filled and placed in the casserole, sprinkle with sugar and bake in a 400° oven for 20 minutes or until they are puffy and brown. Serve immediately.

Artichoke and Avocado Soup
Morue of Beef
Poppy Seed Noodles
Harlequin Tomatoes
Fresh Pears with Gorgonzola
Moulin-a-Vent 1967

Artichoke and Avocado Soup · Serves 8

½ cup butter
1 medium-size onion, chopped
Four friends
2 Tbl. chicken base
½ cup flour
4 cups chicken stock or milk
½ cup chopped parsley
2 cups artichoke hearts, drained
3 ripe avocados, peeled and seeded

Melt the butter in the sauce pan, add the onion and saute until transparent. Then add the four friends, chicken base and flour and stir together. Then add the milk or chicken stock, parsley, artichokes and avocado. Bring to a boil, reduce the heat and simmer 25 to 30 minutes. When cooked, blend in small batches in the blender on medium speed until pureed. (Do not fill the blender more than half full with the hot soup so that it will not fly out and burn you while you are blending. Be sure to have the top on the blender jar.)

When all is blended, return to the heat, stir and bring to the boiling point. Taste for seasoning.

Garnish with **diced avocado or artichoke hearts** and **chopped parsley.**

Morue of Beef   Serves 6 to 8
Piquant Bavarian stew. Game may also be prepared in this manner.

> **1 pound bacon,** diced
> **1 large onion,** chopped
> **2 to 3 cloves garlic,** pressed or chopped
> **3 to 4 pounds stewing beef,** cut into 1 inch pieces
> **Three friends**
> **2 to 3 bay leaves**
> **Ground black pepper**
> **6 to 8 juniper berries or ¼ cup gin**
> **½ tsp. grated nutmeg**
> **½ cup flour**
> **½ cup tomato puree**
> **½ cup currant jelly**
> **2 cups dry red wine**
> **2 Tbl. beef base**
> **2 Tbl. red wine vinegar**
> **2 cups pearl onions**
> **1 pound mushroom caps,** washed, trimmed, acidulated
> **½ cup chopped parsley**
> **Splash of brandy**

In a heavy casserole, cook the diced bacon until half done. Drain off the excess fat, add the chopped onion, and saute until transparent. Then add the diced stewing beef and sear. Add the garlic, three friends, bay leaves, pepper, juniper berries or gin, and nutmeg.

Sprinkle the flour over this mixture, stir, and then add tomato puree, currant jelly, red wine, beef base, and red wine vinegar. Stir, bring to the boiling point, reduce heat and simmer uncovered for one hour or until the beef is tender. Then add the pearl onions and mushroom caps and cook fifteen more minutes. Add the parsley and brandy just before serving.

Poppy Seed Noodles   Serves 8

> **16 ounces medium-cut noodles**
> **½ cup butter**
> **Four friends**
> **2 to 3 Tbl. poppy seeds**
> **2 to 3 Tbl. chopped parsley**

Have a large pot of boiling salted water with **2 Tbl. cooking oil** added, ready. Add the noodles and cook 8 to 12 minutes. Drain and season with butter, four friends, the poppy seeds, and parsley.

Harlequin Tomatoes   Serves 8

Slice the tops from **eight small tomatoes** and scoop out the insides of the tomatoes with a tablespoon.

Put **one cup diced celery** in a sauce pan, cover with **cold salted water,** bring to a boil, and then drain.

Saute **one medium-size, diced onion** in **two Tbl. butter** until transparent. Then add:

> **Drained, blanched celery**
> **½ cup chopped, ripe olives**
> **2 Tbl. chopped parsley**
> **1 Tbl. white wine vinegar**
> **¼ cup diced pimento**

Stuff the cavities of the tomatoes with this mixture. Place in a shallow casserole.

Bake in 350° oven 15 to 20 minutes.

Pears with Gorgonzola   Serves 8

Eight fresh, ripe pears, cored and peeled. Trim off the bottom so they will sit flat. Squeeze fresh lemon juice over them to keep them white.

> **Eight ounces Gorgonzola cheese,** at room temperature **(or any blue cheese type)**

Slice the cheese thinly. Dip your knife into warm water to help keep the cheese from crumbling as you are slicing it.

Arrange one pear and slices of cheese on each dessert plate. Serve with a knife and fork and with plain **Bremner Wafers.**

Olive Salad
Steak au Poivre
Sauteed Mushrooms
Braised Zucchini
Chocolate Cheese Cake
Bordeaux - St. Emilion
(Chateau Trotte Vielle 1964 is special)

Olive Salad   Serves 8

Place in a bowl and mix:
> **1 bunch green onions,** finely chopped
> (green and white parts)
> **One 10 ounce jar, large, stuffed green**
> **Spanish olives,** drained and chopped
> (1½ cups)
> **Juice of one lemon**
> **Ground black pepper**
> **1 Tbl. Dijon mustard**
> **1 cup mayonnaise**
> **½ cup chopped parsley**

Separate and arrange **five or six heads of Belgian endive** in a salad bowl. Add the olive mixture and garnish with chopped parsley, tomatoes, and watercress.

Steak au Poivre

Fillet, sirloin strip, rib eye, or sirloin steaks cut 1½ to 2 inches thick. About one pound per person. Have the excess fat removed.

Bless the steaks with the four friends. With the heel of the palm of your hand, press **coarsely ground, crushed pepper** into the surfaces of the steaks on both sides. Then re-shape the steaks to their natural look.

When you are ready to cook the steaks, heat **one or two Tbl. oil** in a heavy skillet until very hot. Add the steaks and sear on both sides. Then cook until they are as done as you wish.

Flame the steaks with **one or two Tbl. brandy.** Then squeeze fresh **lemon juice** over the steaks. This will cut down the very hot flavor of the ground or crushed pep-percorns. Serve with **brown sauce or Madeira sauce** and **sauteed mushrooms.**

Braised Zucchini   Serves 6 to 8

Eight small zucchini. Wash in warm water, remove the ends, and slice paper thin.

In a saute pan heat:

    2 Tbl. butter
    2 Tbl. olive oil

Add **one medium-size, diced onion,** and saute until transparent.

Then add the sliced zucchini and heat quickly, stirring occasionally, about three to five minutes. Season with:

    Four friends
    1 Tbl. chicken base
    3 Tbl. chopped parsley
    Ground black pepper

You may add, if you wish, **¼ cup Parmesan cheese** just before serving.

Keep the zucchini on the crisp side.

Chocolate Cheese Cake   Serves 8 to 10

In a mixing bowl, beat until light and fluffy:
1½ pounds cream cheese
1 tsp. salt
⅔ cup sugar
2 tsp. vanilla
3 egg whites

Soften **3 Tbl. plain gelatin** in **½ cup cold water.**
Melt over hot water and cool.

Also melt over hot water and cool:
1 pound sweet chocolate
½ cup Creme de Cacao

Stiffly beat **one cup whipping cream or sour cream.**

Add the cooled gelatin and chocolate mixtures to
the cheese mixture. Beat together until well blended.
Then fold in the stiffly beaten whipped cream or sour
cream. Place in refrigerator.

Line a ten inch spring form pan with a crust made of:
Ten ounces Nabisco Chocolate
Wafers, finely pounded (2½ cups crumbs)
½ cup melted butter

Fill the crust with the chocolate cheese mixture.
Cover and refrigerate. May be made the day before. Unmold on a tray and garnish with **whipped cream** and
shaved chocolate.

**Cheddar Cheese and Brandy Soup
Tongue with Madeira Sauce
Spinach with Raisins
Beets and Oranges
Coffee Mousse with Floradora Sauce
Bordeaux
Cru Muscadet**

Cheddar Cheese and Brandy Soup   Serves 8

In a soup pot melt **¼ cup butter,** add **one finely diced onion** and saute until transparent. Add:
>   **½ cup flour**
>   **Four friends**
>   **2 Tbl. chicken base**
>   **1 tsp. curry powder**
>   **1 tsp. paprika**
>   **½ cup finely chopped celery**
>   **4 cups milk or light cream or chicken stock**

Stir, bring to a boil and add:
>   **1 cup dry sherry**
>   **1½ cups sharp cheddar cheese,** grated

Simmer the soup for 30 to 40 minutes.
Just before serving add:
>   **¼ cup brandy**
>   **2 to 3 Tbl. chopped parsley**

Tongue with Madeira Sauce   Serves 8

Place a **3½ to 4½ pound fresh or smoked beef tongue** in a deep soup or stewing pot. Cover with cold, salted water and add:

2 to 3 bay leaves
1 large onion, chopped
2 to 3 ribs of celery, chopped
4 or 5 whole cloves
1 stick cinnamon
1 cup cider vinegar

Bring to a boil, reduce the heat and simmer about one and a half to two hours or until you can easily pierce the root end of the tongue with a fork.

You may have to add more water during the cooking process.

When cooked, remove from the water and let the tongue cool to lukewarm. Then, skin and trim the cartilage, bones and fat from the root end. Cool and thinly slice.

Place the thinly sliced tongue in a shallow casserole and cover with Madeira sauce.

Reheat in a 350° oven 25 to 30 minutes. May be eaten cold with mustard sauce or horseradish.

Mustard Sauce or Mustard Mayonnaise
Mix:

2 Tbl. Dijon mustard
1 cup mayonnaise
Four friends

Spinach with Raisins   Serves 8

Three pounds fresh spinach, washed, trimmed, and wilted. Drain well and chop fine. Place in a sauce pan. **Add ¼ cup butter.** Melt and add **¼ cup finely chopped onion.** Saute. Add:

¼ cup sesame seeds
1 cup white or dark raisins, plumped*
1 tsp. nutmeg
Juice of a lemon
Four friends

Stir until well combined, place in a casserole and bake in a 350° oven for 20 to 25 minutes.

Beets and Oranges   Serves 8

One 2½ can, sliced or small whole beets
2 Tbl. butter
2 to 3 Tbl. finely minced onion
1 small Tbl. dill weed
Grated nutmeg
2 Tbl. arrowroot
1 cup beet juice
Coarsely grated rind of 1 or 2 oranges
1 Tbl. red wine vinegar
Pinch of sugar
2 to 3 oranges, peeled and sectioned
Four friends

In a sauce pan melt the butter and saute the onions. Add four friends, dill, grated nutmeg, arrowroot. Stir off the fire. Add the beet juice and orange rind. Place back on the fire until the sauce has thickened. Add vinegar, sugar, drained beets, and orange sections.

    Add **½ cup orange juice.** Garnish with **chopped parsley.**

---

*Put raisins in a bowl and cover with warm water and let stand 15 minutes. Drain well. This reconstitutes the raisins.

Coffee Mousse with Floradora Sauce   Serves 8 to 10

Stiffly beat **2 cups of whipping cream** and set aside. Separate **8 eggs.** Put the whites in a mixing bowl and the yolks in a bowl you can heat over hot water. Soften **3 Tbl. plain gelatin** in **½ cup cold water** and melt over hot water. Beat the egg whites with **1 tsp. cream of tartar** until stiff. Gradually beat in **2/3 cup sugar** until stiff and add **2 to 3 Tbl. powdered coffee** and a **¼ cup of Creme de Coffee** and the softened gelatin. Put into the refrigerator to slightly set.

When partially set, fold in the stiffly beaten whipped cream with a rubber spatula until well blended. Pour into an oiled quart mold, cover and refrigerate.

Floradora Sauce

To the 8 egg yolks add:

⅔ cup of sugar
2 Tbl. powdered coffee
½ cup Cream de Coffee

Place the bowl over hot water on medium heat and beat gently until the sauce is light and fluffy like hollandaise. Remove from the heat and let cool.

Fold in **one cup stiffly beaten whipped cream.**

To serve, unmold the mousse on a tray and pile the sauce on top. Sprinkle with **candy coffee bean drops.**

Shrimp Newburg
Green Rice Ring
Creamed French Spinach
Apricot Meringue Souffle
Pinot Chardonnay 1970
Pouilly-Vinzelles

Shrimp Newburg   Serves 8

Three pounds of cooked shrimp
Newburg Sauce

See Basic Cooking for classic **newburg sauce.** Add to
this basic sauce, **1 Tbl. chicken base** when you add the
flour and **a splash of brandy** when the sauce has been
removed from the heat and is practically finished.

Add the cooked shrimp to the sauce. Reheat, but do
not boil. Serve in the center of a rice ring.

Green Rice Ring   Serves 8

Line the bottom of a two-quart ring mold that has been
generously **buttered** with a circle of wax paper. Fill the
ring with green rice. (See index for recipe) Tap down
but do not pack firmly. Place the ring in a hot water
bath and bake in a 350° oven 25 minutes.

To unmold, run a knife around the edge of the mold
and turn out on a large tray. The ring of wax paper on
the top helps the rice to unmold easily. Be sure to remove it before filling the center with the Shrimp Newburg.

This may be garnished with **sauteed mushrooms** and **chopped parsley.**

Creamed French Spinach   Serves 8

Two to three pounds fresh spinach, washed, trimmed, and stems removed. Place in a large pot with a little water on the fire and heat until the spinach wilts. Drain, let cool, squeeze out the excess moisture, then chop fine.

In a sauce pan, melt **¼ cup butter,** add **2 or 3 Tbl. finely diced onion** and saute until transparent. Add:

> **¼ cup flour**
> **Four friends**
> **1 tsp. grated nutmeg**
> **1½ cups milk or cream**

Stir, bring to a boil, and simmer for 10 to 12 minutes until thickened. Then stir in the chopped spinach. Simmer for 10 to 15 minutes and season with **ground black pepper** and **salt** to taste.

Apricot Meringue Souffle   Serves 6 to 8

In a sauce pan put:

> **8 ounces dried apricots**
> **⅔ cup sugar**
> **Juice of 1 lemon**
> **Juice of 1 orange**

Add enough water to cover and place on the fire and bring to a boil, reduce heat, and simmer until the apricots are soft and pureed. Be careful not to burn them. Remove from the heat and cool.

Meringue for the Souffle

> **8 or 9 egg whites,** at room temperature

1 tsp. cream of tartar

⅔ cup sugar

Add the cream of tartar to the egg whites and beat them on medium speed in a mixing bowl until stiff. Then, beat in the sugar a little at a time until you have a stiff meringue. You may add a **splash of brandy** and fold in **apricot puree** with a wide rubber spatula.

Pile this mixture into a two-quart souffle pot that has been buttered and dusted with sugar and bake in a 350° oven 20 to 25 minutes or until raised and brown on top.

You can look at this souffle while it is baking. Serve with **whipped cream** and slivers of **candied apricots.**

Lobster Parfait

Saddle of Lamb in Puff Pastry

Ratatouille

Celery Rave Salad

Almond Souffle

Moulin-a-Vent Beaujolais

Lobster Parfait   Serves 8

Two pounds cooked lobster meat, sliced

Sauce

In a blender jar put:

1 pound freshly killed lobster meat (canned or frozen may be substituted)

3 Tbl. tomato puree
1 clove garlic
2 Tbl. lemon juice
1 Tbl. dry sherry
1 Tbl. cognac
¼ cup chopped onion
½ cup dry white wine

Puree on medium speed in the blender, place in sauce pan, and bring to a boil. Reduce the heat and simmer until reduced by one-third. Remove from the heat and chill. When cold add:

2 cups mayonnaise
1½ Tbl. whipping cream
2 tsp. paprika
Four friends

Blend and refrigerate one to two hours.

To assemble in the parfait glasses, alternate layers of the sauce and lobster and **seedless green grapes, cantaloupe balls or seeded kumquats,** ending with the sauce on top.

Decorate the top with stiffly beaten **unsweetened whipped cream** and **sprigs of watercress.**

Not only an unusual first course, but it's great for a summer luncheon, too.

Saddle of Lamb in Puff Pastry   Serves 8

Two boned, trimmed and rolled saddles of lamb, about 2½ pounds each. Your butcher will do this for you.

Place the boned saddles in a roasting pan and season with:

Four friends
2 Tbl. crushed rosemary
Ground black pepper
Juice of a lemon

Roast in a 350° oven 25 to 30 minutes. Remove from the oven, let cool, and drain. When cool, cut and remove the strings and cut away the outside surface fat.

Duxelles (mushroom paste)

In a sauce pan put:

1½ pounds mushrooms, trimmed, washed, acidulated
1 medium-size onion, chopped
¼ cup butter
¼ cup chopped parsley
Four friends
½ cup dry white wine
Ground black pepper

Cover, put on the fire, and bring to a boil. Cook five to eight minutes. Remove from the heat and put in a blender jar to chop by turning the blender on and off for a few seconds. Add **two or three Tbl. whipping cream.** If this paste is thin, it may be thickened with **2 or 3 Tbl. arrowroot,** heated, and then let cool.

You will need about **½ pound puff pastry** for each saddle. Roll out in a rectangle 8 x 12 inches and about ¼ inch thick.

Put the cooled saddle of lamb on the front side of the pastry and coat the top and sides of the lamb with the cold duxelles. Then bring the far side of the pastry up and over the lamb, encasing it in the pastry. Trim off the excess pastry and save it for decorating the outside. Seal the edges with **egg wash** and brush the outside surfaces with egg wash. Using the scraps, decorate the outside with hearts and flowers.

Place on a shallow baking tray. Bake in 425° oven 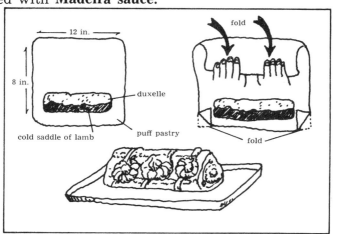 about 20 to 25 minutes or until golden brown. Serve sliced with **Madeira sauce.**

Ratatouille   Serves 8

May be served hot or cold as a vegetable or appetizer.

In a heavy skillet heat **¼ cup olive oil,** add **one medium-size chopped onion** and saute until transparent. Add **one medium-size eggplant,** diced with the skin (about 2 cups) and cook for about five minutes. Then add:

> **4 or 5 small, diced zucchini**
> **2 cups peeled, seeded, diced tomatoes**
> **1 diced green pepper**
> **1 cup diced celery**
> **½ cup chopped parsley**
> **Four friends**
> **½ cup red wine vinegar**
> **Salt**

Ground black pepper
1 to 2 bay leaves
1 tsp. thyme
1 Tbl. sweet basil

Stir with a wooden spoon and cook 15 to 20 minutes. I don't like to over cook this especially if you plan to serve ratatouille cold. Taste for seasoning and transfer to an earthenware or porcelain casserole. Bless the top with **chopped parsley** and a drizzle of **olive oil** and **paprika.**

Reheat in a 350° oven 15 to 20 minutes or serve cold.

Celery Rave Salad   Serves 8

One large celery root, scrubbed and peeled with a stainless steel knife.

Finely julienne the celery root on a mandolin cutter or on a stainless steel grater. Place in a glass bowl and squeeze **lemon juic**e over the celery root. You should have about two cups of the celery root.

Add to the grated celery root:
Four friends
2 Tbl. grated onion
1 cup mayonnaise
Salt
White pepper

Mix well, cover and let stand in the refrigerator for several hours.

Serve on a bed of lettuce and garnish with chopped parsley.

Almond Souffle   Serves 4

4 Tbl. butter

½ **cup sifted flour**
1 **cup milk,** scalded
4 **egg yolks**
1 **tsp. almond extract**
5 **egg whites**
½ **cup sugar**
½ **cup chopped, slivered, toasted almonds**

Melt the butter in a sauce pan and then stir in the flour. Gradually add the scalded milk, stirring over medium heat until thickened. Cook for five minutes. Remove from the heat and stir in the egg yolks. Return to the heat and heat until thickened. Do not let boil. Let cool and then add the almond extract and the chopped almonds.

When ready to make the souffle, stiffly beat the egg whites and gradually beat in the sugar a little at a time until you have a stiff meringue.

Fold the custard mixture into the egg white meringue with a wide rubber spatula. Put into a one-quart souffle dish that has been **buttered** and dusted with **powdered sugar.**

Bake in a 350° oven 25 to 35 minutes. Serve warm with **Vanilla Sauce.**

Vanilla Sauce

3 **egg yolks**
2 **Tbl. sugar**
1 **tsp. vanilla**
2 **cups scalded cream**
1 **Tbl. cognac**

Place these ingredients in a bowl over hot water on medium heat. Stir and cook until thickened.

Beef Cooked in Beer
Bavarian Noodles
Dilled Green Bean Salad
Macaroon Mousse
Dao Portuguese Red
(Grao Vasco, Borges
Colares "Real Vinicola" - unusual and different
wine if you wish to be adventurous)

Beef Cooked in Beer   Serves 8

Great hearty dish that reheats well.

In a heavy casserole cook **½ pound diced bacon** until it is half done. Drain off the excess fat and add **one medium-size, diced onion.** Cook the onion with the bacon until transparent.

Then sear **three pounds stewing beef,** cut into one inch cubes, in the bacon and onion until it is a gray color, not browned. Add **2 or 3 cloves chopped garlic** and sprinkle **½ cup flour** over the meat and stir until the flour has been absorbed. Add:

> **Four friends**
> **½ cup tomato puree**
> **1 small leek,** chopped, washed
> **5 or 6 juniper berries**
> **2 Tbl. beef base**
> **2 cans beer**

Stir, bring to the boiling point, deglaze the bottom of the pan, reduce the heat and simmer, uncovered, 45 to 60 minutes. It also may be baked in a 350° oven, uncovered,

328

45 to 60 minutes or until the beef is tender. Then add:

> **1 pound mushroom caps,** washed, and trimmed
> **½ cup currant jelly or lingonberries**
> **1 cup small pearl onions**
> **2 to 3 Tbl. chopped parsley**

Return to the heat and cook for 15 to 20 minutes. Serve with rice, noodles, or spaetzle.

Bavarian Noodles   Serves 8

Eight ounces homemade-type egg noodles

Cook in boiling salted water with a little **oil** added until tender. Drain and add:

> **2 Tbl. butter**
> **2 Tbl. oil**
> **1 medium onion,** sauteed in the butter and oil
> **Four friends**
> **¼ cup chopped parsley**
> **1 cup seasoned croutons**

Toss together and place in a buttered casserole. Re- heat in 350° oven 15 to 20 minutes.

Dilled Green Bean Salad   Serves 8

Arrange **two pounds cooked, fresh green beans** cut in three inch lengths in a bowl.

Marinate in the following dressing

> **2 Tbl. chopped parsley**
> **1 Tbl. dill weed**
> **Four friends**
> **¼ cup sliced, green onions**

¼ **cup olive oil**
Ground black pepper
Salt

Garnish with **quartered, peeled tomatoes, hard-cooked eggs, chopped parsley.**

Macaroon Mousse   Serves 8 to 10

Butter the sides of an eight to ten inch spring form pan generously and line the sides and bottom with **crumbled macaroons** (about a dozen). Then dust with ¼ **cup slivered, toasted almonds.**

In Bowl I:
Stiffly beat **2 cups whipping cream.**
In Bowl II:
Soften **2 Tbl. plain gelatin** in ½ **cup cold water.** Melt over hot water, then cool.
In Bowl III:
6 egg whites at room temperature
1 tsp. cream of tartar
Beat stiffly and gradually add ⅔ **cup sugar.** Add and fold together:

Juice of one lemon
¼ **cup orange juice concentrate,** defrosted
¼ **cup slivered almonds**
Cooled, melted gelatin
Splash of brandy

Refrigerate until partially set. Then fold in the stiffly beaten whipped cream and **one cup crushed macaroons.** Pour into the lined, spring form mold, cover with saran wrap and refrigerate. To unmold, wrap the mold in a warm towel and turn out on a tray. Release the sides, remove them, then remove the bottom. Garnish with swirls of **whipped cream** on top.

Cornish Game Hens Rudolph with Apricot Sauce
Wild Rice
Puree of Green Beans and Broccoli
Brie Cheese Baked in Puff Pastry
Fresh Fruit in Champagne
French Sauternes
(Chateau La Tour Blanche, Chateau Y'Quem,
Chateau Lafaurie-Peyraguey)

Cornish Game Hens Rudolph   Serves 8

Eight 10 to 12 ounce Cornish game hens, washed, dried and stuffed.

Stuffing

Put into a bowl and mix well:

> **2 cups cooked rice**
> **1 cup chopped, dried apricots**
> **½ cup slivered almonds**
> **¼ cup brandy**
> **Juice of 2 lemons**
> **½ cup chopped parsley**
> **Four friends**

Place the stuffed Cornish game hens in a roasting pan and cover the bottom of the pan with a skim (enough to cover bottom of pan) of **dry white wine.** Brush each hen with **butter.**

Roast in a 350° oven about 45 minutes or until nicely browned.

Pour the **drippings from the pan** into a sauce pan and add **one cup apricot preserves.** Bring to a boil and add a

splash of brandy. Pour the sauce over the roasted hens. Serve with almond rice or wild rice.

Wild Rice   Serves 8

One pound wild rice washed well in cold water.

In a heavy sauce pan melt **½ cup butter,** add **one medium-size, chopped onion** and saute until transparent. Then add:

> **Washed wild rice**
> **Four friends**
> **8 cups chicken or beef stock**

Stir and bring to a boil, reduce heat and simmer until the moisture has been absorbed.

If the rice is old, you will sometimes have to add considerably more stock and cook until the rice is tender.* Normally, it takes about one hour to cook. Taste for seasoning and add **½ cup chopped parsley.**

Puree of Green Beans and Broccoli   Serves 8

> **One bunch broccoli,** cooked
> **Two pounds fresh green beans,** cooked

Cook these vegetables using the recipes given in the book, but add **1 Tbl. rosemary** to the boiling water.

Put the drained green beans and broccoli in the blender with:

> **¼ cup butter**

---

*Rice dehydrates when it is old but it is still usable. It just needs more liquid and needs to be cooked longer. Add more liquid and keep cooking until the rice is tender. A good way to tell if rice is old is by how yellow it has become. The more yellow the rice, the older it is.

Four friends
½ cup heavy cream
Blend on medium speed until pureed. Put the puree in a sauce pan and add **2 Tbl. arrowroot.** Heat until thickened. Taste for seasoning. This puree may be served as is or stuffed into **tomato shells.** Bake in 350° oven 15 to 20 minutes.

Brie Cheese Baked in Puff Pastry.   Serves 8 to 10

>**One 2 pound wheel ripe Brie cheese**
>**One pound puff pastry,** divided in half and rolled out into two circles just larger than the diameter of the cheese.

Place the cheese on one of the circles of the pastry and cover it with the second piece. Moisten the edges with **egg wash.** Seal the edges and cut off the excess pastry. Brush the outside with egg wash and decorate with the trimmings. When done ahead, keep in the refrigerator until ready to bake.

Bake in a 425° oven on a buttered baking tray for 25 to 30 minutes or until the pastry is puffed and brown.

To serve, pass the cheese and let each guest cut a wedge. The cheese will be runny. You may serve **slices of apple or pears** with this.

Fresh Fruit in Champagne   Serves 8

Put in a crystal bowl:

>**1 quart strawberries,** cleaned and stemmed
>**1 pineapple,** peeled and diced
>**2 oranges,** peeled and sectioned
>**1 cup seedless white grapes**
>**½ cup superfine sugar**

1 ounce Grenadine or Cassis
1 ounce Kirsch
½ bottle dry Champagne, chilled
Serve quickly.

Chilean Crab Soup
Boiled White Rice
French Bread
Assorted Cheeses
Bananas Flambe
Vinho Verde - Portugese White

Chilean Crab Soup   Serves 10 to 15
Good after theater chowder. Makes a meal in itself.

In a large soup pot heat ¼ **cup olive oil**, add **one large, diced onion** and saute until transparent. Add:
1 Tbl. curry powder
2 tsp. saffron
Four friends
2 bay leaves
1 Tbl. gumbo file
2 Tbl. chicken base
Heat for two or three minutes until you smell the aroma of the curry. Then add:

2 cups peeled, chopped tomato
1 large, grated sweet potato
2 cups diced celery
1 large green pepper, diced
One 46 ounce can tomato juice
3 cups dry white wine

Bring to a boil and simmer for 30 minutes. Then add:

1 pound King crab meat, diced
1 pound lump crab meat
1 pound tiny shrimps
1 pound diced Haddock
4 diced avocados
1 cup chopped parsley
½ cup dry sherry

Heat and bring up to the boiling point but do not over heat. May be served with boiled white rice and french bread.

Assorted Cheeses
Serve any three of the following cheeses on a platter before or with dessert. Use the same bread you served with the soup.

Danish Blue Cheese
Brie
Boursault
Cheddar or Stilton
Belle Paese
Port Salut

Bananas Flambe   Serves 8

Eight ripe, peeled bananas. Squeeze **lemon juice** over the bananas to keep white.

In a flambe pan or skillet melt ¼ **cup butter** and add
8 Tbl. dark brown sugar. Heat until this mixture melts
or carmelizes.

Then add:

4 Tbl. ground cinnamon
Juice of 2 lemons

Stir and add the bananas, coating them with the
syrup. Heat them for three or four minutes. Pour on **½
cup dark rum** and ignite. When the flame dies out, serve
with:

Vanilla ice cream
Whipped cream flavored with rum
Toasted slivered almonds

Linguini Caruso
Veal Marsala
Gnocchi with Mushrooms
Buttered Fresh Green Beans
Pears with Ricotta
Lambrusco Bianco

Linguini Caruso   Serves 8

Drop **one pound linguini** in a large pot of boiling salted
water with **2 or 3 Tbl. oil.**

Cook 18 to 20 minutes keeping them al dente (undercooked). When done, drain and add sauce.

Sauce

In a sauce pan heat **¼ cup olive oil** and cook **4 or 5 cloves of thinly sliced garlic** until they are lightly browned. Remove from the fire and add:

1 Tbl. anchovy paste
Ground black pepper
Three friends
1 cup whipping cream
½ cup chopped parsley
1 Tbl. sweet basil

Return to the heat and simmer until it has a creamy consistency.

Pour the sauce over the freshly cooked drained linguini. Serve with **Parmesan cheese** immediately.

Veal Marsala

Serves 8

Sixteen scallops of veal pounded very thin and trimmed of fat or heavy tissue. Each piece should be 3 to 4 ounces.

Lightly dust each scallop in **flour** and quickly saute in a combination of **¼ cup each hot oil and sweet butter.** When cooking veal, quickly sear on one side and then turn over and heat on the other side until you see droplets of blood appear on the top surface. This is a sign the veal is cooked through. Remove quickly and place in a shallow casserole. Keep warm. To the drippings in the pan add:

Four friends
Juice of 1 lemon
½ cup dry Marsala

Quickly heat and pour this sauce over the hot sauteed scallops of veal. Bless with **chopped parsley.** Best served immediately.

Gnocchi with Mushrooms   Serves 8
This gnocchi is based on choux paste. It is very light and delicate.

In a heavy sauce pan add:
2 cups water
½ cup butter
1 tsp. salt

Place on the fire and bring to a rapid boil until the butter has melted. Then quickly dump in and stir with a wooden spoon **1½ cups flour.** Cook this over the high heat until the paste forms a mass and leaves the sides of the pan. It should be like clay. Remove from the heat and let cool slightly. Beat **6 eggs,** one at a time, into this paste with a wooden spoon. This takes a bit of doing. Then stir in:
Four friends
⅔ cup Parmesan cheese
½ cup finely chopped parsley

You can put this paste in a pastry bag with a round tip. Squeeze the paste out and cut off in one inch lengths with a knife that has been dipped in water. Continue to moisten knife during the process. Cook the gnocchi in a pan of **boiling, salted water** or **chicken stock** until they float to the surface. This takes about four to five minutes. Skim from the boiling stock or water and place in a shallow, buttered casserole. Do not pile on top of each other. When all are cooked and drained pour **mushroom sauce** over the top.

Mushroom Sauce

In a sauce pan melt ¼ **cup butter,** add one **medium-size, finely chopped onion** and saute until transparent. Add:

> ¼ **cup flour**
> **Four friends**
> **2 Tbl. chicken base**
> **2 cups milk or chicken stock**

Stir and bring to a boil, reduce heat and simmer for 10 to 15 minutes.

Add:

> **1 cup thinly sliced mushrooms**
> ½ **cup dry sherry**

Cook for 10 more minutes. This sauce should not be too thick. Pour over the gnocchi and garnish with **2 or 3 Tbl. chopped parsley, grated Parmesan cheese and paprika.**

Bake in 350° oven for 15 to 20 minutes or until bubbly hot.

Buttered Fresh Green Beans

See receipe in Basic Cooking. Follow those directions adding only the **four friends** for more seasoning.

The beans may be prepared in advance and reheated in a 350° oven for 10 to 12 minutes.

Pears with Ricotta   Serves 8

Eight medium-size pears, cored and peeled. Slice off the bottom so that they sit flat. Squeeze **fresh lemon juice** over them.

In a mixing bowl put:

> ½ **pound soft ricotta cheese**

Juice of 1 orange
1 ounce brandy
1 cup whipping cream

Beat on medium speed until light and fluffy, like whipped cream. Place in a pastry bag with a star tube and fill the centers of the pears ending with a swirl on top. Place the filled pears on dessert plates and put a few **slivered toasted almonds** on top.

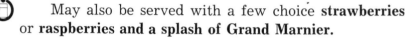

May also be served with a few choice **strawberries** or **raspberries and a splash of Grand Marnier.**

Sole Mousse with Scallop Sauce
Beef Wellington
Madeira Sauce
Vegetable Plank - A French Bouquetiere of
Vegetables
Watercress Salad served with
Brie Cheese and Bremner Wafers
Grand Marnier Souffle
Premium California Chablis
Classified Bordeaux
(Chateau LaFite Rothschild is super)
French Vintage Champagne
(Mumms Cordon Rouge, Piper Heidsieck, Ruinart)

Sole Mousse with Scallop Sauce   Serves 8

Sole Mousse

In a bowl combine and keep as cold as possible:

2 pounds fresh lemon sole, chopped
6 to 8 egg whites
1 cup cold whipping cream
Four friends
1 tsp. dry mustard
Pinch of nutmeg
Salt
White pepper

Blend small batches of this mixture in a blender on medium speed until it is the consistency of whipped cream. Stir all the batches together and taste for seasoning. Place in a two-quart buttered or oiled ring mold, charlotte or fancy fish mold. Cover the top with **wax paper.**

When ready to cook, place in a hot water bath and bake in a 350° oven 30 to 45 minutes. Test as for a custard.*

To unmold, remove from the hot water bath and let stand five minutes. Slip a knife around the edges and then turn out on a tray.

The fish molds will usually throw water on the tray so you will have to soak up the excess moisture with paper towels before you add the sauce and serve.

Scallop Sauce
> ¼ **cup butter**
> **2 or 3 chopped shallots**
> **3 Tbl. arrowroot**
> **Four friends**
> **1 Tbl. paprika**
> **1 tsp. dry mustard**
> **2 cups light cream**
> **1 cup dry sherry or dry white wine**
> **2 or 3 egg yolks**
> **2 or 3 Tbl. chopped parsley**
> **1 pint bay scallops** poached in their juice
> along with the **juice of a lemon** for two
> or three minutes. Drain well.

Melt the butter in a sauce pan, add the chopped shallots, and saute until transparent. Remove from the heat and add the arrowroot, the four friends, paprika, dry mustard, and the cream. Return to the fire, stir and bring to the boiling point. Add the sherry or dry white wine and heat until thickened. Remove from the

---

*Insert knife blade in the mousse. If the blade comes out clean, the mousse is done.

heat and stir in the egg yolks and the poached bay scallops and the parsley.

Heat but do not boil. Pour the hot sauce over the sole mousse. Garnish with **watercress.**

Beef Wellington   Serves 8 to 10

One 4½ to 5 pound (after trimming) beef tenderloin. Cook keeping it slightly more rare than you generally like and cool. See recipe for tenderloin in Basic Cooking.

> **One pound goose liver pate or duxelles paste**
> **Brandy or Cognac**
> **Chopped parsley**
> **Sliced truffles (optional)**
> **1½ pounds puff pastry** rolled out into a 12 by 18 inch rectangle about ¼ inch thick. Keep cold.
> **Egg wash**

Pre-cook the tenderloin and have it cold and ready.

Place the cold tenderloin on the puff pastry leaving about a two inch edge nearest you.

Slice the pate and arrange along the top of the tenderloin. Bless with brandy, the chopped parsley and the truffles.

Fold the front pastry edge up on the tenderloin and fold the ends as you would an envelope.

Reach across and bring the fore edge of the pastry up and over the tenderloin and down the side nearest you. Cut off the excess pastry and seal the edges with egg wash. Make sure the tenderloin is completely encased in the puff pastry. Brush the entire outside surface with egg wash.

Using the cut off scraps of pastry, make decorations for the outside of the Wellington. The egg wash will act as the glue to keep them on. Place the Wellington on a shallow tray.

 This may all be done the day before up to this point. Just keep cold and covered in the refrigerator.

When ready to bake, pre-heat the oven to 425.° Put the Wellington directly from the refrigerator into the oven. Bake 25 to 35 minutes or until the pastry is puffed and brown. Remove and let stand five minutes. Transfer to a carving board or tray.

See illustration of Saddle of Lamb in puff pastry for similar method.

You must let Beef Wellington stand after baking and before slicing so that it will stay intact and not fall apart. Use a long serrated or scalloped slicing knife to cut. Serve with Madeira Sauce.

French Bouquetiere of Vegetables   Serves 8 to 10

> **1 pound fresh green beans,** cooked and cooled
> **1 head cauliflower,** cut into flowerettes, cooked and cooked
> **1 cup defrosted peas**
> **10 or 12 artichoke bottoms,** drained, washed
> **2 cups stemmed cherry tomatoes**

Duchesse Potatoes

> **4 to 5 large, peeled Idaho potatoes** cut into equal size pieces.

Cook until tender and drain. Mash and add:

Four friends
2 Tbl. butter
3 or 4 egg yolks
¼ cup grated Parmesan cheese

Beat this mixture in the mixing bowl until it is light and fluffy. Then place in a pastry bag with a star tube tip. Pipe the potato mixture into the artichoke bottoms and swirl them up into pyramids. Arrange the filled ar-

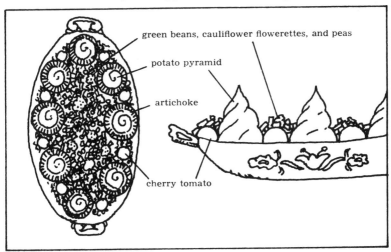

green beans, cauliflower flowerettes, and peas

potato pyramid

artichoke

cherry tomato

tichokes in a shallow, buttered casserole around the outside edge. Arrange the green beans, cauliflower flowerettes, peas and cherry tomatoes in the center after they have been seasoned with:

Four friends
2 to 3 Tbl. melted butter
2 to 3 Tbl. chopped parsley

This may be assembled the day before, covered, and refrigerated.

Bake from room temperature in a 350° oven 20 to 30 minutes.

Watercress Salad

Serves 6 to 8

Three bunches watercress, trimmed and washed. Arrange on salad plates. Serve with **lemon juice** and **olive oil** sprinkled on at the last minute.

Cut wedges of room temperature **Brie cheese** (slightly runny center) and put on one side of the watercress salad.

Pass the **Bremner Wafers** at the table.

Grand Marnier Souffle

Serves 6 to 8

This is my never fail souffle.

Rub the inside of a two-quart souffle pot with **butter,** then dust with **sugar.**

Separate **8 eggs** at room temperature. Put the whites in a copper beating bowl and add a **pinch of salt.**

Put the egg yolks in a bowl that you can heat over hot water. Add **⅔ cup sugar** and the **grated rind of a large orange** to the egg yolks. With a wire whisk, beat the egg yolk mixture over the hot water on medium heat until it is thickened and the consistency of hollandaise sauce. Remove from the hot water and stir in **3 ounces of defrosted orange juice** and **2 or 3 ounces of Grand Marnier.** Then put the bowl in the refrigerator to cool and chill.

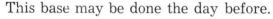

This base may be done the day before.

When you are ready to make the souffle, beat the room temperature egg whites in a copper beating bowl with a large balloon wire whisk until they are stiff but not dry. They will be shiny looking and stand in soft peaks on the end of the wire whisk.

Remove the egg yolk mixture from the refrigerator and stir to recombine if it has separated.

With a wide rubber spatula, fold the egg yolk mixture into the beaten egg whites in the copper bowl. The souffle mixture should look like hollandaise.

Pour this into the souffle pot and bake in a preheated 350° oven 20 to 25 minutes.

I like souffles as the French cook them, soft and runny in the center, not baked through like a cake. Do not open the oven door while baking. Serve immediately when done.

Sprinkle the top with **powdered sugar.** Serve as is or with whipped cream, strawberries, orange sections, or candied violets.

7
Sources

Food

Aglamesis Bros. Inc., 3046 Madison Road, 531-5196. Wonderful ice creams and water ices made in the old world tradition. Their chocolates and hand made candies are superb. Some of the original furnishings in the ice cream store give this shop a special flavor.

Avrils, 33 E. Court St., 241-2433. Another old Cincinnati institution. Fine meats. Especially known for their hams which make super Christmas gifts. You can have them sliced, re-tied and gift wrapped. Their own sausages, made in the back of the store, are personally supervised by the Avril family and are out of this world.

Bengert Poultry, 52 East Court St., 241-0218. Specializes in poultry, game, ducks and geese. Special orders can be filled if given in advance.

The Big Melon, 8424 Vine St., 821-7440. Joe Geraci and Charlie Adams, the amicable owners, are always helpful in suggesting new items and picking out super produce. This specialty store has wines, gourmet items and a cold meat counter that will make party trays. Their produce is top quality (they make up fruit baskets, too) and they have a small refrigerator-type case where you can pick up bunches of flowers to brighten your table. This mini-market can supply all your party or day-to-day shopping needs.

The Big Tree Market, 7811 Montgomery Rd., 891-1097. Other locations — see phone book. Fine quality grocery items and produce. Make gift baskets with advance notice.

Bilker's Food Market, 7648 Reading Rd., 761-6280. This gourmet supermarket has everything you'll need to fill your recipe requirements. Look for notes scattered around the store telling you what new items have arrived and what's good to try. Mr. and Mrs. Nat Reis and their son Harvey continue to provide fine quality foods in this old Cincinnati establishment. Their knowledge of food and wines is superb and their suggestions are invaluable.

If you go there when you're hungry, look out. Chances

are, you'll come out carrying a bigger bag of goodies than you went in for.

Bissinger's Candy, Carew Tower Arcade, 241-0600. These candies and confections are based on recipes dating back to the time of Napoleon. They are made in the finest old world tradition.

Bracke Meats and Produce, 1010 Delta Ave., 871-1515. Long established quality in meats and produce. The Caboose has a fine selection of wines, imported and domestic. They have charge accounts, too!

Busken Bakery, 2675 Madison Road-Main Office, 871-2114. Ten other suburban locations — check your phone book. Joe Busken, Sr. and Joe Busken, Jr. make quality bakery products of all kinds. Special orders are filled if given in advance.

The Busy Bee Food Shop, 2707 Erie Ave.-Hyde Park Square, 871-2898. Joe and Jean Sumner own this lovely shop which is the basis of my cooking world. I can always find new cooking treasures there from around the world. They have great gourmet items.

The wine shop is one of the best I know and Jean's advice is always treasured.

Cape Cod Fisheries, Inc., 118 West 6th St., 241-5878. One of the few remaining fresh fish stores in town. Selection depends on availability and weather conditions where the fish are flown in from. You will most likely find whatever fish you need right there. Cape Cod will deliver.

Clifton Meat Market, 324 Ludlow Ave., 861-2561. Harry Jaeger and his son Paul run a top quality meat market. This long-established shop also has poultry, fish, ducks, geese and oysters. And will charge and deliver to many parts of the city.

They are a great source of cooking advice — you call with a recipe and they'll send you the meat you need or you can pick the meat and they'll tell you how to cook it.

Diet Center, 3214 Linwood Ave., 321-7015. Everything for the restricted diet as well as special diet cookbooks. They have all kinds of rices and hard-to-find cooking oils like seasame oil.

Earth's Bounty, 707 Main St., 651-5043. Specializes in health and organic foods. Has organically grown fruits, vegetables and meats which are hard to find locally. Has books and cooking equipment, too.

C. Eberle Sons Co., 3222 Beeckman Street, 542-7200. Wholesale frozen fruits, vegetables and prepared foods in commercial and household sizes, by the case.

Erie Ave. Fruit Market, 2730 Erie Ave., 321-1884. This market has everything from high quality fruits and vegetables to canned and frozen items. Will charge and deliver.

F and F Fruit Market, 3444 Edwards Rd., Hyde Park Square, 321-0953. Tom and Elsie Fukunaga and Mary and George Fukuwara have a shop filled with fruit and vegetable treasures as well as Oriental condiments. These friends have seen me through many cooking needs and they will you, too. Their special service is a delight.

Farmers' Market, Kellogg and Wilmer Ave. at Lunken Airfield. A market near Lunken Airfield where area farmers bring their produce. You buy from the backs of their trucks in almost any quantity you wish. It's so hard to resist buying, you find yourself happily going back to your two room apartment with a truckload of eggplant or zucchini. There are great bargains — and its fun just to see.

The Findlay Market, Findlay Street, Wednesday and Saturday, 8 to 6. Cincinnati's super open air market — open year round. Individual shops and booths. One can find all kinds of fresh meats, fruits and vegetables, just like the great European markets. You can browse and buy and have a wonderful time.

Fred's Meats, 2730 Erie Ave., Hyde Park Square., 321-4008. Fred Halmad has fine quality meats, poultry, ducks and fish. Racks of lamb are his specialty. He couldn't be nicer about answering questions and will charge and deliver.

Graeter's, 2145 Reading Road, Main Office. Special orders. 721-3323. See phone book for seven suburban locations. Graeter's uses the French pot method for making some of the world's best ice cream. In season, Dick Graeter makes fresh fruit flavors that have no rival. Their chocolate, too, is diet destroying.

With advance notice, you may order special flavors in quantity.

Hickory Farms, 2736 Erie Ave. 321-3522. Other suburban areas, too — check your phone book. The best selection of finest quality fresh cheeses from around the world. Great gourmet food items of all kinds. Mr. Rowe, Louise, Millie, Thelma, Joan and Glenna are always ready to give you friendly service.

Party trays and special gifts made up with advance notice.

Hitch Meat and Produce, 6209 Corbly Road, 232-1939. Top quality meat, produce and prepared food. This lovely shop is located in the Mt. Washington area.

Hitching Post Chicken, 3708 Edwards Road, 631-8553. Fine quality fried chicken that is always fresh. I find this place very helpful when I need fried chicken for large parties. Sure makes entertaining easier on the hostess!

Hot Baegels, 7378 Reading Rd., 731-9118. Nine varieties of hot bagels. They make bialys, too. Baked fresh daily, they're great for brunch or breakfast. Retail or wholesale.

Ruth Howard, 1733 E. McMillan, 281-5063. Individual cooking lessons by advance reservation. Ruth is a Cordon Bleu graduate and a great teacher. It's a joy to cook in such lovely company looking out on a beautiful river view in a home filled with antique treasures.

Huber Meats, 2719 Erie Ave., Hyde Park Square, 871-4272, 3504 Erie Ave., 321-4328. A world of quality and service. Nothing is too great or too difficult for Larry, Bob and Red to do with advance notice.

Finest meats, poultry, fresh fish and shellfish. You can buy excellent prepared foods such as stuffed pork chops, meat loaves, ham loaves, spare ribs and chicken Kiev.

Al Huber and his staff have seen me and my students through many trials. It's a marvelous place.

Hyde Park Food Shop, 3700 Edwards Road, 531-6666. Pete Minardi specializes in Italian and Greek foods. There you can find the ingredients for lots of our international recipes.

Jansen Nut Company, 204 West Court St., 621-2831. A world of fresh and roasted nuts of all descriptions. (The nuts are roasted there!) One of the few places you can get shelled pistachios. The varieties here are endless!

King Duffy, 2708 Erie Ave., Hyde Park Square, 321-4600. Fine groceries and meats. Will deliver.

Kramers Grocery, 6102 Madison Road, 271-0575. One of our fine independent groceries on the east side of town. Charges and will deliver. Finest quality meats and groceries. Many specialty items.

Lang's Finer Meats, 6212 Montgomery Rd., 731-2561. Top quality meats here. They have fantastic values on tenderloins — super good at reasonable prices. They will lard and season them for you too! You can buy Beef Wellington ready for the oven and Shish-kebab made up for the grill. Lang's delivers.

Lippert's Bakery, 2719½ Erie Ave., Hyde Park Square, 321-5471. Emily and Walter Lippert operate a great German bakery. They make my favorite breads and hard rolls, super macaroons and a myriad of pastries. They are wedding cake specialists. Special orders will be filled if given in advance.

Nettuno Italian Delicacies, 129 East Court St., 762-9592. Elena and Angelo have a special shop that carries food from 32 nations. Their largest collection is from Italy, Greece, Spain and India. They have wines from every region in Italy and other countries too.

Elena will cook special dishes for parties if you order them a week in advance. Some she is famous for are antipasto, lasagna and ravioli. You must pick them up at the store.

Quality Fruit Market, 8621 Winton Rd., 522-2740. George and Irene Koenig run this shop filled with dazzling fruits and vegetables. You can find not only great variety but also the best quality produce here. They carry a great deal of Chinese vegetables. They have a wine department stocked with choice selections to complement your table. Betty Klug, another asset to the store will answer questions and give advice as will George and Irene about what's best, what's good and how much of what you may need.

Railroad Salvage Food Outlet, 6012 Madison Rd., 272-0172. You'll find broken cases, discount prices and many commercial-sized items. Great fun for bargain hunters and easy on the budget.

Frank Sansone, 2719 Erie Ave., Hyde Park Square, 321-0106. Frank, Mrs. Sansone, and mean Lil and Jill are there to help you.

Fine quality fresh fruits and vegetables year round. Always come to the rescue on my special orders. Their great and varied selection includes keeping watercress in stock — always.

John F. Schoeny Co., 415 Plum Street, 721-5503. A great wholesale produce house which handles some canned goods by the case. They're a great help when you are cooking for large groups or stocking the larder.

Servatii Pastry Shop, 2838 Observatory Ave., 871-3244. Bill Gottenbush is a great European pastry-maker. His pastries are delicate and beautiful and enhance any table.

They make fantastic baskets out of bread — these filled with rolls and bread make a delightful party centerpiece. You must order them a week in advance.

Schmidt's Meats, 8621 Winton Rd., 522-4443. William Schmidt runs this meat market located in the back portion of the Quality Fruit Market. High quality meats and homemade soups are found here. They take orders for live lobsters early in the week, in season, and you can pick them up later that same week when they're flown in.

Soya Food Products, Inc., 2356 Wyoming Ave., 661-2250. A Far Eastern paradise for fresh, dried and canned foods. All kinds of cooking and servicing equipment for Oriental cooking. Ben Yamaguchi is a fund of knowledge and can answer questions about what, how much, and how big.

Tony Sparto's Fruit Store, 23 E. Court St., 721-7776. Wonderful selection of top quality fruits and vegetables. They have a licorice-tasting celery called finocchio which is a variety of fennel and in season you can buy big baskets of grapes if you're interested in jelly-making.

Spatz Health Foods, 607 Main, 621-0347. Cincinnati's original health food store. Has whole grains, vitamins and health foods from around the world. There is a health bar where you can eat lunch. Yogurt mixed with wheat germ is good and filling and helps you keep on your diet. Their peppermint tea is heavenly.

Swallen's, 3700 Red Bank Rd., 272-1300. Their discount food department carries commercial-sized cans of food you might not find elsewhere. Handy for big parties and big families.

Vinos' Inc., 4704 Montgomery Rd., 731-4027. Harry Tuemler has an intriguing collection of top quality wines, including many treasures. He has great knowledge of the world's vineyards and you can always rely on his suggestions.

Virginia Bakery, 286 Ludlow Ave., 861-0672. One of Cincinnati's fine old bakeries located in Clifton. Especially noted for their breads and pastry. Their Christmas cookies are beautiful.

West India Coffee Co., Inc., 1506-1508 Republic St., 721-0795. This restaurant supplier of special coffee blends will mix almost any combination of beans to suit the most demanding coffee buff's taste. You can buy by the pound for a little less than at the supermarket.

Equipment

Abbey Rents, 7151 Reading Road, 351-7000. All your party needs can be found right here. They can supply your party whether you're serving two, two hundred or two thousand people.

Acme Tinning and Lead Coating Co., 1126 Marshall Ave., 541-1712. One of the few tinner's left — it's a vanishing art. They do a super job of retinning your copper pots and pans quickly and inexpensively. Estimates given.

Ace Runte Hardware, 3439 Michigan Ave., 321-6027. Mr. and Mrs. Runte run a real old fashioned hardware store. They offer helpful advice on all household problems and have a good selection of cooking equipment.

America Rents, Inc., 2900 Gilbert Ave., 221-7200. You can rent everything you need for your party at America Rents. The people are helpful and will assist you in handling any party problems.

Aronoff Galleries, Inc., 15 East 8th St., 241-3230. A wonderful antique shop for silver and china. Pat Halleran and Joe Aronoff are the people to see.

Louis Aronoff Auctions, 711 Sycamore St., 721-2144. Our "Park Bernet" in Cincinnati — one always comes away with a find for the table from some great estate. Catalogues on request.

Samuel Aronoff Enterprises, 3275 Erie Ave., 871-2233. A myriad of world treasures, old and new — for your table, home, and garden.

Boxwood Inc., 2713 Erie Ave., Hyde Park Square, 871-3031. A tiny shop filled with tasteful gifts. You'll find treasures for your table, and party equipment, too.

Cappel Display Co., 920 Elm, 621-0952. If you're having a party with a theme, you can find everything you need to carry it through at Cappel's. From flags, paper flowers and beads to table decorations for baby showers to the Fourth of July — its all here — at reasonable prices.

Children's Hospital Thrift Shop, 16 E. 12th St., 721-2767. Somebody else's overflowing cupboard may set your table. Sometimes, grand old silver finds, pots and pans and odds and ends. You have to dig to look for treasure, but then, that's most of the fun. Catherine Hull who knows all the merchandise there, will be glad to help direct your treasure hunt.

Cincinnati Bakers Supply, 655 Evans, 921-6682. A world of bakery tools — anything and everything needed for the serious baker. They're friendly, too, in helping you find what you need.

Cincinnati Enquirer, 617 Vine St., 721-7200. Pat Williams, the food editor of the Enquirer provides information covering every facet of planning, preparation and entertaining. Read her column for new ideas that you can adapt to your own style of entertaining. When we said earlier in the book to be a clipper of columns in magazines and newspapers for ideas — here's a good place to begin.

You may ask specific questions by mail. Send a self-addressed stamped envelope for a prompt reply.

Cincinnati Gas and Electric Co., 139 East 4th St., Ann Holiday, 632-2824. This wonderful service of C. G. & E. Co., offers helpful information on food storage and preparation and the use of appliances. They will even consult with you on kitchen design. If you buy a new appliance, they'll send someone out to show you how to work it. They have so many services. Call and find one that can aid you.

A. B. Closson, Jr. Co., 407 Race St., 621-1536, 7866 Montgomery Rd., 891-5531. Closson's has beautiful furnishings for your kitchen and all your entertaining needs.

Helen Schoenebaum who buys for the gourmet shop, glassware, china and silver will be glad to answer all your cooking questions. They stock French tinware such as fish and lobster poachers and have fine quality Spring copper utensils — made in Switzerland. There are copper au gratin dishes and fry pans.

There are big, heavy aluminum stock pots, Sabatier knives and wonderful three-tiered vegetable stands so that your kitchen can be organized and beautiful at the same time.

Closson's has everything for the gourmet cook. All their stock is fine quality and good looking — you just can't miss.

Cowperthwaite Florists, 8404 Beechmont, 231-7158. Mrs. Cowperthwaite and her sons have a wonderful collection of rare plants, unusual garden treasures, and herbs. You can get knowledgeable advice from a real gardener.

M. Dunsky and Co., 37 East Court Ct., 621-8041, 721-9363. This restaurant supply house will sell retail. You can find endless varieties of commercial equipment. They have china and glassware at prices that will fit your budget and varieties of kitchen equipment to start you cooking.

Fancy This-Fancy That, 8416 Vine, 821-0844. You can find all the supplies you need for your party here. They have marvelous invitations, paper plates and matching napkins, serving equipment, inexpensive flatware, dishes and aprons (long and short). There are lovely wicker baskets, glass and tin cannisters, kitchen-wall organizers and just about anything else you may need to make your kitchen and your party beautiful.

Connected with the gift part of the shop run by Miriam Pease is a handicrafters heaven run by Ann Bloom. You can pick up some needlepoint to do while your pots are bubbling away on the stove.

The Fig Leaf, 7710 Shawnee Run Rd., 561-5699. An intriguing shop in Madeira that always has unusual gifts. You can take them along with you to a party to make your hostess happy. There is cooking equipment and table accessories to make your parties memorable.

Flowers by Marjorie, 1971 Madison Rd., 321-8977. This lovely shop does wonderfully creative flower arrangements and has the knack of making your party individual-looking and exciting. There are always many intriguing gifts, too, for the gourmet and his kitchen.

The Garden Center of Greater Cincinnati, 2715 Reading Road, 221-0981. A membership in the Garden Center is invaluable if you are interested in growing things. The staff there will come up with answers to all your gardening questions and their library is available for reference use.

Annually, there is an herb sale in May where you can find wonderful plants and support the Garden Center at the same time.

Gattles, 3456 Michigan Ave., 871-4050. Beautiful table linens, placemats and napkins. Finest quality, beautiful service and a lovely store to browse through. Their dishtowels can't be beat. They last forever, don't need ironing and brighten up your kitchen. They make marvelous gifts, too!

Sources

The Glass Barn, 1516 Reading Road, 733-4121. A warehouse of all kinds of glass at low prices for bargain hunters. You can find everything from fish bowls to bird baths, as well as drinking glasses. Zanesville stoneware at bargain prices is a real find.

Greenwich House, 2126 Madison Rd., 871-5204. Beautiful serving and cooking pieces, new and antique. Great kitchen planning and decorating from Walter Farmer, one of the finest decorators in America.

Hamilton County Extension Service, 11100 Winton Rd., 825-6000. Good source of information about food. Call if you're stuck for an answer on something and they'll try to help you out.

The Heart Mart, 5917 Madison Rd., 271-7323, 2702 Vine, 751-4469, 718 Wyoming Ave., 761-0420. Constant searching will yield untold treasurers. A good place to find bargains on all household items, appliances, antique china, silver serving pieces, old linen, pots and pans.

Herschede, 4 W. 4th St., 421-6080. Suburban locations — check phone book. Brides have started their collections at Herschede's for years — and still do. Everything for the table — from fine quality to more casual styles at one of Cincinnati's fine old stores.

Jones the Florist, 1037 E. McMillan, 961-6622. Frances Jones Poetker is a world famous artist and author whose creations are unequaled.

Her staff (Jim Simmons is super terrific) answers millions of questions, are very accomodating, and suggest flowers that best suit the occasion or the type of party you are giving.

You can't go wrong with one of their unique arrangements to complement your table decorations.

Mabley and Carew, 5th and Vine, 241-7400. Check phone book for suburban stores. Mabley's has a complete line of housewares and kitchen appliances. There is a great variety of pots and pans, electric appliances, kitchen linens, gadgets and accessories. You should be able to stock up on many staples here.

McAlpins, 13 W. 4th St., 381-4400. Other suburban stores — check phone book. Complete line of housewares and decorative accessories. You can find all your staple kitchen needs here along with electric appliances, kitchen linens and notions.

The Miller Gallery, 3453 Edwards Rd., 871-4420. Norman and Barbara Miller provide art for the kitchen. They have one-of-a-kind non-lead casseroles, ceramic mugs and will frame paintings or drawings to make your kitchen happy. Their Tubino crystal bowls are especially beautiful.

Nann's Florist and Greenhouses, 7954 Cooper, Montgomery, 791-3811. Mrs. Nann has high quality plants, flowers and garden care products. Her herb plants are super. Helpful advice abounds and questions from novice planters are handled amicably.

Newstedt-Loring Andrews, 27 W. 4th St., 621-6898, 2714 Erie Ave., 321-3604. Fine china, crystal and silver. Have more informal serving pieces and stainless steel flatware too. This old Cincinnati tradition carries on good taste and quality in everything it offers in its store.

Normolle Green Houses, Marburg and Wasson Roads, 321-4395, 321-7223. Henry Normolle has superb house and garden plants, flowers and herb plants.

Odds & Ends Thrift Shop, 115 East 12th Street, 721-0915. This is another one of those over-the-Rhine places where you stumble into more exciting buys for the kitchen than you can dodge. A recent trip turned up a lovely double waffle maker for $2.00 and a super, genuine, turn-of-the-century silver service. Other locations are 2809 Woodburn Ave., 861-2656 and 925 E. McMillan, 281-1155.

H. & S. Pogue Co., 4th and Race St., 381-4700. Check phone book for suburban locations. Marge Valvano, the wine buyer at Pogue's is one of the most knowledgeable people in the city. She runs a fine department full of exciting wines in various price ranges to fit your inclination and your budget. The people in this department will be glad to assist you in any way.

The gourmet shop has a full selection of cheese and

specialty food items. Here you can find Indian Tap sauce and candied violets and Mailliard chocolate. They'll be glad to help you find those hard-to-find items!

The houseware department carries Graham Kerr Cookware which is rolled steel covered with pocelain in designer colors. They have copper equipment, Farberware, Club Aluminum and will special order Kitchen-Aid mixers and carry Mixmaster and Hamilton Beach in stock. Oster and Waring Blenders are plentiful.

Their placemats and napkins are super and you can find great combinations for creative tables. Pogue's has all gadgets — such as skimmers, whisks — whatever.

Its a complete store full of fine quality merchandise. You can't miss.

Post and Times Star, 800 Broadway, 721-1111. Fern Storer, the food editor, is a fund of information on every aspect of food buying, preparation and entertaining. Her columns always provide instruction and helpful advice and a look at what's new in the food world. Here's a good place to keep abreast of what's happening and to gather ideas for your own parties.

For answers to your specific questions, send a stamped, self-addressed envelope and you will be promptly taken care of.

The Pot Shop, 936 Hatch, Mt. Adams, 651-1612. You can find imported Cordon Bleu cooking equipment, copper pots and pans, large free standing butcher blocks and hanging pot racks. There are French souffle pots and the best peppermills you can find made by Moulin. There are coarse salt and chocolate mills too! Its a fun shop stocked with excellent equipment.

Saalfeld Paper Co., 2701 Spring Grove Ave., 542-7100. This wholesale paper company is the place to buy cases of paper and plastic supplies for large parties. They have one of the largest selections in the city.

Scandanavian Art Handicraft, 7696 Camargo Rd., 561-6785. Mrs. Greta Peterson is the Swedish Consul in Cincinnati and owns and operates a fascinating Scandanavian shop filled with yarns, needlecraft, weaving and rya rug supplies.

Mrs. Peterson also carries a big stock of Scandanavian cookbooks including the most complete one: *The Great Scandanavian Cookbook* by Karin Fredrikson. It's a delightful shop to visit and browse through — and you may find a friendly cat or two snoozing amidst the goodies.

Shillitos, 7th and Race and Shillito Place, 381-7000. See phone book for suburban locations. You can find just about everything you'll need all in one great store.

There's a gourmet food shop that carries 75 or more different imported cheeses — along with all the specialty food items you'll need for your recipes. There are sausages from Milwaukee and across the way you can buy breads, rolls and pastries.

They have a fine wine department with French wines and others to complement any table.

Their housewares are endless! You can buy virtually any item from a huge selection of different brands. They carry Copcoware and Decoware — heavy enameled iron pots and casseroles. There are wooden chopping boards, Robinson knives, Farberware, Magnalite pots and pans — you name it — its there.

Miss Hughes will be happy to direct you in kitchen appliances and will take special orders for Kitchen-Aid mixers. Oster and Hamilton Beach blenders are kept in stock.

Elsewhere you can pick up aprons, dish towels, gadgets — endless amounts of kitchen things that tickle your fancy.

This most complete store can supply your most basic needs, all the way up to special gourmet items.

The Square Box, 2001 Madison Road, 871-1100. Beautiful dried arrangements and creative flowers of all kinds. Will fill your own containers with their special creations.

Tomar Gifts and Imports, 2757 Observatory Rd., 871-2044. Tomar is one of the most creative shops in Cincinnati. There are so many treasures, old and new, it is impossible to list their stock.

They have everything you'll need for a party from paper

plates to matches. There are glasses, dishes, mugs, trays, candles and innumerable beautiful items.

Tom Bryant has fantastic imagination. Go upstairs and see some of the tables that he sets up. He sometimes uses bells as napkin holders, uses egg candles in egg holders at each place as decorations — he'll give you advice and ideas on what to use and you can trust his taste — it's sensational.

Just browsing through the shop will give you ideas — so plan enough time for that when you go there.

The Village Viking, 8386 Vine, 821-7730. This shop specializes in Scandanavian imports. They have beautiful mugs, dishes and serving platters and lovely George Jensen placemats. Their most spectacular display of Marimekko fabrics is certainly welcome in Cincinnati! There are placemats and napkins to match, kitchen mitts and potholders. Best of all, you can choose any fabric you wish (all are stunning) and have long or short pinafore-type aprons made up in your size. Maria Frey, the delightful owner of this shop, says the fabrics and vinyls are super for tablecloths too!

Harry B. Weber Co., 118 West 3rd St., 721-4560. This restaurant supply house will retail if you go there knowing what you want to buy. They will sell you commercial equipment or supplies by the case. They have excellent knives and omelet pans.

The Woman's Exchange, 3507 Michigan Ave., 321-5303. Old Cincinnati institution offering hand-made items on a consignment basis. They have some linens, pot holders and specialty cooking items and a good collection of regional cookbooks.

Out of Town

Bazaar Francais, 666-668 6th Avenue, New York, NY 10010. This long established firm has a huge warehouse full of cooking equipment where you can buy anything you will ever need. You can shop by catalogue, too. It's very complete and their shipping is super-efficient and prompt.

Everything they carry is top quality, so you can be sure

you are investing wisely when you buy from them.

Bloomingdale's, 59th Street and Lexington Ave., New York, NY 10022. You can spend an hour or a day or a week browsing and buying at Bloomingdale's. From cooking equipment to cookbooks — they have it all. They carry virtually every brand and offer a huge variety of anything you may need to cook, to serve, and to set your table. You can even find something smashing to wear at your next party.

Bonniers, 605 Madison Ave., New York, NY 10022. Bonniers carries designer equipment. Their stock is beautiful — from inexpensive flatware to more expensive crystal. They carry European pottery you can't find anywhere else and wicker placemats and baskets that are knockouts. Their stock looks like it is of museum quality, and is exciting to use in your home.

Bullock's, Broadway & 7th St., Los Angeles, CA 90014. Beautiful domestic and imported foods and equipment of all kinds in one of California's most prestigious department stores.

The Cannery, Beach and Hyde Streets, San Francisco, CA. 94109. An amazing shop for great California wines, foods, and kitchen equipment.

Le Cordon Bleu, 24 rue de Champ de Mars, Paris VII, France. The classic French cooking school. You may attend cooking classes on a short or long term basis. Write for a program.

There is a pot and pan shop in connection with the school.

Cost Plus, near Fisherman's Wharf, San Francisco, CA. A great wholesale circus where you can find anything for the house and home. There are three huge warehouses full of wine, plants, glassware, furniture, ad infinitum from around the world. You name it and its there at reasonable prices.

Cross-Imports, Inc., 210-212 Hanover Street, Boston, MA. 02113. Serves the Italian, French and gourmet cook. A world of everything for any cuisine. Catalogues on request are 25¢ per copy.

La Cuisiniere, 903 Madison Ave., New York, NY. 10021. A treasure box of a store jammed with beautiful cooking equipment and sensational things to make your table beautiful. Their antique copper is dazzling. There's not a thing in the store that isn't a delight. Catalogue on request.

Elizabeth David, Ltd., 46 Bourne Street, London S.W.I., England. Elizabeth David is England's Julia Child. She has cooking classes — you can take her course or sit in on just one class. Make reservations in advance. You can also buy cooking equipment from her stock of wisely chosen wares, too.

The Golden Lamb Gift Shop, The Golden Lamb Inn, 27 South Broadway, Lebanon, OH. Fascinating collection of gifts. Many cooking and serving pieces to enhance your table. It's fun to amble through the old inn, too!

Hammacher Schlemmer, 147 East 57th Street, New York, NY. 10022. Hammacher Schlemmer is always a wonderful source of new ideas and the place to buy the old stand-bys that last forever

This lovely store deals in cooking equipment, china, silver, linens, wines, specialty food items and gadgets, just to mention a few. Catalogue on request.

George Jensen, 601 Madison Ave., New York, NY 10022. One of the most exciting stores for cooking and serving equipment and ideas. Their china, silver, glasses, and stainless steel are fantastic.

Walk through the store and notice the tables they've set up. They're so imaginative and beautifully done, you're bound to come home full of fresh ideas.

Maison Dehillerin, 18 & 20 Rue Coquilliere and 51 Rue J. J. Rousseau, 75-Paris, France. Located in the former market district of Les Halles in Paris. This shop is filled with virtually every utensil used in classic cuisine. It's *the* place to buy copper (by the kilo) in Paris. They will ship merchandise.

Paprikas Weiss, 1546 Second Ave., New York, NY 10028. A fascinating shop specializing in Middle European foods and cooking equipment.

Fresh Hungarian paprika is a true find here as well as many other culinary delights. Will send catalogue on request.

Pampered Kitchens, 21 East 10th Street, New York, NY 10003. Just as the name implies, this store always features the unusual in kitchen equipment. Catalogue on request.

Pottery Barn, 231 Tenth Ave., New York, NY 10011. This huge warehouse has three floors of cooking equipment, glasses, plates, stainless steel, furniture — everything you can imagine — and at low prices. They carry discontinued stock from other stores and therefore can sell it cheap.

Their teak trays and salad bowls are a real buy as are their wine glasses.

Tarpy's Beverage and Delicatessen, 1805 Kingsdale Center, Columbus, OH 43221, 488-7901. A great selection of domestic and imported wine. Good advice given. There is also a delicatessen offering well prepared foods and things done to order. *Tom Tarpy's Market,* 2140 Tremont Center, Columbus, OH 43221, 488-1838. A gourmet's world of food; imported and domestic, fresh and canned.

Wasserstrom Wine Import and Restaurant Supply Co., Inc., 77 West Fulton Street, Columbus, OH, 221-7744. Stewart Wasserstrom will retail great kitchen equipment and supplies.

The wine import company is one of the midwest's best. Many of the world's great wine houses are represented. Retail and wholesale.

Epilogue

Cincinnati Experience, E .St. Clair and Jefferson, 861-3354. Open Wednesday 12-5 p.m. Saturday and Sunday 10-5 p.m. How about recycling all the bottles and cans you'll be buying now that you're going to be cooking all of these exciting recipes? Separate your bottles and cans and bring them (and your newspapers, too) to Cincinnati Experience. Not only are you eliminating waste, but Cincinnati Experience uses the money they get from selling the bottles and cans to push for environmental action!

INDEX

376

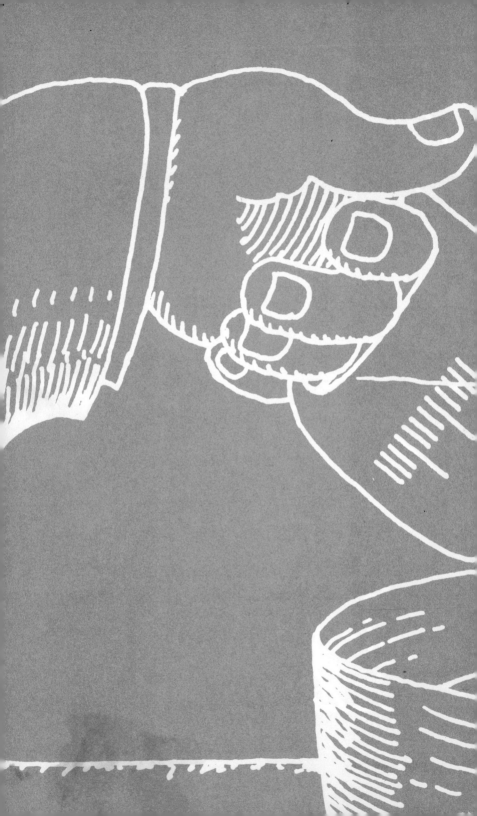